One Hundred Years
of Fire Insurance

Being a History
of the
ÆTNA
Insurance Company
Hartford, Connecticut
1819–1919

By HENRY R. GALL
and
WILLIAM GEORGE JORDAN

1919

William George Jordan

William George Jordan was born on 6 March 1864 in New York City, USA. He took his university education at the *City College of New York* and began his literary career as an editor of *Book Chat* in 1884. After a brief spell (1888-91) editing *Current Literature* - a magazine offering an eclectic combination of literature review and contemporary commentary, Jordan relocated to Chicago. It was here that he first lectured on his system of Mental Training; although not with any great success. In 1897 Jordan moved back to New York and was hired as the managing editor for *The Ladies Home Journal*, after which he moved on to edit *The Saturday Evening Post*. This substantial editing career is not Jordan's best known achievement however – his essays and thoughts on education and 'mental training' have garnered the most attention. In July 1891 *The Chicago Inter-Ocean* printed an interview with Jordan on his 'mental training'. After the article was published he received so many inquiries that he scheduled a long lecture tour on the subject. *The Inter-Ocean* reported that 'during the past few weeks the calls from Chicago have been so numerous, enthusiastic and positive for lecture courses and private society classes that he has concluded to resign his position in New York and come to Chicago.' In 1894, Jordan published a short pamphlet; *Mental Training, A Remedy for Education*, which opened with the following lines; 'here are two great things that education should do for the individual—it should train his senses, and teach him to think. Education, as we know it to-day, does not truly do either; it gives the individual only a vast accumulation of facts, unclassified, undigested, and seen in no true relations. Like seeds kept in a box, they may be retained, but they do not grow.' Jordan's allegorical style was widely utilised in all his works, and he penned his first book, *The Kingship of Self-Control*, in 1898. This was followed by a further nine texts, all on the subject of self-improvement; a theme which he continued writing on for the rest of his life. *The Majesty of Calmness* (1900) was perhaps his most popular self-help book. Despite these successes, Jordan's most influential writing was actually a political tract. In *The House of Governors* (1907), he aimed to 'promote uniform legislation on vital questions, to conserve states' rights, to lessen centralisation, to secure a fuller, freer voice of the people and to make a stronger nation.' The work was circulated to each state governor and to President Theodore Roosevelt, and was incredibly well received. His ideas were put into practice and the first 'meeting of the governors' was held in Washington, on 18 January, 1910 – with Jordan as its secretary. He was dropped as secretary a year later, but nevertheless, this group is a key part of his legacy.

At the age of fifty-eight, Jordan married Nellie Blanche Mitchell, in New York City at the Grace Episcopal Church. The marriage was a happy one, for the short time it lasted, but sadly Jordan died just six years later of pneumonia on 20 April 1928, at his home in New York.

ILLUSTRATIONS

	FACING PAGE
THOMAS K. BRACE, First and Third President,	30
SECTION OF ORIGINAL PETITION FOR ÆTNA CHARTER,	32
ORIGINAL ENTRY IN FIRST RECORD BOOK,	36
SEAL OF ÆTNA INSURANCE COMPANY,	38
FIRST ÆTNA ADVERTISEMENT,	42
HENRY L. ELLSWORTH, Second President,	52
PAGE FROM CORRESPONDENCE BOOK NO. 1,	58
ÆTNA POLICY NO. 1,	74
ÆTNA OFFICE BUILDING, 1837 TO 1867,	78
ISAAC PERKINS, First Secretary, and SIMEON L. LOOMIS, Second Secretary,	82
OLD FARM HOUSE WITH "ÆTNA" TIN SIGN OVER THE DOOR,	90
EDWIN G. RIPLEY, Fourth President,	96
THOMAS A. ALEXANDER, Fifth President,	102
ÆTNA OFFICE BUILDING, 1867 TO 1903,	108
LUCIUS J. HENDEE, Sixth President,	114
JOTHAM GOODNOW, Seventh President,	124
HENRY E. REES, Vice-President; ALMERON N. WILLIAMS, Vice-President; EDGAR J. SLOAN, Secretary,	130
ÆTNA'S PRESENT OFFICE BUILDING,	136

ILLUSTRATIONS

	FACING PAGE
EDWIN S. ALLEN, GUY E. BEARDSLEY, and RALPH B. IVES, Assistant Secretaries,	142
LOVING CUP PRESENTED TO PRESIDENT CLARK,	146
OLD OFFICE BUILDING OF ÆTNA AT CINCINNATI, OHIO,	182
THOMAS E. GALLAGHER, General Agent, and LOUIS O. KOHTZ, Assistant General Agent, Western Branch, Chicago,	186
GEORGE C. BOARDMAN and GEORGE W. SPENCER, former General Agent and Assistant General Agent, respectively, Pacific Branch, San Francisco, California,	190
WILLIAM H. BREEDING, General Agent Pacific Branch,	196
WILLIAM F. WHITTELSEY, Marine Vice-President, and RAYMOND E. STRONACH, Marine Secretary,	214
ÆTNA "ROLL OF HONOR,"	222

ONE HUNDRED YEARS
OF FIRE INSURANCE

CHAPTER I

THE DAWN

IN tracing the history of any idea, institution or subject, it is a bit daring and self-confident to stick a pin into a certain date or incident and to say that there was its actual beginning. The origins, in every phase of life and thought, are shrouded in the haze of tradition or controversy. There is often the germ of a great idea, or the recognition of a real need, followed by tentative and inadequate efforts to meet it, yet no more like its present state of development than the first hot-air balloon is like a 1919 model in airships. So it is in the long evolution of fire insurance into a well-organized, modern business.

Away back in the old days in Assyria and the East, about twenty-five hundred years ago, as we learn from the inscriptions on clay tablets and cylinders dug up from the ruined cities, there was a primitive kind of insurance. In case of fire, the magistrates, judges and priests of the town or district were empowered to make up the loss to the individual by assessing all the members of the community. This method, in a modified form, still exists in China and in parts of Russia. It seems also to contain the germ of state fire insurance as practiced, to a degree, in the bureaucratic and autocratic Germany of yesterday.

During the Middle Ages there was some kind of security against loss from fire and other hazards in connection with the Anglo-Saxon and German guilds. The members of these guilds made contributions regularly to a common relief fund, somewhat in the manner of our modern benefit societies.

There is little doubt that marine insurance, covering fire at sea and other risks of traffic and travel on the waters, preceded land insurance. In the twelfth century marine insurance was either conceived or rediscovered by the Italians, as claimed by the historian Villani. The earliest of these policies of insurance now known is dated September 20, 1547, on the ship *Santa Maria de Venezia*, covering her trip from Cadiz to London.

It is from the Italians that we get our word *underwriter*, for they began their contracts with the equivalent of "We the underwriters." The custom was to divide a large risk among a number of people, who agreed to share in the hazards and in the profits of the enterprise in proportion to the subscription made by them, each writing *under* or below the contract, his name and the amount of risk he would assume. The word *policy*, too, seems to have come from Italy, probably being derived from the word "polizza," meaning "promise," though some authorities claim for it a different origin.

In the year 1609 we have the first clear statement of an actual system of fire insurance as we understand it today. It was a proposition made to Count Anton

Günther, who has been described as the "wisest prince" that ever ruled Oldenburg, one of the grand-duchies of Germany. It was proposed that he offer, for the sum of a dollar a year on every hundred dollars of valuation, to guarantee his subjects against loss by fire, the misfortunes of war alone excepted. He gave considerable thought to the plan, which he believed could be made successful, but finally turned it down for two reasons: he feared it might seem that he was willing to make money from the sorrows of his people, and, more important to him, it seemed a tempting of Providence.

But good ideas often move slowly, and for a quarter of a century the subject lay dormant. In 1635 a petition was presented to Charles I of England "to ensure all your Majesty's subjects whomsoever for so much of their estates combustible as they themselves shall conceive in danger of Fire." This seems to have been pigeon-holed, for three years later a similar petition was favorably received; and on October 16, 1638, the King ordered the Attorney General to prepare a patent for such a company, to run for forty-one years, and to "await his royal signature." But the King soon became engrossed in taking care of his royal political fences, and the insurance project was forgotten. Other attempts, made later, also failed.

Then came the great fire of London in 1666, which burned over 435 acres and destroyed over 85 per cent. of the buildings, with a loss of about ten million pounds. This conflagration advertised graphically and tragically the need of protecting individuals against loss by fire.

In the year following, Nicholas Barbon, one of the first and most important builders of London, opened an office where he individually proposed to insure buildings. He had some success, and in 1680 he formed a partnership and established the "Fire Office" at the "back side of the Royal Exchange." This concern insured houses to a stated amount for a fixed premium; namely, 2½ per cent. of the yearly rental for brick houses and 5 per cent. for frame houses, the rental being assumed to be 10 per cent. of the value of the property. The capital of the firm was £40,000, or about $200,000 — to be increased by £20,000 for every 10,000 houses insured. It was believed that the interest of the fund would pay all losses and leave a good margin of profit. They must have had luck, for although their plan seemed to leave no opportunity for discrimination in risks, and there were few facts to go by and only most crude statistics, yet somehow the business prospered. Possibly their recent calamity had taught the people caution, and thus reduced the probability of fire to a minimum.

Within a year the very success of the new venture threatened to kill it. Envy and opposition were followed by a socialistic demand that such profits should not go to a private concern, but should accrue to all the people. The Common Council voted to do the business at a lower rate than the Fire Office, and books were opened and policies issued. Realizing that they could not stand against this opposition, which had so coolly appropriated their idea when it promised prosperity, Barbon and his associates, facing disaster and ruin, fought for the life of their concern. Many fair-minded citizens, who believed in rewarding and encouraging individual initiative and enterprise, joined with them. The battle, carried on by means of public meetings, pamphlets, and articles in the "Gazette," proved warm and spirited.

In a year or so the city abandoned the project. The "Fire Office" at the back of the Royal Exchange was thus left alone in the field. Its symbol or trademark was a phœnix amid flames; and as it placed a badge with this device on all buildings it insured, it soon became known as "The Phœnix Office." Later, when it aged, it was called the "Old Phœnix," much as the Ætna Insurance Company centuries later became popularly and affectionately known throughout the Western world as "Old Ætna."

Then came upon the stage of action the first of the mutual insurance associations. It was the Friendly Society, with its device of a sheaf of arrows. The plan of this new organization was different. The assured had to meet three conditions — first, the payment of a small sum yearly, varying in amount as his building was of brick or frame; second, he deposited a sum equaling five annual payments in advance to guarantee future assessments; and third, he agreed to contribute toward the settlement of each loss of the Society by fire, up to and not exceeding thirty shillings on each hundred pounds of his insurance. The policy-holders were thus responsible for one another's losses.

The Phœnix promptly began to fight the Friendly, tooth and nail. It applied to the Lords of the Privy

 ONE HUNDRED YEARS OF FIRE INSURANCE

Council for the exclusive right of "making and registering all assurances, policies, and contracts of houses from fire for thirty-one years." Its greedy demand was not satisfied, but it was granted the entire field free from competition for one year; after which the Friendly Society could do business for three months and rest for three months, and so on by alternate quarter years of business and retirement. As a part of this decision, given in 1687 in the presence of King James II, the Phœnix was required to pay the government for its work in putting out fires, the amount being fixed by the King for each individual fire.

In 1688 the political and business atmosphere of England began to clear; there was greater freedom from petty restrictions, and underwriting no longer required a special license. In 1696 a new form of mutual insurance was started by an organization which had many names during the ensuing century, among them the "Amicable Contributionship," but since 1776 has been known as the Hand-in-Hand Company; deriving its name from the device of interclasped hands, which from the beginning it had used as its emblem on all the buildings it insured. This Company grew rapidly and prospered. It is now the oldest mutual fire insurance company in the world, but confines its operations to London and its suburbs. The original plan of the Hand-in-Hand had as one element a deposit to be paid back, less expenses, on the termination of a policy. Profits from interest on invested funds, less losses and expenses, were to be distributed among the stockholders, and the rate of

 THE DAWN

assessment was to be determined annually by the Board of Directors.

Up to the dawn of the 18th century, insurance on dwellings, stores or other buildings had covered only the structures themselves, and not the contents. In 1704 "Lombard House" was organized for the insurance, among other things, of household and business goods. This was the first company to enter this field, as it also was the first to institute a salvage corps, for the rescue and saving of goods at fires. The proposal to insure household furniture was at first met with loud and merry ridicule, but it soon became popular.

It was about this time that Charles Povey, who seems to have been an energetic hustler, with a streak of the Yankee in his composition, made his appearance in the fire insurance field. He had no money, but apparently plenty of nerve, for he formed an organization and opened an office in London to insure buildings against fire. This venture not succeeding, he formed another organization to insure household furniture and merchandise throughout Great Britain and Ireland. Although he was long on hope and short on funds, the laughter incited by his efforts did not daunt his courage and determination.

The second venture not proving any more successful than the first, Povey conceived the idea of a third organization; and here he seems to have foreshadowed the "holding company" of the nineteenth century, for his third organization was to own the other two. It was known as the London Insurers, but soon adopted the name of the Sun Fire Office. There was one difficult phase of his problem — he had no capital to pay losses. This, however, was only an incident to the young Napoleon of finance. He solved that difficulty to his satisfaction by stating in his policies that one-half of the premium received would be set aside as a reserve fund from which losses would be paid, with the added proviso that when this reserve became exhausted the company was not to be held further liable. His reserve fund must not be confused with that carried by our modern fire insurance companies, which is a wise, safe guarantee in addition to their entire capital; the reserve fund of the Sun Fire Office, or Mr. Povey, as you prefer, represented his only capital.

Insurers somehow did not take over-kindly to this scheme, with its lottery atmosphere of chance and with the odds all against them. Later, the company announced that it would make its promise to pay unconditional, and in 1726 a capital fund of £48,000 was secured. The company remained a partnership and never incorporated. Begun in 1710 on a shoestring, it succeeded and it still exists, flourishing today as the oldest non-mutual fire insurance company in the world.

There were by this time a number of companies in operation, doing a profitable business. Fire insurance had vindicated itself as a real need; and the prosperity of these companies tempted men, some impractical, some over-optimistic and others unscrupulous, to enter the field. In 1720 began an era of flimsy, speculative companies, which flooded the market, somewhat like the wildcat concerns that proved such a menace to safe, sound and conservative underwriting in our own country at different periods during the last century.

The air of England, in the early part of the eighteenth century, seemed surcharged with get-rich-quick schemes. The people were wild over the possibilities of the great "South Sea Company," organized in 1711 to capture what was claimed to be the untold wealth of South American trade. Enthusiasm grew to frenzy, mad, unreasoning and unreasonable; every class of society from the King, who was its Governor, down to the humblest peasant, was in the Company, or was begging or borrowing or stealing money to get in.

For valuable concessions and privileges, the Company offered to take over the entire national debt of England, amounting to over £50,000,000. There were tricks, and wheels within wheels, in this scheme; but Parliament nibbled at the bait and then swallowed it whole, and the offer was accepted despite the opposition of the Bank of England, which offered £5,000,000 for the same privileges. The business was prosperous for years or was made to seem so; big dividends brought in bigger investments, and shares rose from £100 to £1,000 in a brief time. Then at the very height of speculation Sir John Blount, one of the promoters, sold out. This started an avalanche of unloading, and the beautiful "South Sea Bubble" burst. Thousands who dreamed themselves millionaires were actually beggared, and the whole fabric of trickery, knavery and corruption was revealed.

The speculative mania inspired during the life of

 ONE HUNDRED YEARS OF FIRE INSURANCE

the "Bubble" affected fire insurance. It was the time of the promoter's paradise, and prospectuses breathed of romance and wealth, and luxury for one's whole lifetime, to be easily secured by merely investing in a few shares of some new company.

Shortly before the collapse, when the "Bubble" was showing its most iridescent hues, Overall's Insurance Company invited stock subscriptions to the tune of one million pounds sterling. Their prospectus read like a page from Monte Cristo; they were going to do wonders, but really they did not, for they too went down in the crash. Other companies were started with calls for capital of from one to three million pounds each. One of these proposed a scheme to combine insurance and building.

This saturnalia of frenzied finance eventually came to an end. The wreckage was great and the mourners were many; but after it was all over, legislation stepped in to safeguard insurance in the spirit of modern business. There was a steady increase along normal lines, new companies being formed as needed, until in 1856 there were seventy-two corporations or companies recognized by the government, and insuring property to an amount aggregating over nine hundred million pounds sterling.

Fire insurance as a business was still in its infancy when it was transplanted to America. The first company in this country of which we have record was started in 1752 in Philadelphia. Like its prototype in England, it had a long, cumbersome name which it succeeded in shortening and living down; it was "The

THE DAWN

Philadelphia Contributionship for the Insurance of Houses from Loss by Fire." Benjamin Franklin was one of its most enthusiastic promoters. It was modeled on the Amicable Contributionship, or Hand-in-Hand, of London, and adopted its name, plan, seal and badge—four hands clasped. Under the name of the Hand-in-Hand this company still continues in business.

In 1783 the Company passed a by-law refusing to insure houses surrounded by shade-trees, on the ground that the trees impeded the putting out of a fire. This stand aroused opposition, and many of those insured by this institution seceded and organized a new company known as the "Mutual Assurance." Its housemark was a green tree, made of lead, fastened to a wooden shield and affixed to all houses insured by the company.

It was not until 1770 that there was even an attempt to organize a fire insurance company in the city of New York. Though proposed and discussed under the dignified chaperonage of the Chamber of Commerce, discussion soon languished into inactivity and the whole plan petered out. It was not until seventeen years later that the first company in New York was organized (though not incorporated until 1809) under the name of the Mutual Insurance Company and later changed to the Knickerbocker Fire Insurance Co. In the same year, 1787, the New York Insurance Company was also started; in 1801 the Columbian Insurance Company; and five years later the Eagle Fire, now the oldest stock fire insurance company in New York. In 1799 the Providence-Washington began

 ONE HUNDRED YEARS OF FIRE INSURANCE

business at Providence, Rhode Island, and still continues in successful operation.

During the closing years of the eighteenth century in this country, thirty charters for insurance companies were granted, most of them being for marine and fire insurance. They were distributed as follows: Maryland seven, Massachusetts six, New York four, Pennsylvania four, Connecticut three, South Carolina two, Rhode Island two, New Hampshire one, and one in Virginia.

Fire insurance existed in but a crude, experimental form in the eighteenth century. Though based on a genuine need, in its practice even the broad fundamental principles were not recognized, and there were no statistics and no precedents of value. Early colonists who came to this country brought over the idea from England; but in the working out, the development and improvement of the thought into finer, practical detail, it was more American than British. In this field no State did more important work than Connecticut, and Hartford early achieved prominence that later came close to pre-eminence.

The early underwriting in Connecticut, as in the other colonies, was generally of an individual or partnership character, even partnerships not coming in until near the close of the eighteenth century. Early in 1794, Peleg Sanford and Daniel Wadsworth opened an office in Hartford, for the insurance of houses, merchandise and furniture. A year later they formed a copartnership, taking in Elias Shipman of New Haven, who was made agent for that city, for the purpose of

THE DAWN

underwriting on vessels, merchandise and stock, under the firm name of the "Hartford and New Haven Insurance Company." In 1797, Shipman withdrew from this firm and established a new business, under the charter of the New Haven Insurance Company, which was devoted exclusively to marine insurance and was carried along until 1833, when it was discontinued.

The oldest insurance company in Connecticut, and the first to be incorporated in the State, is the Mutual Insurance Company of the City of Norwich, which received its charter in May, 1795. Each person joining agreed to pay on the sum insured, for the first year one-half per cent., for the second year one-third, and for each subsequent year one-quarter per cent. It continues to do a small business and has never attempted to branch out into larger activities. A similar company was organized in 1801 in New Haven, under the name of the Mutual Assurance Company, but it did not succeed and soon died a natural death.

In 1810 the Hartford Fire Insurance Company was organized with a capital of $150,000, with the privilege of increasing to $250,000. The first President was Major Nathaniel Terry, who headed the company for twenty-five years, resigning in 1835. It was in 1813 that the Middletown Fire Insurance Company was incorporated. It somehow did not strike the right gait, as it survived its organization by only six years and then passed out of existence. Two brief mentions complete the record of insurance in Connecticut up to the year 1819: the Norwich Fire Insurance Company, which was organized in 1819 and was wiped out by the Chicago fire; and the New Haven Fire Insurance Company, started in the same year as the Norwich Company, and surviving only a few years.

Fire insurance in America had now merely made a good start; it was in a tentative, learning, struggling stage. Its real vital history, as a business reduced to principle, system and wise and scientific underwriting, was still to be written in the years to come in the nineteenth century, which at this time was still an infant in its swaddling clothes.

CHAPTER II

BIRTHPLACE OF THE ÆTNA

THIS country of ours, during the few years preceding 1819, was passing through stirring times of storm and stress, of wars and peace, of alternating depression and prosperity. Underneath the surface of conflict and confusion there was, however, the pulsing throb, the freeing of mighty formative forces, and the reaching out toward greater things. Though the States were not in close sympathy, and while there were sectional jealousies and inharmonies and the threat to split on vital issues, yet notwithstanding, it was the real dawn of a national spirit in America. The people began, because of the unifying pressure of conditions, to think and to act in terms of a nation, and not of a mere union of States.

In 1814 we had two wars on hand at the same time—the hard conflict with England and the war with the Creek Indians in Alabama which, when settled, ended the power of the red man east of the Mississippi. The South favored the war with England, but the North bitterly opposed it. The presence of British troops holding on land a large part of Maine and the southern portion of Massachusetts, and by sea blockading the ports, roused the indignation of the people of New England to fever heat against the Federal Government, which they held responsible for these conditions. The shipping interests, which had been the pride and prosperity of the people, were completely ruined. Massachusetts, Connecticut, and Rhode Island refused the levy of troops to the government and threatened to secede from the union. The people of Nantucket declared themselves neutral and under the protection of England. The famous Hartford Convention of 1814, with delegates from all the New England States condemning the war and the administration of President Madison, was a vent to the angry feelings of the people, but it accomplished nothing but the ruin of the Federalist Party that called it. In August, 1814, occurred the burning of the White House and of the unfinished structure of the Capitol, containing the archives and books of the Congressional Library. This disaster led to the flight of the President and his wife, the popular "Dolly" Madison, who hid in the woods beyond the Potomac to escape capture by the British.

It was in this year, too, that the "Star Spangled Banner" was written by Francis S. Key while detained on a British ship during the bombardment of Fort McHenry. Money was scarce, business was paralyzed, and an oppressive and unpopular war-tax was levied on caps, hats, boots, watches, household furniture and other articles. Henry Clay was leader of the new Democracy, gloating over the downfall of the Federalists. Nearly all the banks in the country suspended specie payment, and at the close of the year the national debt had reached what was for the people at that time the appalling sum of about one hundred million dollars.

Then came the war with Algeria, and a year of depressed spirits and empty pockets. The painful work of reconstruction, with all its irritating and perplexing problems and tangles, did not begin till after the election of President Monroe in 1817. It was President Monroe who, six years later, in his annual message to Congress, enunciated in a few sentences what was later to become famous as the "Monroe Doctrine." He declared that the United States would regard as "unfriendly" any attempt by any foreign power to extend its territory on this side of the Atlantic or to meddle with the political affairs of the two Americas. This declaration was inspired by the war which Spain was then carrying on against her revolting colonies. It was given new life by President Cleveland in 1895 in his message concerning the Venezuelan question.

In the beginning of the Monroe administration the rechartered Bank of the United States resumed operation with a capital of $35,000,000, and long-languishing business began to revive. The first savings bank in America was opened in Philadelphia; Congress abolished all internal taxes and enacted a high protective tariff to encourage American industries.

We were just beginning to breathe freely the air of peace when we were plunged into a new war, the eighth in our history — this time with the Seminole Indians of Florida. The great West began to open up under the Government encouragement to settlers to buy public lands, and the guarantee by the States of immunity from taxation on these lands for several years. Endless picturesque processions of prairie wagons passed through New York and Pennsylvania on their way to the prairies, which soon became dotted with little settlements, the germs of future cities and towns.

It was the "Era of Good Feeling" in politics (for by this name was the period from 1817 to 1823 popularly known), and party lines were in general broken down. Henry Clay was prime mover in an attempt to unscramble the eggs of slavery, by forming the African Colonization Society to return negroes to Africa, when the year 1817 was nearing its close. The slavery question was much in evidence; there was violent agitation and vigorous resistance incident to the petition of Missouri for admission as a slave State. The Union was now evenly divided into eleven free and eleven slave States; the South threatened secession if its demands were not satisfied. Our pension system, which was to assume such gigantic proportions in later years, was at this time begun with the first grant by Congress of pensions to needy veterans of the Revolutionary War. It is interesting to note in this connection that in the Great War, a century later, the Government abandoned the time-honored pension scheme of relief for soldiers and their dependants, and adopted a plan based on the principle of insurance.

There were many parallels between those times and the present. In order to counteract the use of ardent spirits among the people, Secretary Calhoun prohibited the use of liquor altogether in the United States army; we went a step further just one hundred years later when it was forbidden in both army and navy, with the resulting final plunge into national prohibition.

When in 1819, John J. Crittenden of the United States Senate resigned "because he could not get bread for his family on $900 a year," which was a Senator's salary in those days, it was a close parallel to the resignation in 1919 of Secretary of the Treasury McAdoo and Attorney-General Gregory, because they needed more money than the $12,000 a year they received from the Government. The people were then suffering, as are we today, from the high cost of living; they, in that year, suffered from a scourge with its wide swath of mortality — yellow fever, which claimed as one of its victims the hero of the memorable battle of Lake Erie, the famous Commodore Oliver Hazard Perry, at the age of thirty-four; we, a century later, faced the horror of a greater scourge, the Spanish influenza, with a higher mortality than our entire losses in the great world war.

In 1819 the country faced its first national financial crisis. The stringency and hard times were, to a degree, due to the contagion of the bad times in England, but also to our own extravagant speculations and reckless over-confidence following the reorganization of the United States Bank.

During 1819 and the five years preceding, there were inventions, discoveries and events, not of great immediate importance, but big with possibilities in the future development of the ideals and industries of the country. Beside those already referred to, brief mention may be made of the erection of the first cotton mill, the first rolling mill to puddle iron and roll iron bars, the first lighting of a city by gas, the erection of a city water-works at Philadelphia, the opening of part of the Erie Canal, the introduction of anthracite coal, the beginning of stereotyping and printing from stereotype plates, the first use of steam power applied to cabinet making and paper making, the invention of steel-plate engraving, the first transatlantic packet line, beginning of the United States coast survey, first steam vessel to cross the Atlantic, manufacture of porcelain and patent leather, first canned goods, first school for deaf mutes, at Hartford, the invention of the sewing machine, the organization of the first peace society — the first in the world — established in New York, and a host of other important events.

At this period Connecticut was a farming and trading community; there was no manufacturing except that of coarse goods in general demand. The larger towns, like New Haven, Hartford, New London and others, were collecting and distributing centers. Through the country roads and lanes came creaking wagons, laden with wheat and peas in bags, kiln-dried corn in barrels, tierces of beef and pork, tons of hay, baskets of beans, onions, potatoes and turnips, firkins of rich butter, great cheeses, cases of tobacco, flour, corn and corn-meal. Sometimes the big wagons were filled with lumber or piles of pipe-staves of spruce or hickory-hoops from some place away back in the woods. Then there were the droves of horses and cattle for the plantations.

These processions moved picturesquely townwards, for there were no prosaic railroads in those days. What was not needed for local use was loaded at the busy docks for shipping to Martinique, Barbadoes and other islands in the West Indies. When the vessels came back after their long perilous trips they brought valuable cargoes of rum, sugar, salt or molasses.

The West India trade meant much to the people of Hartford in these early days — more indeed than a mere lucrative industry. Many of the young men, energetic, adventurous and anxious to make their way in the world, entered this service. Work on these clipper ships was no sinecure, yet it was splendid training. The open-air life under trying conditions made them strong and sturdy in body. They had to be prepared for any responsibility that might suddenly be thrust upon them, to meet emergencies on the instant, to have courage and fearlessness; the life not only made boys sailors but made them men. There was, too, the tang of romance in their contact with the civilization and manners and customs of the West Indies, so different from their own, and they were forced to see and to think in broader terms than those of merely provincial interests.

There was still much of the pioneer spirit in New England, and of close hand-to-hand grappling with the problems of life. There was hard work, with little money and few luxuries. It was a living that made for

individuality and initiative, and a fine sane sturdiness. There was no machinery, as we know the word today; the manufacturing was of the simplest, and the spirit of real hand-craft still breathed over a piece of work. If a man built a boat there was thoroughness and solidity in every plank and bolt, if a house it could be guaranteed to defy time and the weather for generations; the cooper put no defective stock in his barrels and the blacksmith made sure of his iron before he forged it. There was individual work and individual responsibility. The communities were small, and every man knew every other; character was a real asset and could not well be counterfeited.

In New England at this period, was the only real democracy in the country; there the people truly ruled. The "town meeting" decided matters for the town; every citizen went to meeting, knew what were the issues and problems, formed his own opinion and spoke his own voice. They often were narrow and bigoted and obstinate, but they were free and they gloried in their freedom, as did the old Greeks in Athens.

The schools had not reached the elaborate curriculum that we know today; but the small amount taught was drilled into permanency and thoroughness; it tended to make clear, shrewd, practical thinkers rather than scholars. The New Englanders were not stained-glass saints, but they were men of character, strong, sturdy, individual, and with a tinge of conservatism that made their progressiveness safe and sound.

Hartford was then a town of about 6,900 people

and nine hundred dwelling houses. It was a prosperous growing young city of culture and enterprise, and stretched along the banks of the Connecticut River. Grouped near the river were the importing houses and principal business places, and beyond them was what real-estate agents today like to term "the residential section." The whipping-post still stood in the public square, the Puritan strain of religion had not quite faded out; the Sabbath began on Saturday evening at sunset and ended at dusk on Sunday, when the freedom of week-day activities began, except as to the theatres, which, though tolerated, were not considered good-form.

There was no prohibition noticeable in Hartford then, for it would have had hard work to compete with the rum from Barbadoes and the fine wine from Madeira. Lotteries still were popular and respectable and were legalized by charter. Money being scarce, a dollar was venerated and a penny treated with respect, and not permitted to wander far away unnoticed; but, perhaps partly because of this, the people were in the main scrupulously honest and strict in money matters, and debt was considered a reprehensible thing.

The newspapers in Hartford at this period devoted most of their space to news from London and foreign countries, extracts from other papers, and little essays on morals, public and private, on economy, industry and other virtues. There was little or no local news, perhaps because in a small town every one might be supposed to know the news anyhow. Such items as are today considered of personal, social or business interest, were then paid for and appeared in the advertising columns.

One of the real institutions of the time was the coffee house. It was the club of the period; a place for business and sociability, one where public problems and grievances were discussed freely, and where plans for progressive movements, civic and commercial, could be made in an atmosphere conducive to clear thinking and free expression. One of the most popular of these houses was Morgan's Exchange Coffee House, 33-35 State Street, where the post-horses of the stages were changed.

Morgan's was a centre of social activities too; for here was held, among other "functions," the annual "election ball," where dancing kept up to an early hour and the receipts for liquid refreshment mounted high. On the third floor was the dancing hall, with a special "spring floor," and recessed seats where the beaux and belles could say sweet things to their hearts' content. The splendors of the room were enhanced by heavy hangings at the windows, and a large oval gilt-framed 'mirror at each end of the room. There was a generous space for the musicians, while overhead were three chandeliers, with crystal pendants, appropriately holding numberless wax candles.

Joseph Morgan, the proprietor, was one of the important men of the town; a man of high character, keen mind and energy, and a genius for finance which he handed down to his son, Junius Spencer Morgan, the great London banker, and to his grandson, the famous J. Pierpont Morgan. Joseph was of the third generation from Miles Morgan, who, with his two brothers, James and John, came to America from Wales in 1607. Miles settled in Springfield, Mass., in 1636, and had four sons, Isaac, Jonathan, Nathaniel and David. Nathaniel died in 1773, survived by eight children, one of whom was Joseph, the father of Joseph of Hartford, who was born in North Parish, West Springfield, on January 4, 1780. He spent his early years on the home farm, and in teaching school for several winters after his fifteenth year. In 1807 he married Sally Spencer and in the same year purchased for ten thousand dollars Asa Goodenough's coach line and tavern on the west side of the green in Westfield, Mass., and started in the hotel business there. Six years later, on the death of his father, he was left in possession of a farm of 112 acres and other property worth eleven thousand dollars.

In November 1816, Morgan bought a brick house and a barn on the north side of State Street in Hartford, and on New Year's Day of the year following he opened in this house what came to be known as Morgan's Exchange Coffee House, and the birthplace of a great American institution.

Chapter III

STARTING A GREAT ENTERPRISE

IN the early days of 1819, there was a subject of spirited discussion at Morgan's Coffee House, among a few of the merchants and business men of Hartford, that seemed but a trifle of irritation at the beginning, but, fanned by heated protest, burst into a flame of revolt. The first Secretary of the Hartford Fire Insurance Company was Walter Mitchell, the uncle of Donald G. Mitchell of New Haven, the beloved "Ik Marvel" of American literature. Walter Mitchell was a handsome looking gentleman with a head like that of Daniel Webster. He was one of the legal lights of the town and lived in Wethersfield, a village three or four miles out of Hartford. Those who wanted to take out a policy had to seek Mr. Mitchell and at whatever hour best suited his convenience. He had a habit of closing his office at three or four in the afternoons and on Saturdays at noon. He did not count time or appointments as serious and had a way, too, of putting off till tomorrow what might be done today.

The trip out to Wethersfield along a clayey road, sometimes swamped by rains or rutted by drought, was an exasperating journey at the best, and many citizens of Hartford made this trip when unable to find Mitchell at his little office near Ransom's Inn, close to the present site of the Hartford *Courant* building. Merchants or business men who wanted insurance did not relish the "Gone for the day" sign that greeted their eyes so often on the door of his office. They pooled their discontent in a general protest and they felt that something radical must be done to mend matters.

The leader and moving spirit in the revolt was Thomas K. Brace, who proposed the organization of a new fire insurance company. Brace knew something of the business, for he had been a director of the Hartford Fire Insurance Company when it was organized in 1810, and had left the directorate in 1817 with David Watkinson and Ward Woodbridge. He was the son of Jonathan Brace, Mayor of Hartford from 1815 to 1824 and was graduated from Yale College in 1801 at the age of twenty-two. He was now the head of the wholesale grocery and commission firm of Thomas K. Brace & Co., who were also agents for a line of packets plying between Hartford and Boston. This packet line was established immediately after the war of 1812 and consisted of five topsail schooners used for carrying freight and passengers, said to be very handsome boats and specially fine in their furnishings and equipment.

Mr. Brace was described as having rather thin features, high forehead and firm mouth which showed him to be keen, energetic and aggressive, with the courage of his convictions, an excellent executive and the type of man that puts things through. He was a firm believer in Hartford and its future and ever backed his faith by his actions. Prominent as a merchant, there were few vital activities in the town in which his hand as organizer or director did not appear. He was one of the founders of the Society of Savings, incorporated in 1819, and also interested in the promotion of the American Asylum for the Deaf and Dumb and the Retreat for the Insane.

Mr. Brace's regular business did not so absorb his boundless energy that he could not at the same time be a Director and Vice-president of the Phœnix Bank, a member of the Common Council, Justice of the Peace, Director of the United States Branch Bank, a Member of the Committee to Abate Taxes and a few other things. In after years he also served in the Connecticut Legislature, as Mayor of Hartford and as President of the Hartford County Savings Bank.

When a man like Thomas K. Brace decided that he wanted to organize a new insurance company, it was a safe wager that he would put it through. He associated with him, in the preliminary work of the practical details, Isaac Perkins, a lawyer who had his office in Morgan's Exchange Coffee House. Perkins seems to have been an active, dependable, hustling kind of man, with a large acquaintance and a habit of making good in whatever he undertook. There were frequent meetings at Morgan's between these two and other prominent men of the town who were

 STARTING A GREAT ENTERPRISE

interested, and they finally petitioned the Legislature for a charter.

The movement for a new fire insurance company was not limited to a few people, nor is it wholly fair to say that the cause of the organization was the Mitchell episode we have cited; it may have been merely a talking point to focus a general, diffused consciousness of a real need. This seems to be proved by the wording of the original petition, which, because of the clearness of its presentation, its conciseness and the occasional quaintness of its phrasing, is worth quoting in full:

TO THE HONB. GENERAL ASSEMBLY OF THE STATE OF CONNECTICUT, to be holden at Hartford on the first Wednesday of May, A. D. 1819, the subscribers, inhabitants of said State, respectfully represent — that there is a great deficiency of Fire Insurance Capital in this State, there being but four offices and the whole amount of their capital but six hundred thousand dollars. It is also believed that an increase of capital would tend but little to render the public safe without an increased number of offices; and it has ever been found expedient, if not necessary, to the establishment of proper premiums, to allow Insurance Offices to take risques to any amount, whilst the stockholders are rendered liable only to the amount of their capital. From this principle results the necessity, for the safety of the assured, of multiplying the number of incorporations. Risques will be effected in smaller amounts, and the customers of each office being spread over the whole state, losses by an extensive fire, in any section, will fall on several offices and be less likely to render them unable to pay to the sufferers the amount of their policies.

It is presumed that each of the existing offices have undertaken risques to an amount greater than the capital of them all, and should a conflagration take place, in some of our towns, as disastrous as has been experienced in many places, it is greatly to be feared many of the sufferers would too late discover their insecurity. It is also a well known fact that the Insurance Offices in the neighboring states, sensible of the deficiency of our

ONE HUNDRED YEARS OF FIRE INSURANCE

Capital of this kind, not only maintain agents in many of our towns, but are enabled, so great are the calls for insurance, to render the business equally profitable with those companies which have been empowered by your Honors — Wherefore your Petitioners pray your Honors to grant to them and their associates an Act of Incorporation, with all powers and privileges necessary and convenient to the business of insurance against losses by Fire, — and your Petitioners as in duty bound will ever pray.

Hartford, April 19, 1819.

This petition was signed by one hundred and thirty-seven men, leaders in the business and social life of the town, and included in this list were the names of nearly every one of the eighty-seven original stockholders of the new company. (See Appendix.)

The first sign of life in the Legislature on the subject of the incorporation was an obscure item, stowed away in the Hartford *Courant* of May 18, 1819, in a long dry account of the session, to the effect that "Messrs. Olcott, Hitchcock and Griffin were appointed a committee on the petition for a new Fire Insurance Company in this city." On June 8, the *Courant* stated that "A bill for incorporating a new Fire Insurance Company in this city, was read a second time and referred to a committee for examination." A little further down in the same column were the words: "The following acts were passed during the session on June 5: No. 38 — An act to incorporate the Ætna Insurance Company."

The name of the new corporation, for some reason not given in the petition, was, as set forth in the title of the act, to be the Ætna, happily taken from the famous old mountain of that name on the east coast

STARTING A GREAT ENTERPRISE

of Sicily, which "though surrounded by flame and smoke is itself never consumed."

In this modest and unostentatious fashion was ushered into American life, an organization which was to write its name large in the insurance world during the circling years to come. The capital stock was placed at $150,000 with the privilege of increasing to $500,000. It was not necessary for the full amount of the minimum capital, though subscribed, to be paid in at once. Custom, at first due to the small amount of money circulating because of the poverty of the country, made it possible to float new ventures on a small initial investment, to be paid a few weeks after incorporation, leaving the balance in the form of notes properly secured by property. Sometimes these notes bore interest, sometimes they were paid directly, but usually they were lessened and finally canceled by special dividends. But the notes always had the guarantee behind them that made them collectible and safe in a crisis.

Subscribers to the Ætna stock were required to pay five per cent. within thirty days after the first meeting of the corporation; five per cent. more thirty days later; and the remaining ninety per cent. in promissory notes, secured by mortgages on real estate or by other surety approved by the President and the Directors, and payable thirty days after demand. Each stockholder was entitled to one vote for every share up to fifty, and had no higher voting power no matter what his holdings. Both corporate and personal liability were limited to the amount of the subscription. It was further stated that "for misconduct or fraud, the person guilty thereof shall be personally liable to said corporation, or to the insured, as the case may be."

In the issues of June 8th and 15th, the following advertisement appeared in the *Courant:*

>The General Assembly of the State of Connecticut, having incorporated the Ætna Insurance Company with a capital of $150,000 with liberty to increase the same to $500,000, for the purpose of insuring against loss or damage by fire, and having authorized the subscriber to call the First Meeting of the Company, Notice is hereby given that said First Meeting will be holden at Morgan's Exchange Coffee House in this city of Hartford, on Tuesday the 15th inst., at 2 o'clock p. m., for the purpose of organizing under the charter and to transact other necessary business.
>
>Gentlemen desirous of obtaining stock are requested to apply at the office of Isaac Perkins, Esq.
>
>June 8.   Thomas K. Brace.

On Tuesday the 15th of June, 1819, one of the large rooms at Morgan's was filled with the stockholders of the new Company. How many of the eighty-seven who made up the roll of the original stockholders were present is not given in the records. Promptly at two o'clock the first meeting was called to order, and Mr. Brace was appointed Moderator, or as we term it today, Chairman, and Isaac Perkins was made Clerk.

In a few earnest words Chairman Brace sketched the conditions that had led to the organizing of the Company, and spoke of its future. He believed in the future of Hartford, in the splendid body of stockholders present at this launching of the new business; the country itself was growing rapidly, and national growth meant increase in population and in wealth, a larger field for greater needs. Fire insurance was a real need; they had part of the increasing business in Hartford as their possibility, but there was no reason why it should be limited to Hartford or even to Connecticut; it could spread into other States. This would mean broadened business and a safe distribution of risks. Fire insurance, he felt, was in its infancy; there was much to be learned, much to be formulated and reduced to system; and it was his sincere belief that the company would do its part in this work.

Mr. Brace also emphasized the fact that the business had its special hazards, but, while the risks were large, the success could be correspondingly great; few lines of enterprise were so absolutely dependent on the character, energy, enterprise and tireless devotion of its officers as a company engaged in fire insurance, and he urged those present earnestly to consider this in electing their Board of Directors. The business should be handled with conservatism yet in a spirit of progress, with economy, with liberal faith toward those insured, with strict adherence to broad fundamentals of principle, an avoidance of conflict that might reflect on the honor and prestige of the company, and fine co-operation within the organization that would guarantee success.

His straight-from-the-shoulder talk seemed a foreshadowing of the great future of the Company. It was the right note, and it won instant response in the election of the first Board of Directors. Those chosen were: Thomas K. Brace, Thomas Belden, Samuel

Tudor, Jr., Henry Kilbourn, Eliphalet Averill, Henry Seymour, Griffin Stedman, Gaius Lyman, Judah Bliss, Caleb Pond, Nathaniel Bunce, Joseph Morgan, Jeremiah Brown, James M. Goodwin, Theodore Pease, Elisha Dodd and Charles Babcock.

An account of the first meeting of the new directors, which immediately followed that of the stockholders, can best be given in the report of Secretary Perkins, as entered by him in the original Record Book, which is still carefully preserved in the vaults of the Company:

At a meeting of the Directors of the Ætna Insurance Co. at Morgan's Coffee House, June 15, A. D., 1819.
Thomas K. Brace, Esq., chosen President.
Isaac Perkins, Secretary.
VOTED: That the business of the Co. shall in future be done at the office of Isaac Perkins, Esq.
VOTED: That Eliphalet Averill, Thomas K. Brace & Isaac Perkins, Esq., be a committee to design & report to some future meeting of the board an engraving, a seal & a form of Policy, stock notes, certificates, etc., & a system of By-Laws.
VOTED: That the two first installments on the Stock of the Company be secured by notes with or without security.
VOTED: That the form of notes shall be similar to the notes of the Hartford Fire Insurance Office.
VOTED: That the business of the Office shall be done at the Phœnix Bank.
Attest:
Isaac Perkins, Secy.

President Brace was right in emphasizing the importance of having the best men for this work. That they should be men of character and integrity goes without saying; but in addition it was essential, he felt, that they have energy, sound business judgment and devotion. Upon them devolved the task of the determination of all risks in those early days when

At a meeting of the Petitioners praying for an Act of Incorporation to insure against loss or damage by fire owned by Thomas K. Brace Esqr & others at Morgans Coffee House in the City of Hartford on the 15th day of June 1819 agreeable to the 13 Sec. of the Charter Granted on the prayer of said Petition

Thomas K. Brace Esqr. Chairman

Isaac Perkins Clerk

The amount of stock required by said Charter having been taken up, the meeting proceeded to the choice of officers when the the following Gentlemen were chosen by the members to be duly chosen Directors for the year ensuing.

Viz Thomas K. Brace
Thomas Belden
Samuel Tudor jun'r
Henry Hudson
Charles Boswell
Henry Seymour
Charles Sigourney
Chas Lyman
Josiah Bliss
Caleb Pond
Nathaniel Bunce
Joseph Morgan
Jeremiah Brown
James M Goodwin
Edward Pease
Elisha Dodd
Charles Babcock Esquires

Meeting adjourned without day

Attest Isaac Perkins CP

ORIGINAL ENTRY IN OFFICIAL RECORD BOOK GIVING ACCOUNT OF FIRST MEETING OF INCORPORATORS OF THE ÆTNA INSURANCE COMPANY ON JUNE 15, 1819

fire insurance was largely guessing, for there were neither statistics nor precedents of value. A few blunders might readily have wrecked the Company in the period of its infancy; they had to make their decisions on sound principle rather than on formulated rules. A brief glance at the record of the personnel of the Board is therefore of interest. They were all prominent business men who were identified with the civic, business and financial institutions of Hartford.

Thomas Belden was a merchant and one of the directors of the first Board of the Farmers and Mechanics Bank of Hartford.

Samuel Tudor, Jr., wholesale drygoods dealer, and director and an organizer of the Phœnix Bank.

Henry Kilbourn, merchant, inspector of roads, captain of a Hartford engine company, member of the Connecticut General Assembly, director of Marine Insurance Company and of the Hartford Bank.

Eliphalet Averill, merchant, member of the Fire Sack Company, organized in 1818 for the purpose of taking charge of goods at fires, director of the Phœnix Bank and of the Farmers and Mechanics Bank.

Henry Seymour, merchant, justice of the peace, city alderman and member of the General Assembly of the State.

Griffin Stedman, lumber merchant and director of the Phœnix Bank.

Gaius Lyman, lumber merchant and city alderman.

Judah Bliss, physician.

Caleb Pond, stock and exchange broker, member of the Common Council and of the Fire Sack Co.

 ONE HUNDRED YEARS OF FIRE INSURANCE

Nathaniel Bunce, dealer in West Indian goods and groceries.

Jeremiah Brown, wholesale grocer and dealer in West Indian goods, director of the Phœnix Bank and of the Hartford Marine Insurance Company.

James M. Goodwin, wholesale grocer, who later became secretary of the Ætna.

Charles Babcock, publisher of the Hartford *Mercury* and a member of the Common Council.

Elisha Dodd, dry-goods merchant, active in local affairs as auditor of accounts, rate maker, and a member of the committee to abate taxes.

Major Theodore Pease, a leading merchant, died in August, 1819, before the Ætna actually began business.

Ten days after the first Directors' meeting, the by-laws of the Company were adopted and the committee submitted a design for an official seal. This device, with minor changes during a century of use, has become familiar to countless thousands in every State of the Union. An excellent description of the seal, with an enthusiastic and appreciative interpretation of its symbolism, was given in 1911 by the "Insurance Index":

The insignia of the Ætna Insurance Company, of Hartford, Conn., is a composite, representing strength, energy, defence, perpetuity, justice, protection, safety, security and progress in fire insurance underwriting.

The sun stands for strength, physical and thermal. He is the conserver, maintainer and underwriter of all things visible, but not the creator. Like the Ætna, he shines for all. He is the master clock of the universe, and without him nothing that is could exist.

The burning mountain is Mount Ætna — at once a type of

safety and combustion. It is one of the safety valves of the earth; a natural chimney which carries off the gases generated by subterranean caloric.

The sea is the Mediterranean, which knows no tide, and therefore, like the Ætna, has no ups and downs.

The shield is the shield of Agamemnon with its gules argent on a white field, which denotes singleness of purpose, dignity and derring-do, graces which add lustre and glory to their possessor. The shield is also an emblem of defense, not defiance, and of protection, vital and instant when needed.

The sword means that the Ætna can not only defend itself against the total depravity of inanimate things, but that sword and shield constitute a combination of invincible protection. The fact that the sword is unsheathed assures the thousands insured by the company that the Ætna is always ready to defend and protect their interests from destruction by the common enemy.

The two rings mean perpetuity in fire and marine insurance. The Ætna's chain is perpetual as to both of these lines. The rings, therefore, symbolize an all-round institution, compact and cohesive, gathering strength with the circling years, and of that infinite variety which age cannot wither nor custom stale.

With the adoption of the by-laws and the acceptance of the seal, the Ætna was now ready to start on the career that has been so successful and so important in the general history of fire insurance.

Chapter IV

BUILDING FOR THE FUTURE

IN the little office of Secretary Perkins, with its walls well covered with shelves of law-books, reports and dusty pamphlets, the Ætna Insurance Company began business in what was destined to be its home for many years. There was no expenditure for fine furnishings and extras. It was like taking desk-room in an office already in operation, where things are to be accepted as they are without any radical change. The secretary simply cleared up the top of his desk a little, emptied two drawers for Ætna papers and records, and was ready for work.

When the Board had its first meeting there, ten days after its organization, the first business to dispose of was the adoption of by-laws. In order to divide and distribute the work among the directors, they were arranged in four groups of four each; each group was to be on duty for one month at a time. This meant real service too, for the director in those days had a man-sized job on his hands. He had to examine and survey all local risks, pass upon all applications sent in by the various agents, visit and examine agencies, attend the scenes of fires and adjust losses; in short, the early fire insurance company director was a composite of the director, surveyor, examiner, auditor, investigator, adjuster and special agent of today. At this meeting, also, the Directors adopted as a form of policy the form then used by the Merchants Insurance Company of New York, with such additions or changes as might be deemed expedient.

In the *Courant* of June 22 appeared the following notice to stock subscribers:

ÆTNA INSURANCE COMPANY

The stockholders in the Ætna Insurance Company are notified that the 1st installment of $5.00 on a share of said stock is payable on Thursday, July 15th, at which time or before, gentlemen are requested to offer security for the other installments of said stock, agreeable to the provisions of the charter.

Hartford, June 20, 1819.   Isaac Perkins, Sec'y.

This money was not permitted long to remain idle, for on the same day that the first installment was due the Company voted to make its first investment in twenty shares of the stock of the Connecticut Branch of the United States Bank, which was then located at Middletown but which, in 1824, moved to Hartford. This investment, a little less than $2,000, was quickly followed by the purchase of twenty-nine shares of the stock of the Phœnix Bank of Hartford. This institution was the official depository of the funds of the Ætna. The two companies had many directors in common, and for the century that followed the cordial relations between the two corporations were unbroken.

The call for the second installment of five per cent., due August 15th, was advertised in the *Courant* of July 26, and in the same issue appeared the first advertisement of the Company soliciting business. It was three-quarters of a column in length, enumerated the different classes of hazards, names of officers and directors, and rates of premiums, with the announcement that the company would be open for business on August 19th and every day thereafter except Sunday. Applicants for insurance were directed to apply at Morgan's Exchange Coffee House. This advertisement continued through successive issues for some time.

Secretary Perkins' heart was cheered at this time by the vote of the Directors that signers of notes for stock "shall pay to the Secretary fifty cents for his extra trouble if they fail to pay their notes when due," and two weeks later he was voted sixty dollars for his preliminary work in the organization of the Company. On the 14th of August, on the death of Major Theodore Pease, one of the directors, Henry L. Ellsworth was elected to fill the vacancy.

Though the Company had advertised August 19th as the date upon which it would be ready to transact business, Joseph Morgan forestalled the opening by two days by taking out the first policy, one for $6,000 on his Coffee House, and paid the premium of forty-five dollars. It seemed a happy omen that the first business should come from one who was to remain for so long a devoted friend of the Company and worker in its interests, and the first member of four generations of Morgans serving as directors. The next three insurers were Frederick Bangs on August 20th and Samuel Kellogg, Jr., and Thomas S. Williams on the day following. So the wheels of business began to

REPRODUCTION OF THE ÆTNA'S FIRST NEWSPAPER
ADVERTISEMENT ON JULY 26, 1819

turn in the direction of its future great success, then unknown in the keeping of the years.

The country at this time began to feel acutely the pressure of bad times which had been growing worse for months. It was to a degree a back-wash from the money tightness in England and to a degree the extravagance and inflation in our own States. Niles' *Weekly Register*, in August, 1819, put the situation graphically in a few words:

> From all parts of the country we hear of severe pressure on men in business, a general stagnation in trade and a large reduction in the price of staple articles. It is estimated that there are 20,000 persons daily seeking work in Philadelphia, 10,000 in New York and 10,000 in Baltimore.

How these conditions directly affected the Ætna may be seen in this brief note:

ISAAC PERKINS, Secretary of the   HARTFORD, Sept. 27, 1819.
Ætna Insurance Company.
    Sir: In consequence of my pecuniary embarrassments I hereby resign the Presidency of your Institution. You will please notify the Gentlemen Directors that the office is vacant.
    I am sir, respectfully
        Your obd't Sev't,
           THOMAS K. BRACE.

There was more real feeling beneath these few lines, short and direct almost to the point of curtness, than was apparent on the surface. Mr. Brace, as a wholesale grocer and dealer in goods from the West Indies, had suffered severely the embargo on commerce during the years of the war of 1812. The shipping of New England, then demoralized, was only beginning to recuperate; but with the storm of "bad times," in addition, he felt fearful of the outcome. The Ætna meant much to him, more than a mere investment; it was largely his project and his idea, and he had dreamed in a big way of its future. Whatever the fate of his personal fortunes, he did not wish any failure of his to cloud the name of the Ætna or to handicap its progress. So he resigned, but happily he weathered the gale, and, though out of the Presidency of the Company for a while, he returned later, so that his interim of retirement seemed only a vacation, not a breaking off in the continuity of his service.

Henry Leavitt Ellsworth was elected second president of the Company to succeed Mr. Brace. He was a son of Oliver Ellsworth, Chief Justice of the United States Supreme Court, and twin brother of William W., and was born on November 10, 1791. He was graduated at Yale in 1810. He studied law and had been practicing his profession at Windsor, Connecticut, closing out his business there to move to Hartford in June, 1819, and had been in town only about three months before becoming president of the Ætna.

President Ellsworth wore the regulation dress of the period, which is worth noting as contrasted with our present more sombre garb. His black broadcloth "cutaway" coat was somewhat similar to our "evening coat" though not so close fitting; white lace ruffles for cuffs — a survival of the colonial dress; green waistcoat, soft ruffled shirt, a high collar which came up well above the chin, and loosely-tied black bow tie, made up his costume, and he wore a heavy seal ring and seal watch fob.

President Ellsworth resigned from his office in 1821, though he continued for sixteen years a director of the Company. In 1832 he went to Arkansas as Indian Commissioner, for ten years was head of the Patent Office at Washington, and later, as United States Land Commissioner, settled at Lafayette, Indiana, where he became one of the largest farmers in the West. He died at Fair Haven, Connecticut, on December 27, 1858, leaving the bulk of his large estate to Yale College; the will was contested and the matter ended in a compromise.

William W. Ellsworth, the twin brother, practiced law in partnership with Thomas S. Williams, who was a nephew of one of the signers of the Declaration of Independence, and who became attorney for the Ætna in 1826. Mr. Ellsworth married Emily, daughter of Noah Webster, who in 1828 published the first edition of his world-famous dictionary. In 1827 Mr. Ellsworth was made a Director of the Company, serving for eighteen years, and two years later was elected its first General Counsel. He held this position for a little over a year and from 1838 to 1842 was Whig Governor of Connecticut.

In the fall of its first year, the Company issued a booklet entitled "Instructions and Explanations for the Use and Direction of the Agents of the Ætna Insurance Company." It was prepared by Secretary Perkins, and the idea that inspired it was later adopted by other companies. It was the first book of the kind ever published by an insurance company. The *Insurance Register*, nearly a century later, said:

> As far back as September, 1819, the Company issued a book of instructions for the use of its agents; classifying risks, fixing

the rate of each, and excluding some as non-insurable. It insisted on correct surveys as serving to expose frauds, prevent law suits and secure truthfulness. Buildings and fixtures were not to be estimated above their actual cash value, and any proposal for more was of itself a cause of suspicion; the rule, however, was not to be enforced against merchandise and other personal property liable to vary in kind and quantity. The insured was entitled to no more than the value of the property proved to have been destroyed. It is interesting to observe that the correctness of the rules appearing on the pages of this little book — (believed to be the oldest of its kind in the country) — has never been successfully assailed, though attempts for the encouragement of robbery have been made through valued policy laws and other vain schemes.

The Ætna early pinned its faith to the building of business through agents. It was realized at the very beginning that the local field, shared as it was with another company, would be small, and that it would be essential to stimulate outside business through carefully selected agents. In the latter part of the year Gurdon Robins of Fayetteville, North Carolina, and a former resident of Hartford, was appointed the first agent in the South.

In October, 1819, the Ætna assumed all outstanding risks of the Middletown Fire Insurance Company, founded in 1813. These risks, aggregating $69,500, consisted of twenty-one policies. The Ætna put up an indemnity bond for $200,000 and received a total premium of $286. This was the first known case of re-insurance, which has now reached tremendous proportions and has become a business in itself.

In the evolution of re-insurance the phase where one company took over all the risks of another corporation was followed by a division of individual risks, wherein a company assuming a risk higher than it seemed prudent to carry, re-insured part of it in some other company. A germ of this later development in the system of re-insurance may be found in an instance which occurred in 1821, when the Ætna received an application for a policy for $15,000; the Directors decided that this was more than they were willing to carry, so the secretary put the matter before the Hartford Fire Insurance Company and it was arranged that each company should take half of the $15,000 risk. This, of course, was not re-insurance, but it was a groping in that direction.

In October, 1819, there appeared in the *Courant* a letter signed "Watchman," calling attention to a recent fire and saying: "This suggests very forcibly the necessity as well as the propriety of a night watch. Seasonable attention to this subject is of the utmost importance to the welfare of this place. The expense of it is too trifling to defeat so prudent a measure." This matter seems to have been taken up by the city authorities, for on December 12, the Board of Directors of the Ætna voted to pay $12 to the night wardens of Hartford for defraying the expenses of the night watch of the city for the ensuing year.

The event seems trivial, yet it was important as showing the dawning of recognition by fire insurance companies of the need of preventive measures to safeguard against fires occurring at all, just as modern medical practice seeks not only to cure disease but by proper regulation and hygiene to prevent it. Whatever reduces the liability of fire occurring, or lessens its spread, or quickens putting it out, increases protection to all risks and lowers premium rates; but greater than all, it is an invaluable service to the community in the preservation of life and property.

It was perhaps with this thought in mind, that Secretary Perkins wrote to an agent at Troy, N. Y., in 1820, concerning the rate of premium on a cotton mill, stating that if the owners kept a night watchman on the premises the premium would be one-half of one per cent. lower. On March 5, 1827, the Board voted "that in consideration of an agent's service in securing a fire engine for Newcastle, he be allowed, in addition to his regular 5% commission on premiums, 3% commission on the business he secures during the ensuing year."

About this time and later the Company had frequent calls to contribute to a fund, in one town after another, to buy hose, or an engine, or some other item of fire paraphernalia. An occasional contribution as a gift might be pardoned, but when requests came thicker and faster and the request had somehow the atmosphere of a demand, the Company began to chafe under the obnoxious system and finally shut down tight on the whole scheme. They rightly held that the fire department of a town is essentially a public service for the good of all and one to be sustained by the town itself. All these reachings out to better conditions have since been largely stimulated by the work of local boards and the activities of the National Board of Fire Underwriters.

When, on December 15, 1819, the Ætna closed the books on its first six months of life, though only

BUILDING FOR THE FUTURE

its fourth of actual business, the directors felt that the excess of receipts over expenses justified them in declaring a dividend of $900, this being six per cent. on the $15,000. When a balance was struck on May 31, 1820, the total receipts were $3,646.42, and the total expenditures, exclusive of dividend, were $451.82. They paid no enormous salaries in those days, for Secretary Perkins, who seemed to be the general active mainspring of the business, received only $225 for his six months of service and the rent of his office. The President of the Company received no pay whatever. Ezra Colt, the Town Clerk, probably felt that the $20 voted to him for recording the charter, opening the stock-ledger and for *et ceteras* that ran into considerable detail, was a goodly sum to get all at once.

Business was conducted in those days in what would seem a crude, slow, primitive way. The letters were all carefully written out with a quill pen and then transcribed in one of the old letter-books, not by a "process" but again by pen. These books, jealously treasured by the Company, are growing yellow at the edges of the pages, and the writing is gradually growing fainter and more difficult to decipher in places. The handwriting was not always of the best, and this further complicated correspondence, as one may judge from a letter written by Secretary Perkins to an agent in which he said:

I notice the contents of your favor of the 23rd inst. The name of our President is Thomas Kimberly Brace. You will from his name thus written at length understand his abbreviations. It has sometimes been made a question of our Board of Directors which writes worst — mark, *worst*, not best — and they have with great judgment, and seriously, decided that as the President never makes any marks found in the Alphabet, he can never mislead, but that as the Secy., by accident, sometimes does — the President does not write *best*, but the Secretary does write *worst*.

In the early correspondence there were constant references to the difficulty of sending packages of policies to agents at a distance. These were nearly always sent by "private conveyance" and had to be held up until some one was found who chanced to be traveling in the direction of the agent's town. In a letter to Gurdon Robins of Fayetteville, North Carolina, Secretary Perkins wrote on February 5, 1820:

> I have anxiously looked for an opportunity to remit more blank policies. As no opportunity direct presents, I propose to send some by way of New York and Wilmington, if you can obtain them from Wilmington, and will direct to whose care they shall be sent.

The postal rates were high and the service unsatisfactory. The charge ran from twelve cents for letters within a radius of forty miles, up to thirty-seven and one-half cents for over five hundred miles. Early agents were remiss in the matter of specifying amounts on buildings and contents and failed to supply other details. This necessitated more correspondence and long irritating delay. There was not a single mile of railroad in the United States, and travel was by stage-coach or by boat; which may have romance to us as a relic of bygone days, but then meant discomfort and slow journeying.

There was no fine, steel safe in the office of the Ætna, for the records were all kept in an old, hair-covered trunk which remained the "safe" for the first nine years of the Company's business. On January 1, 1828, the Board of Directors, waking up to the need of fire protection for their own records, voted "that hereafter the small trunk containing the stock securities and notes belonging to the Company be kept in the Phœnix Bank and in no case be permitted to remain in the office over-night." These were some of the smaller, though none the less trying, phases of conducting the business during its early years.

The Board of Directors was proceeding most conservatively, taking no unnecessary or unsafe hazards in its policies nor in the expenditures and in the general conduct of the Company. While rates of premiums were specified in the policy, agents were instructed to vary rates according to location or character of construction, and largely to use their own discretion. At the same time they were instructed to send a complete survey of each proposed risk, on which the Ætna directors passed. The limit of risk to agents was $5,000. In February, 1820, the Board voted that the Company would not insure any amount exceeding $10,000 on any single risk, other than for policies already issued, "except by unanimous vote of the Board, and for this purpose a quorum shall not be less than nine."

It was characteristic of Perkins to write good "selling" letters to the agents; he kept in close personal touch with them, dropping in a word of encouragement here or of inspiration or counsel there, ever emphasizing the basic principles and policies of the company, advising in favor of distributing risks and of watching the character of applicants for insurance, booming the standing of the officers of the Company and the soundness, safeness and solidity of the Ætna. There was a fine spirit breathed through it all, and he never lost an opportunity to make his own confidence and enthusiasm contagious.

On May 5, 1820, the Board voted to petition the General Assembly for a charter amendment to permit the writing of life insurance, and on May 26 this was granted. Though the Board voted to issue $50,000 additional stock to be set aside as a separate fund for life insurance, no further action was taken in this direction until the middle of the century. The second dividend, 12 per cent. on the amount paid in, was voted June, 1820, and six months later the third dividend, of 15 per cent., was declared. In September of this year, Secretary Perkins, who had now been made a member of the Board, fell dangerously ill with typhoid fever, and James M. Goodwin, a director, acted for some weeks as secretary pro tem.

A long letter written in November, 1820, by the Secretary, to an agent, contains two or three sentences worth quoting, as showing the principles and practices of the Company:

> The Ætna Company do indeed consider the practice of older and well regulated companies and endeavor to derive instructions from their greater experience. The Board of Directors disclaim all interference with other companies, or underbidding upon their premiums. A fair competition is all we aim at, and rely on our economy, prudence and liberality for success.

Further on in the same letter he states that the Board of Directors consists of seventeen members,

HENRY L. ELLSWORTH
1819 · PRESIDENT · 1821

most of them from among the largest stockholders, all within a few minutes' walk of the office, and whose attention to the business is assiduous. One of the important regulations, he says, is "refusing to vest the funds of the company in large sums in the hands of individuals, however perfect the security, or in small sums except on ample security, and payable in sixty days. It is also a primary consideration with them to distribute their risks in such a manner that any single fire, though extensive as any that has desolated our cities, would not destroy the Company."

As to the financial solidity of the corporation, he says: "The capital stock of the Ætna Insurance Company is $150,000, of which 90 per cent. is secured by notes, with mortgage or personal security, payable in thirty days after demand, and by the terms of our charter the stock is pledged to the surety and to the Company. No person, therefore, can transfer his stock while indebted to the Company. These notes are constantly under the eye of the Secretary and are reviewed by the Directors every sixty days. There is now not a doubted debtor to the Company. With the exception of one instance there is not a stockholder that owns over fifty shares (shares are $100)."

The Board, at all times, carefully scrutinized all risks and watched zealously every expenditure. The success of the Company was not due to luck or chance; it was the natural result of character and brains concentrated on every problem, judging each, not by hard, unchangeable rules, but on its individual merits. This was shown when in May, 1821, the agent at

ONE HUNDRED YEARS OF FIRE INSURANCE

Providence made application for a policy for $17,000. There was a buzz of excitement and an air of earnest discussion and debate round the Directors' table the day that application was before the meeting. It did seem like putting a good many eggs in one basket, but much could be said, too, on the other side of the question. The matter was threshed out to a finish; the Board finally decided to take the plunge into higher risks, and the nine Directors, to a man, voted in favor of it.

President Ellsworth, who could not spare as much time from his personal affairs as the demands of the Ætna required, and who may have felt his presidency as an interim-filling of a vacancy caused by the business pressure on Thomas K. Brace, resigned on March 6, 1821, and Mr. Brace, who had come bravely through the national financial storm, was re-elected President. He seemed really glad to be back in the harness; he started in with the glow of enthusiasm, and spoke much of the glorious future in store for the Company. The Directors felt that the foundations had been laid on the lines of solid, true principles, that real progress was now to begin, and that they were all prepared to work with zeal to make their great vision a reality.

CHAPTER V

THE ÆTNA BEGINS TO SPREAD

IT really seems at times that just when we are feeling elated and grateful that things are running along so smoothly we bump into some little snag that disconcerts us a bit. It may not amount to much after all, but it serves to remind us that we are human and that sunshine is transitory, not perpetual. Thus it was with the Ætna. The Company, which was now twenty-three months old, seemed to have led a charmed life in its immunity from losses; it seemed too good to be true; it was like running a fire-proof fire insurance business. Secretary Perkins rubbed his hands together with glee when he wrote on March 17, 1821, to one of the agents: "Truly you may say the Company is prosperous. It is two years next May since they were chartered, and no loss of any kind, except a two-dollar counterfeit bill, has occurred."

Whether it was that Perkins' premature joy broke the spell, or that a fire was bound to take place some time, will never be definitely known, but the two years were destined not to be completed. The first fire loss occurred in May, 1821. It was on the store of

Shepherd & Co. of Northfield, Massachusetts. The amount was $4,000, but Perkins faced disaster as smilingly as he had met prosperity, for he referred to the mishap with airy nonchalance in a letter in which he said: "Four thousand dollars loss is no great affair, nor in fact is it any more loss than the lava of Ætna is when it runs down upon the shepherds." This was the greatest loss until 1824, when $10,000 was paid on the burning of a steam sawmill at Darien, Georgia. The year following saw two fires in Providence in November, which consumed over $15,000 of the Company's money.

The Ætna, while having strong confidence in the power of agents to build up the business, did not scorn the power of printer's ink. Agents were permitted to advertise at their discretion and the Company paid the bills. The agents were urged to be as liberal as possible to all insurers and to endorse permission to them to do certain things not specified in the contract, wherever they seemed reasonable and when consistent with the spirit and purpose of the policy.

New inventions, relating to lighting and heating, might affect policies for better or worse, and the Ætna Directors felt they should be consulted if the innovation modified the contract in the least. In 1826 kerosene was first used as an illuminant; the year following the manufacture of fire brick was begun at Baltimore; and in 1829 friction matches were first used — all elements in considering risks.

As an instance of the modifying of a policy, it might be that a progressive tenant or owner had

THE ÆTNA BEGINS TO SPREAD

desired to put stoves in his house when his contract with the Company specified "fireplaces," and in one such case the Secretary wrote:

> When stoves were first introduced they were looked upon as much increasing the risk, but this opinion has now passed away and our officers consider them as no more hazardous than fireplaces; still it is perhaps best for the insurers and the insured, in order to avoid the possibility of a misunderstanding, to mention stoves, when they are used, in the survey.

The Company's watchfulness in the matter of finances was shown in every detail of the conduct of the organization. The salary list was limited to the Secretary and a clerk, who was also Clerk of the Town, and who seems only to have helped out in emergencies, for which service he was paid forty dollars a year. The President received no pay until December, 1821, when it was voted to pay Thomas K. Brace fifty dollars salary for the six months preceding.

The Directors were cautious, conservative, feeling their way in the hazardous uncharted sea of risks and rates. They felt the need of collecting data and statistics on which to base an intelligent method of writing insurance. The first real move in this direction was the request made to the Secretary to register in a blank book all losses by fire he should chance to note, designating the place, the kind of property, the loss, and whatever details might seem necessary; and for this service an extra compensation was promised him. He was requested to subscribe for one New York and one Boston paper, and to purchase a gazetteer to aid him in the work. This might well be the beginning of what is now an elaborate system, which has placed fire insurance underwriting on a more or less scientific basis.

Prior to the entry of the Ætna into the field, the practice of the few American companies in operation was to confine their efforts almost entirely to such local business as could be secured by the executive officers. In the very beginning, however, the Ætna inaugurated a policy, then regarded as radical and revolutionary, of planting agencies far afield and of entrusting its agents with discretionary powers and authority theretofore jealously reserved to officials and Directors at the Home Office.

In March, 1822, Secretary Perkins was sent on what was then considered a long trip, to Norfolk, Virginia, to adjust and settle a loss by fire on the woolen factory of Earl P. Pease. This was the first journey of a Company official to adjust losses. On his return he was requested "to journey on the seaboard of Massachusetts, New Hampshire and Maine, and from there, through the interior of the country, home, and establish agencies; and for his services he shall be allowed his expenses and two dollars a day." This per diem allowance was not in addition to salary, but took its place.

The success of this trip led, three years later, in October, 1825, to the bolder action of the Board of Directors, authorizing the President and the Secretary to employ a suitable person to travel through Pennsylvania, Ohio, Indiana, Illinois, Missouri and the southern states for the purpose of establishing agencies. William L. Perkins, of Ashford, Connecticut, who had

Hartford Jan 28th 1821

I. C. Bates Esq.

Sir Inclosed I send a Check for four thousand Dollars, which is designed to satisfy the loss of the Aetna Ins. Co. on their Policy to the Messrs. Shepherds. As the Co. have now the money ready to them, they thought they might without inconvenience accomodate the Messrs. Shepherd — If agreeable to them please to pay the loss with the check upon their entire discharge to the officer in'd. dly.

Your &c
Isaac Perkins Secty

Hartford Jan 30th 1821

Isaac C. Bates Esq.
Sir
The Directors of the Aetna Ins. Co. have this day heard that three days ago Shepherds Factory was again on fire, & that there is every likelihood or no doubt but that some incendiary is determined to destroy the Messrs. Shepherds. The Directors think it desireable to employ a watch for the remainder of their insurance upon the Factory — For this purpose of watching the bearer Mr. Samuel Bottsfords, a trusty man, is sent to Northampton. Should he need aid he is directed to call upon you as our agent & the Directors expect you to afford him any advice & assistance of which he may be in need — We hope all yet is and will be free & it is desir'd the watchmen only should be employed til the ruin of the Messrs. Shepherd. The bearer will also take a letter to the Messrs. Shepherd who will be requested to give you a circumstantial account of the last fire & we also desire a letter from you.

A few days since I wrote a letter py the

PAGE FROM CORRESPONDENCE BOOK No. 1
LETTER AT TOP RECORDS PAYMENT OF THE ÆTNA'S FIRST FIRE LOSS

been serving as local agent there, was appointed; therefore he might properly be called the first Special Agent of the Company.

In line with its policy of extending its agency business and thus securing a greater distribution of its risks, the Ætna had early entered the Canadian field; having, on December 22, 1821, appointed Abijah Bigelow agent at Montreal. The first loss there was on a building occupied by Holt & Co., which was destroyed by fire caused by gunpowder stored on the premises. In this connection an incident occurred which showed the spirit inspiring the Ætna, and also how important a factor in the early success of the company was Secretary Perkins, and how cordially the Board bowed to his judgment.

On April 23, 1822, President Brace, in a letter to Bigelow, advised him to dispute the claim and to contest it in court. He left to Bigelow freedom of action, but it was clear that in his honest indignation he felt a contest was fair. He would never consent "that any honest sufferer insured in the Ætna should," as he expressed it, "be choused out of a just claim by a subterfuge or mere legal lack." But in this case the *powder*, he pointed out, was the sole cause of the destruction, and "as we took no premium on this extra hazard, we cannot think that justice or equity requires us to pay the loss." There was a postscript to this letter which read, "Isaac Perkins, Esq., left town yesterday on a journey. Thomas C. Perkins is appointed Secretary pro tem."

About three weeks later, on May 15, the Secretary pro tem. wrote to Bigelow as follows:

At the date of our President's communication to you, our Secretary, to whose sole judgment the Directors had submitted the settlement of Holt & Co.'s loss, was absent on a journey, from which he has not yet returned, and it is only within a day or two that I have been able to hear from him and learn his views of the subject.

He is decidedly of opinion that a lawsuit is to be avoided unless the case is beyond all question in our favor. To gain the reputation of a litigious office would be death to our success, and even if law and equity were clearly in our favor the mere fact that we had disputed a loss must to some extent fix upon us that character.

You will therefore consider it as the earnest wish of the Directors that a lawsuit may be avoided and the matter amicably adjusted, and particularly that the loss should be paid unless on investigation you are satisfied that you can demonstrate to the Court not only that the conditions of the Policy have been violated, but also that the insured either fraudulently caused the fire, or wilfully & understandingly deviated from the conditions of the policy to the enhancement of the risk.

Respectfully your Obt. Servt.,
THOS. C. PERKINS, Secy. pro tem.

The incident was closed a few weeks later when the case was settled without litigation for a little over four hundred dollars. But the Ætna learned its lesson too, for some months afterward when new blanks were sent to Bigelow, they were accompanied by a significant little note to the effect "that the principal difference in the blanks from those which you have had, consists in the direction that powder is not insurable and that over-valuation by the insured shall render void the policy. These alterations require no comment."

Though the Company consistently avoided litigation, it had no fear of it and did not hesitate to

 THE ÆTNA BEGINS TO SPREAD

dispute claims in which fraud was strongly suspected. One of the first of such cases occurred in connection with the claim of one Flanders in 1823, when the attitude of the Ætna was completely vindicated by a verdict in its favor on the ground of fraud.

The growing needs of the Company at this time demanded more capital; but it was also realized that fresh blood would be helpful too, and would tend to lessen the likelihood of getting into a rut or of having the weight of a rapidly increasing business bear unduly on the shoulders of a few men. When it was decided, therefore, in 1822, to increase the capital stock from $150,000 to $200,000, it was provided that the new stock should not be offered to the existing stockholders, but sold, so far as possible, with a view to interesting new people in the Company. The corporation was moving ahead on such safe and solid financial lines that the stock was offered, not at par, but at a premium of five per cent.; fifteen dollars to be paid in cash on each share, and the balance, ninety dollars, in well secured notes.

In the correspondence with agents as given in the yellowed and faded old letter-books which form so valuable a part of the archives of the Ætna, there was no let-up in the constant iteration and reiteration of the principles and policies which were making the business so successful. These talks on paper, not *form* letters, but close intimate explanations, put the agents in close touch with the home office, no matter how far removed in mere mileage. They furnished arguments to be used with prospective customers or applicants for insurance, though this was never so stated.

Here is a characteristic bit from one of Perkins' letters about this time, explaining the Company's policy of distributing its risks:

> I conceive that office is safest which, having its risks duly dispersed, does the most business — if the business to a given extent is deemed profitable, the profits of further business must undoubtedly be considered a guarantee of the funds of the Co. Note, the argument for extension rests on the proper location of risks — if an office with a million of capital should insure to the amount on every building in a compact part of Philadelphia, its exposure to ruin would be much greater than that of our Office with a capital of two hundred thousand dollars, insuring $100,000 in each of ten towns. The disparity of these examples is great, & almost forces the conclusion that the system of doing business is of more importance to the insured than the magnitude of the capital; in the one case, with an increased business, millions may be exposed to a single conflagration; in the other case, it is not in the experience of any man that the whole capital of $200,000 would be lost.
>
> The business of the Ætna Co. is scattered throughout the United States & the Canadas. Thus the risks being detached, the losses come singly upon us, & tho it is possible it is incredible to suppose we shall at one period incur so many losses as to endanger the existence of the Co.
>
> These remarks are not intended to discredit other offices — necessity or rather the want of business at home, compelled us to take a wide range — a range unknown to any other American office, & now experience & reflection concur to convince us that the course we pursue makes assurance doubly sure, not only to the insured but also to the stockholders of the Co.

When Lafayette made his memorable visit to Hartford in 1824, and the city went wild to do him honor, there was ringing of bells, booming of cannon, fine street decorations, a parade of eight hundred school children who strewed the General's pathway with flowers, a review of the troops, and music and feasting

THE ÆTNA BEGINS TO SPREAD

without stint. Prominent among organizers of the great festivities were members of the Board of Directors of the Ætna. There were Henry L. Ellsworth — one of the two men deputed to meet Lafayette at the State line and to bring him, with a military escort, to the city — Gaius Lyman, James M. Goodwin, Henry Kilbourn and Charles Babcock.

One of the policies of the time that had a sentimental interest and historic association was one issued by the Ætna in 1825 on Yale College, for the sum of twenty thousand dollars. By its terms the policy was always to be continued in force, the Company being authorized to draw on the Treasurer of the college for the premium each year when it became due. It was provided that should either the insured or the insurer desire to cancel the contract, it was necessary to give six months' notice. The policy was kept in force at least twenty-six years, for it was renewed in 1851 by John G. North, who became an agent for the Ætna the year before. The agency started by North is still in existence, and has the original of this policy on its walls. This old policy suggests many comparisons and contrasts between the methods in vogue in 1825 and those of nearly a century later.

The continued prosperity of the Ætna led it, in a spirit of natural expansion, to petition the Legislature in 1826 for a charter amendment to permit the writing of insurance on inland navigation. There was opposition from some marine insurance company, which must have been vigorous and influential, for it succeeded in deferring favorable action for thirteen years.

ONE HUNDRED YEARS OF FIRE INSURANCE

The custom of the Ætna, which was, indeed, a practice among companies at this time, of sending officers or Directors on special missions in the interest of the corporation, was evidenced in 1827 by the appointment of Joseph Morgan as special agent, to go to Canada to investigate the business of the Company and to settle the losses on a fire which had occurred a short time before at Quebec. This was the first of many such trips for investigation or adjustment of losses, which Morgan was to make for the Company.

At the close of this period, which immediately preceded the first real crisis in the history of the Ætna, the Company had become not only a national, but an international institution; and all this accomplished in less than eight years. Its agencies extended as far north as Quebec, reaching out to Saco, Maine, on the east, and as far south and west as Louisiana and Michigan. The Company had made a splendid start; there was a fine spirit of harmony and co-operation among its officers; the name Ætna had begun to stand for strength and security and to inspire a confidence that was to grow but stronger with the passing years.

CHAPTER VI

FACING ITS FIRST CRISIS
1827–1845

AFTER eight years of prosperity the Ætna was now to meet the first crisis in its history. Financial conditions were bad throughout the country in 1827; idle factories, inactive trade, poor collections and frequent bankruptcies attested the seriousness of the times. The Company had a series of fires, none of severe loss, but in the aggregate taxing heavily its resources. In July the Directors voted to sell the stock owned by the Company in the United States Bank, the Phœnix Bank of Hartford, Merchants Bank of New York City, and the State Bank of Albany.

The summer of 1827 was passed through without special strain, when in November came the news of a big fire in Mobile, Alabama, with reported loss of a million dollars, a startling sum in those days. What the Ætna's share in this calamity was, did not immediately appear. Perkins wrote at once to Thaddeus Sanford, the agent at Mobile, to proceed as rapidly as possible to collect information as to the amount of the Ætna's losses, and said that he himself would go to Mobile to assist in the final adjustment. Two days later he was on his way, empowered to settle claims and to establish or suspend agencies.

While in Mobile, Secretary Perkins was scrupulously alert not to incommode the Company a bit more than was necessary, for he drew at thirty days for money needed instead of by sight draft as was customary. The adjustment was long and tedious. While he was doing his best at the southern end of the line, the Directors in Hartford were grappling earnestly and efficiently with a most serious problem, for the very existence of the Company trembled in the balance. A committee, composed of President Brace and Directors Henry L. Ellsworth and Stephen Spencer, appointed to devise ways and means to meet the losses, were fully alive to the gravity of the situation. Their prescription was heroic, but it met the crisis.

First, all the bank stock of the Company, having a par value of $21,750, was to be sold, except $1,500 in the Eagle Bank of Providence. Second, all loans, amounting to $6,780, were to be collected as rapidly as possible, without inconvenience to the borrowers. Third, all agents were pressed to remit premium funds in their hands. These three measures would, it was thought, bring in about $30,000. Fourth, the remaining funds necessary were to be secured from local banks on paper endorsed by some of the Directors, the Board guaranteeing to protect the endorsers.

That was the plan proposed by the Committee which, accepted by the Board, saved the day. The seriousness of the situation will be realized when we remember that the investments and losses referred to by the committee constituted the entire paid-in capital and accumulated profits. Up to this time the bulk of the Company's assets consisted of stockholders' notes for ninety per cent. of the par value of their stock. It was not deemed advisable to demand payment of these notes at this time, nor to make an assessment on them.

The action of the Board was typical of the way the Company faced the crises and calamities that shadowed some of its later years, calmly, coolly, and in a fine spirit of courage and co-operation that never faltered. There are some thin slips of paper in the vaults of the Ætna, — notes browned with age, and the writing growing dimmer, — that tell today how Brace and Morgan, individually and jointly, signed their names during the dark months of the winter of 1827, and long into 1828, to promises to pay amounts aggregating $103,000 to preserve the Company's life and its honor.

One great lesson from the Mobile fire was the realization of the need of a reserve fund or surplus, slowly accumulating, as a resource in a crisis. There had been a happy optimistic feeling theretofore that a premium paid in was a profit and as such should be divided. But the Directors who had gone through this ordeal, with its perilous stress and strain, were not likely to face willingly a repetition, when a surplus would prevent, or at least reduce, the force of the blow of a heavy loss; so they began work to this end.

It was the character and credit of the Board of Directors that pulled the Company through, not ordinary assets. Part of the money raised was needed to pay other losses, for 1827 seemed a hoodooed year to all insurance companies, losses being four times in excess of the normal. The long after-effects were shown when on June 1, 1828, the Ætna account was found to be overdrawn $2,163.90 at the Phœnix Bank, which had stood bravely by in the crisis. The loss at Mobile was finally determined to be about fifty thousand dollars.

The solvency of the Company was questioned by enemies during this dark period, and James M. Goodwin, Secretary pro tem. in the absence of Perkins, was kept busy answering personal inquiries and letters from all over the country, from agents and other anxious seekers for information. The Company's promptness in paying all losses, dollar for dollar, as it ever has during its century of existence, soon dispelled all doubts.

The Mobile fire had one result that was to grow with the years. It was in 1827, the coming together in conference of the three Hartford companies — the Ætna, the Hartford, and the Protection — to compare experiences to the end that the business should be stabilized by means of equitable and just rates. This was an early, if not the first move of insurance companies to combine their wisdom on questions of vital and common interest and to agree on certain details — a movement which later broadened into the splendid work of the local boards and of the National Board of Fire Underwriters.

The Protection Insurance Company, just mentioned,

was organized in 1825, and its first President was W. W. Ellsworth, a Director and later general counsel of the Ætna; subsequently Eliphalet Averill, another Ætna Director, became President of the Protection. The spirit between the two companies ever remained cordial, and often they had joint agents.

About the middle of March, 1828, Secretary Perkins returned from the South, after a hard, anxious, four months' trip, weary in body and mind. He realized that the growing business of the Company was making it extremely difficult for him to attend to his diverse secretarial duties and, in addition, carry on his law practice. Four months of absence had seriously disturbed his legal business, and it became imperative for him to choose between the law and insurance as his permanent profession. The result of his decision was his resignation as Secretary on June 9, 1828. For the last year of his service to the Company his salary, including rent, had been reduced from $1,000 to $750 in consideration of allowing him to use the "front office" for his legal business.

In the withdrawal of Perkins the Company lost an intelligent and loyal worker. After leaving the Ætna he continued to practice law in Hartford for some time, being a partner of Thomas Clapp Perkins, one of the leading lawyers of the state. Isaac Perkins served as State's Attorney of Connecticut in 1839, a year before his death, which occurred on August 18, 1840. Fifty-four years later, Frederick Perkins, surviving son of Isaac Perkins and administrator of his estate, filed papers in court for the distribution, among the heirs, of $127.58, which was discovered as having been left by his father, at the time of his death, in the Society of Savings of Hartford. In 1908 the Ætna received from the family of Isaac Perkins an oil portrait of the Company's first Secretary made the year of his death.

After the Mobile fire the Ætna seems to have been even more than usually watchful of its risks; it drew sharper lines of distinction between the buildings it insured, as to their construction, proximity of other buildings, and the kind of business carried on within their walls. The letters to agents at this period had frequent reference to such questions, and rates were increasing. New England agents were instructed not to renew any risks on buildings occupied for cotton, woolen or paper manufacture without having the rate specifically fixed by the home office.

Beginning in June, 1828, the Company, which for nine years had paid rent to Perkins, now paid it, at the rate of $175 a year, to Joseph Morgan. In the year following, Morgan sold his Exchange Coffee House to Selah Treat, and then leased the City Hotel at Hartford, which he disposed of in 1835, and permanently retired from the hotel business, devoting the remaining years of his life to the affairs of the Ætna. He made shrewd real-estate investments, notably on Farmington Road and Asylum Avenue in Hartford, which increased greatly in value in later years.

In the early days of Morgan's Exchange Coffee House, or, to be more exact, the year which saw the organization of the Ætna, Joseph Morgan employed as an assistant a youth of sixteen years, named James Goodwin, whose son, Rev. Dr. Francis Goodwin, and grandson, Charles A. Goodwin, a century later, were to be among the active Directors of the Company. James — who, by the way, should not be confused with James M. Goodwin, successor to Perkins as Secretary of the Ætna — was an aggressive lad. His bent and later activities in life were disclosed when, at the age of twenty-one, he purchased a stage-coach line running out of Hartford. This young student of transportation later was to be prominently identified with the development of steam and street railroads in New England. It was a proud moment in his life, many years after, when he performed the ceremony of driving the first horse-car along the newly-laid rails of Hartford's first street railroad system. In 1832 James Goodwin married Lucy Morgan, the daughter of his early employer, thus cementing a relationship between two families that have made their impress upon every period of American life for more than two centuries.

After retiring from the hotel business, Joseph Morgan made many trips for the Company, establishing agencies, investigating risks and adjusting losses. To his diaries, begun when he was only twelve years and kept up without a break till three weeks before his death, we are indebted for interesting details of his trips in those early days, when travel was slow, roundabout and tiresome.

In and between the lines of these diaries may be glimpsed much of the history of the Ætna during the first quarter century of its existence, for during those years Joseph Morgan was closely and continuously connected with its progress. Like President Brace, in time of crisis he was a tower of strength, and more than once the magic of his name on company notes enabled the Ætna to meet serious losses fully and promptly. Likewise, behind the brief entries in his diaries, we can see the Ætna growing and extending its activities in the north and south and west, keeping pace with, and oft-times leading, the constructive and civilizing forces that built the inland cities and towns of America and Canada as we see them to-day.

An excellent account of some of these trips is given by Frank Farnsworth Starr, the well known genealogist of Middletown, Connecticut, who says:

On Mr. Morgan's first journey, in 1827, he went to Quebec to adjust losses from a fire, and ten years later made a trip to St. John, New Brunswick, necessitating an absence of three weeks, and covering 1100 miles of stage and steamboat travel, excepting the distance by rail from Worcester to Boston. Three years later, on a Southern trip, he touched at Norfolk and Portsmouth, Va., Wilmington, N. C., also at Petersburg, Richmond and Fredericksburg, where he visited the grave of George Washington's mother.

An extensive and interesting trip was that of April 21st to June 30th, 1842, on which he visited New York, Trenton, Phila., Harrisburg, Pittsburgh, Wheeling, Zanesville, Chillicothe, Columbus, O., Dayton and Cincinnati. In Cincinnati he visited Lane Seminary, of which Dr. Lyman Beecher was President. Having left that city, he saw from the boat while en route to Louisville the home and burial place of President Wm. Henry Harrison at North Bend, Ohio. Arriving at Lexington, having left Louisville and Frankfort, he called on Henry Clay.

By the 18th of May he had returned to Louisville and boarded a steamer for Natchez. Making interesting and instructive notes in his diary, he went to New Orleans by boat. His passage from New Orleans to Vicksburg, and thence to St. Louis, was retarded by sand bars in the river, breaking of paddle wheels and other injuries to the machinery. Pausing to note 50 steamboats in the river near St. Louis, and commenting on the prosperous appearance of that city, he traveled cross-country to Springfield and Peoria, Ill., thence by stage and steamboat to Chicago — then a place of 5000 souls — and thence by boat to Detroit, Cleveland and Buffalo.

After visiting Toronto he came East, stopping at Rockport, Rochester, Auburn, Syracuse, Utica and Albany: "thus," as he says in his diary, "having performed a journey of 6099 miles in ten weeks, viz: 4330 by s. boats, 743 in stage-coaches, 716 on railroads, and 310 in canal packet boats. The whole legitimate expense of which — $3.83 for every hundred miles, including board, etc., it being per day for every expense $3.29, and being for every twenty-four hours including lying still, etc., about eighty-three miles of travel."

A comparatively local trip occurred in 1843, when, at the age of sixty-three, he visited Brattleboro, Windsor, Montpelier and Burlington, Vt., Montreal, Ogdensburg, Kingston, Toronto and Rochester. In the summer of the following year a nine weeks' trip embraced Central New York, Southern and Central Michigan, Illinois, Wisconsin, Iowa, Western Virginia and Maryland. His last extensive trip on insurance business was confined to Canada, where he stopped at Halifax, Nova Scotia, and St. John, New Brunswick.

In the offices of the Ætna are many interesting souvenirs of the life of the organization. Among them is a crudely printed invitation "to sup with the President and Directors of the Ætna at Morgan's Coffee House on December 13, 1833." That they made merry, and that "to sup" was but the modest deprecation of a host's over-modesty, is proved by Joseph Morgan's bill for this little celebration. It itemized forty-two dinners at six shillings each, and that meant one dollar a plate; and to show that the "drys" were not then in the ascendant, there were seventeen bottles of champagne, twelve bottles of sherry and ten of Madeira, at twelve shillings per bottle. The Ætna still preserves this mute memorial of its reckless extravagance, with Joseph Morgan's signature, acknowledging payment of one hundred and twenty dollars. How Perkins must have shivered at the enormity of the outlay, if he had chanced to be present on this festive occasion!

There were heavy losses during the winter of 1832-33 amounting to $56,000 in three months. The Company was doing an unsatisfactory business in New York, as was shown in a letter to one of its agents in May, 1834, written by Secretary Goodwin:

> I am perplexed and discouraged with our business in your State (New York). We are now minus about a hundred thousand dollars since we commenced with Mr. Van Rensselaer (1828), and it is growing worse. Our business in New York swallows up our earnings everywhere else. Our whole scale of premiums must be advanced from a third to a half. If that cannot be done, we had better withdraw.

The Ætna was doing little business in New York City, for foreign offices did no extensive underwriting there until later. There was keen competition and reckless slashing of rates that made foreign companies steer clear of the city, as the prudent man avoids becoming mixed up in a street fight. This rate-cutting was not a new thing, for even in 1819, the very year of the birth of the Ætna, an organization was founded in New York — one of the early local boards — known as the Salamander Society, the members of which were pledged to adhere to established rates. It did not seem to have accomplished much, for the bitter rate-war went on. *Foreign* companies, as the term originated during the period of the War of 1812 when anti-British sentiment ran high, meant only those whose home

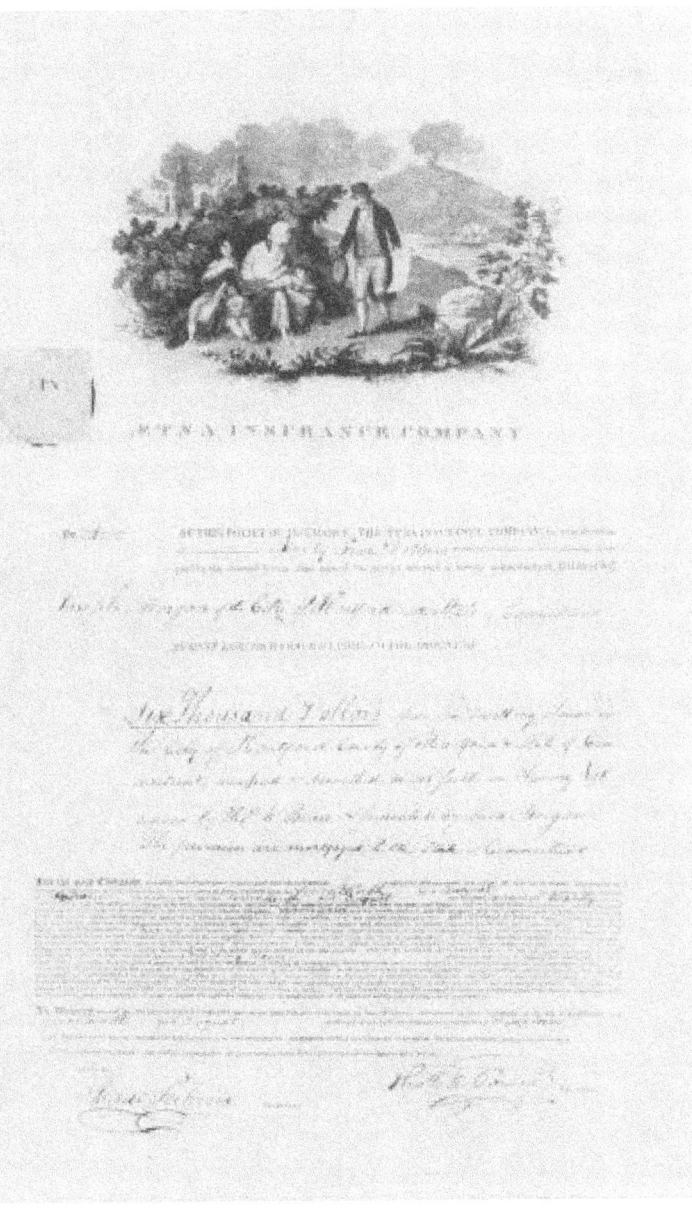

ÆTNA POLICY No. 1
ISSUED TO JOSEPH MORGAN, AUGUST 17, 1819

office was in a foreign country, and such companies were forbidden by law to operate in New York State, though foreign companies, restricting the term to those from other States, could operate, but had to pay a premium tax of ten per cent. The rate-cutting, combined with the tax, made New York City an undesirable territory for outsiders.

When the terrible fire broke out there on December 16, 1835, the Ætna had reason to congratulate itself that its risks in New York City were but trifling. For three days the fire raged, with a strong north-east wind blowing; hydrants were frozen and out of commission; the water drawn from the river froze in the hose. Finally the flames were extinguished only by blowing up a number of buildings by gunpowder, leaving a vacant space the fire could not overleap. Nearly the whole of the business section of the city around Hanover Square, Pearl and Wall Streets, comprising 648 houses and stores with their contents, entailing a loss of $18,000,000, were destroyed. It burned over fifty-two acres and was the greatest fire the country had known up to that time. Twenty-three of the twenty-six local companies failed as a result.

But New York learned its lesson; the people now realized that payment of losses was more important than low premiums, and that soundness was the first question to be considered in relation to an insurance company. The wiping out of the New York concerns made it essential to secure immediate protection, new local companies were organized, and the tax on those of other States was reduced from ten to two per cent.

This action made it possible for the Ætna to enter the field in earnest.

The Company was merely "singed" by the fire to the amount of ten thousand dollars. In response to numberless inquiries, Secretary Goodwin responded: "The Company was never in better condition. The calamitous fire in New York has brought us an accumulation of business which has kept me constantly occupied." The Board of Directors voted to send a representative to New York City to investigate with a view to appointing an agent there and also to write risks while there "at his discretion, not to exceed $8,000 on any single risk." Some of the Board voted against the general proposal.

In April, 1835, the Directors, feeling the necessity of expansion due to increased business, authorized the purchase from William H. Imlay, of the lot and buildings west of Treat's Exchange Coffee House (formerly Morgan's) for $9,570. This deal was put through, and a committee being appointed to supervise the erection of a new building, the Ætna moved to its second home, No. 53 State Street, after having spent its first sixteen years in the Coffee House. The year following they bought this too — the lot, building and furniture — from Selah Treat for $30,000.

A curious note of interest relating to this second home of the Ætna was published in the *Courant* on July 15, 1913, over three-quarters of a century later. This item read as follows:

Workmen yesterday removed a sign over the entrance to No. 134 (originally 53) State Street and discovered the old sign

 FACING ITS FIRST CRISIS

"Ætna Insurance Company" in gilt letters in two large slabs of sandstone. It was put up in 1835, when the Ætna moved into its own property. It occupied the first floor of the building as offices until 1867. The old vault in the offices had a door of sheet steel three-fourths of an inch thick and thick walls of brick.

The financial prosperity of the Ætna at this period is shown by the fact that dividends of one dollar per share were paid semi-annually from June, 1831, to December, 1834, when the rate was increased to five dollars; only one dividend had been passed since the organization of the company, and that was following the Mobile fire. By May, 1836, the situation of the Company was so strong that the Board voted a dividend of $50,000, being twenty-five per cent. of its capital, to be applied towards the liquidation of the notes of the stockholders. Money was coming in rapidly, and the Directors made many new investments, putting as much as they could safely afford in railroad stock. Getting into these enterprises on the ground floor, when a new road was chartered, they paved the way for the increasing prosperity of the Ætna in the later years when the success of the railroads made their original stock of great value. The first purchase of this character was three hundred shares of the proposed New Haven & Hartford Railroad Company.

In January, 1837, there was a big fire at St. John, New Brunswick; $50,000 was voted to pay losses, and Secretary Goodwin was sent to direct the adjustment. This fire practically wiped out the cherished surplus of the Company. Later in the year Joseph Morgan was also sent to St. John to investigate and to clear up any loose ends remaining unsettled.

Secretary Goodwin, who was now receiving $1,500 a year, had accepted an offer to become secretary of the Protection Insurance Company of Hartford, and resigned from the Ætna in April, 1837. Whether he was wise in making the change from the Company which he had served since 1828 may be problematic; at any rate he remained with the Protection but a brief time and then became Hartford local agent for the Washington-Providence Insurance Company. He died at Hartford on March 30, 1870.

Simeon L. Loomis, who had been with the Company as an assistant to Goodwin since 1833, was appointed Secretary. Loomis was a picturesque figure in the life of the Ætna in the years to come. He was individual, forceful, direct, rapidly grasping the details of a problem and resourceful in seeing the way out. He was shrewd, diplomatic, adroit, and there was a live-wire quality and a sparkle and tang in whatever he wrote, with a delightfully human touch, that makes it hard to resist quoting each of his letters in full, as they come up in the records.

It may seem, in this story of the Ætna, that while we hear much of the secretaries we hear little of Thomas K. Brace, the President. This is, however, perfectly natural, for the hand that performs is in evidence, apparent to all, but the head that directs and controls is 'way back in the silence, behind closed doors, just as we see the chauffeur who runs the car but not the motive force that moves it. It was round the conference table of the Board of Directors that Brace really revealed himself. Cool, keen, even, calm

STATE STREET OFFICE OF THE ÆTNA INSURANCE COMPANY
1837–1867

and quick to grasp a situation, and safe and sound in his decisions, there he was a real force. Had it not been for his clearness of thought, his dynamic energy and inspiring leadership, the history of the Ætna might be vastly different from what it is to-day. The final outcome of all discussions was the "vote of the Directors," with his voice merged with the others.

But truth to tell, the Secretary of the Company, at this period, was the real executive, so far as underwriting was concerned, while the President confined himself principally to financial matters, as was manifest in the attitude of the Board in deferring to Perkins' judgment over the decision of Brace in the proposal to litigate a fire loss at Montreal early in the Company's history. It is also illustrated, in the wise, fatherly words of counsel written by Secretary Loomis to President Brace when the latter was in Washington, in February, 1838, suggesting that he go to Baltimore and try to settle a claim in litigation. There is a touch of the worldly wisdom of Chesterfield's letters to his son, in these lines, and a suave deference which counsels while seeming merely to restate what the other already knows so well:

> It has been suggested that an offer from you, made unconditionally, of a greater sum than hitherto offered them, might prejudice our cause and retard a settlement. It is, as you are well aware, a case which requires the best address, and a good share of adroitness, to manage; and the duty of treating it skillfully and with success could not have devolved on one better qualified than yourself. Dignified reserve, with no apparent solicitude, yet a countenance beaming with fairness, an open ear to all their statements, treasuring in your memory everything, or recording it, with occasional assurances of the disposition of the Board to be just unto all, may draw from them altogether

better terms than have yet been submitted. When you get them to the right *notch*, you may, if you please, assure them of your influence with the Board in their behalf. Make them put on paper their terms, and at the same time authorizing their attorney here to receive the pay and close the matter forever.

About two weeks later these lines were sent to President Brace by Loomis:

We will add but a word in relation to a final settlement with Dawsons, i. e. no offense will be taken by Directors if you settle with them at $500, $1000 or $3000 less than you are authorized to by vote.

The Directors had authorized Brace to settle, but not to exceed $5,000. But, in the words of Robert Burns, "the best laid schemes o' mice or men gang aft a-gley," for despite Loomis' coaching, or perhaps because Brace had not acquired true diplomatic technique, the eventual settlement cost nine thousand dollars.

In May, 1838, the President's salary was reduced to $600 a year, at his own request, on account of his employment of a clerk at $800 per annum to assist him. A month later President Brace was authorized to make an inspection tour of agencies in New York, New Hampshire, Maine, Montreal and St. Johns. His letters to Loomis are filed in the archives of the company, and his journey, which could now be made in a week, was then made in a leisurely way from mid-June to the first of September.

The question of an amendment to the charter, permitting the writing of inland navigation insurance, which the Company had first made an effort to secure in 1826, now came again to the fore. The Board suddenly grew active on the subject and voted to appeal again to the Legislature, and on May 8, 1839, the amendment was granted. Though the Directors were anxious to secure the right to write inland marine insurance, they did not actually begin the new line of business till 1843, four years later. This postponement of action was characteristic of the care and caution evidenced in every step of the progress of the Company. With the authorization to enter this field, they could watch and wait for the most opportune hour for beginning the work.

The years from 1837 to 1839 were rather severe times for the Ætna. The loss of over $51,000 at a fire in St. John, New Brunswick, in 1837, was serious at the time. Two years later, in addition to smaller blazes it had five large fires, with heavy losses. These were Richmond, Virginia, $15,000; Stonington, Connecticut, $24,000; at St. John, New Brunswick, $33,500, and two in New York, one for $45,000 and a second two months later for $12,000. These fires hit the Company's finances a hard blow. The Board had a special meeting in October, 1839, to consider ways and means to settle outstanding losses, and to protect the credit of the Company. For some reason, doubtless wise and prudent, the Directors worked out their own plan of relief when under special financial stress without calling on the stockholders to pay up on their notes. Such a course might have affected the general credit of the Company by giving undue publicity to a merely temporary stringency. So President Brace was instructed to borrow the money from the banks or if necessary to mortgage the real-estate of the Company. Much of the money needed was secured on his personal notes, guaranteed by the Ætna. This borrowing was frequent from 1839 to 1843, though it did not interfere with the paying of some dividends.

In December, 1839, the Board voted to join with the other Hartford companies in agreeing upon a new regulation of rates, and to hold meetings at stated times to discuss ways and means of protecting their common interests. Two years later the Directors decided that the Ætna would write no more policies on distilleries or theatres.

One feature of the life of the Company constantly evident in studying its record is the persistence of fundamental principles from the very beginning; secretaries may come and go, but the Ætna principles seem to run on forever. When we read this note of Loomis', written to the agent at New Orleans in 1843, it might almost seem that we had picked up one of Perkins' letters of 1820 or so:

> We have ever found a wholesale, liberal policy good enough — and we have no wish to pursue any other. Doubtless we have many times paid more than there was a righteous claim for — and in some instances paid when there was no *just* claim upon us. But we hold it better to be sinned *against* than to *sin* — and what any man gets unjustly does *him* no good.

And the old Perkins touch of inspiration and counsel is manifest in this Loomis letter to an agent who was moving from New York to Milwaukee. We now begin to realize it is not merely the voice of the Secretary but the voice and spirit of the Ætna and the Directors:

> We learn that the town of Milwaukee is a smart flourishing place. Now it would be the part of wisdom, when these new cities

are going up, to plan for the best possible security of their property when the population should become large. In putting up blocks let there be thick entire walls between each tenement, or every alternate one, extending through the roof, say two feet, so that one might burn without destroying the adjoining. We trust you will exert a good influence on such matters when on the ground.

This is an example of the early stages of the work of "safeguarding America against fire," which has since assumed such great importance under the direction of the National Board of Fire Underwriters.

The broad spirit, the confidence of the Ætna in its agents, and its willingness to vary rules as need might occur, as being only wise modifications of principles that did not change, as well as its closer supervision of the work of agents, are shown in a letter from Loomis to J. C. Peasley, agent at Burlington, Iowa, in October, 1844:

It was formerly a custom to furnish agents with a "Book of Instructions & Tariff of Rates." There were difficulties attending it — agents were governed by it when their own good judgment ran counter to the directions, and we found on personal investigation of risks at the several agencies, that a tariff could not be made which would operate justly — and hence we preferred to submit the conduct of the agencies to the prudence and discretion of agents, rather than bind them to arbitrary rules. Now we mean to visit them once a year.

The best risks are dwelling houses; the worst risks are cabinet and joiners' shops. Risks of an intermediate character are the ones on which we do the most, as stores and shops.

We would have our dealings, as far as possible, with men of integrity. Let rogues stand their own underwriting.

The Ætna had now completed its first quarter century, and the Directors felt that they could look back on the history that they had made, with pride and congratulation. The business had successfully passed through the perils of the pioneer stage; experi-

had been converted into experience with the golden harvest of fuller wisdom; the principles upon which the Company had been founded had proved themselves true, safe, and sound; there had been critical times, it is true, but all had been lived through, and severe storms had all been weathered in safety. The Directors felt heartened by the prosperity that had been attained, and they faced with a sense of serene confidence the future of the Company.

Chapter VII

"OLD ÆTNA'S" GROWING PAINS

THERE was consternation in the office of the Ætna on the afternoon of July 19, 1845, when the captain of one of the boats plying between Hartford and New York rushed in, and demanding to see Secretary Loomis, shouted the alarming news that New York City was on fire.

"When we pulled out of the slip this morning," he said, "the whole lower part of the city was covered with thick clouds of smoke through which we could see angry tongues of flame, seemingly in a dozen places at one time. Never did I hear such a clanging of fire bells; we could see at various points crowds of people running frantically up the streets; the city was in tumult, and we heard men on the docks calling out that New York was doomed this time."

Thus did the Company receive its first news of the great conflagration known as "the Broad Street fire," which was to threaten the very life of the Ætna and bring it face to face with its second crisis. The Directors had congratulated themselves in April, just three months before, that they had escaped the big fire in Pittsburgh that nearly burned the town off the map; now they were to meet a more serious disaster.

When Secretary Loomis wrote, with his airy optimism, "we are probably in for a cool fifty thousand dollars," he did not realize how he was under-estimating the loss. It was soon discovered that it would run over $100,000, and final settlements brought it up to $120,000. There were grave faces round the Directors' table when it was discussed. It was a big loss to meet, but of course it had to be met, and yet the way was not immediately clear. But the spirit of courage and resourcefulness that had tided the Company over its first great crisis in 1827 was strong and energetic in pulling it through its second critical period.

President Brace made a hurried trip to New York to survey the damage and estimate the losses. He returned to Hartford and called the Directors together. There was no possible misinterpretation of the single sentence in which he told of the tragedy:

"Gentlemen," he said, "our entire surplus has been wiped out and our capital seriously impaired."

"What are we going to do?" asked one of the anxious Directors.

"Do?" exclaimed the President, without a second's hesitation, "Why, we're going to pay every loss in full — dollar for dollar — and we are going to do it at once."

Then, reaching into his inside coat pocket, he pulled out a sheaf of blank notes, with different amounts filled in on each one, and passed them across the table, saying, "Morgan, you sign this, Woodbridge, sign

this," and so on until in front of each of the seventeen Directors was a significant bit of paper. President Brace had carefully calculated in his mind the relative ability of each Director to pay, and had made out each note accordingly. There was no questioning, no hesitation; each man quickly read the amount allotted to him, dipped his pen into the ink and signed his name. The President put his personal endorsement on each note and was ready to go directly to the banks to discount them — and such paper was as good as gold. It had all taken but a brief time, yet there were long breaths of relief when the tension was over.

The needed amount was quickly forwarded to New York. Every claim was paid. This instant action on the part of the Ætna, in the face of failing companies on every side, was the final turning point in the affairs of the Company. Its reputation as a reliable and paying corporation was so firmly established that, for many years afterward, numerous New York City insurers would place their insurance only with the Ætna. New business came in so rapidly that within a year the Company was in as strong a position financially as before the fire. Thus, what threatened to be a calamity for the Ætna proved really to be a blessing in disguise.

The New York City agent at this time was Thomas A. Alexander, who later became President of the Ætna, and who, on the very day of the breaking out of the New York fire, had succeeded Augustus G. Hazard, who had represented the Company in the metropolis since 1836, the year following New York's earlier fire.

Alexander did good work in adjusting the losses, with the splendid co-operation of Joseph Morgan, who had been sent from Hartford "to be on the ground."

Secretary Loomis' skill and charm as a letter writer were strikingly demonstrated during these troublous times. He was in his element, calming the fears of excited agents over the country who feared for the Ætna the same fate which had befallen so many other companies. Had he owned the whole company, he could not have felt more pride and enthusiasm than he showed in his correspondence at this time. His excited fervor is revealed in this letter of July 24th, in response to a suggestion which he repudiates with these words of magnificent scorn:

> You suggest the expediency of our coming out with a statement in the public journals just to let the people know that "Old Ætna" is alive and kicking and is going to make such a splashing in insurance as the Gothamites never dreamed of before? Pshaw, man — don't you know that we are old-fashioned folks, not given to dry vaporing and puffing? Perhaps you can do nothing in the big city unless under the influence of hot brains and feverish excitement. Here, our motto is "Keep Cool" — bear adversity with fortitude and prosperity with meekness. We see no occasion for blustering away in the papers; it is not in keeping with our genius. We go in for the "solids" and there is an unction about the word "ready" that cannot be expressed in all the newspaper paragraphs in New York. All we have to say is — Go ahead with prudence, don't get too many eggs in one basket, and we will pay as fast as claims are established.

In August, 1845, occurred one of those minor fires in the history of the Company, which one refers to merely because of associations. This was the burning of Henry Clay's bagging factory at Lexington, Kentucky, insured in the Ætna for $2,500. Thomas

 "OLD ÆTNA'S" GROWING PAINS

Dolan, the Lexington agent, was instructed to "pay as soon as the statement is rendered."

The growing business of the Company required more capital, and the Directors in 1846 were justified in voting to increase the capital stock by $50,000, payable half in cash and half in notes, bringing the amount of capitalization up to $250,000, and three years later a further increase of $50,000, payable in cash, brought the figure up to a full round $300,000. That the Company was now moving along easily and serenely seems evident, for the big fire at St. Johns, Newfoundland, in 1846, with its loss of $77,000, was met as a mere matter of routine, without a ripple of disturbance or anxiety, although it was less than two-thirds this amount which threatened the life of the Company at the time of the Mobile fire less than twenty years before.

By this time the name of the Ætna had become nationalized; it had come to mean not merely the well-known title of the Company, but all that the Company stood for — safety, solidity, generous treatment and sure and prompt payment of losses. The little tin signs bearing the single word "Ætna" tacked on the walls of thousands of farm houses, stores, dwellings, and factories throughout the country, told the passers-by that the owners rested secure from the fear of loss by fire because they were protected by the big insurance Company that bore that name away off in Hartford, Connecticut.

Apropos of this familiar old sign, it was told a few years ago that a little girl traveling in a carriage through the country roads out in Ohio, noting the number of houses thus marked, asked her mother why there were so many places called "Ætna." The mother told what the five letters meant, and added:

"I remember asking my father the very same question when I was a little girl like you, and when he answered me he told me that he, too, remembered as a young boy asking that question of his father."

It was on July 23, 1847, that the Company had a real loss — this time not by fire, but in the death, at the age of sixty-seven and a half years, of Joseph Morgan, who had been so devoted to the Ætna from its very inception. He was, for those times, a wealthy man, for the value of his estate was over a hundred thousand dollars. He left two children — Lucy, married in 1832 to James Goodwin, and Junius Spencer Morgan, who was the second of the Morgans to become a Director of the Company, a few years later.

During many periods of stress and storm Joseph Morgan had been a pillar of strength to the Company. He lived to see the silver lining of the cloud which cast its dark shadow over the institution in 1845. The tremendous increase in Ætna business which followed closely on the heels of the New York fire made it possible within a few years finally to cancel, through the payment of extra dividends, the notes which the stockholders had given in subscribing for their stock. At the time of Morgan's death the capital of the Company was $250,000. Of this sum the actual amount of cash paid in by the stockholders was $45,000, plus the bonus of $2,500 paid on the stock issue of

AN OLD FARM HOUSE WITH THE FAMILIAR TIN SIGN "ÆTNA"
TACKED OVER THE FRONT DOOR

1822, which had been sold at five per cent. premium. This left $205,000 due on the notes. The process of cancellation began in 1836, with a special dividend of $50,000; this was followed two years later with one of $10,000, another in 1843 of $20,000, two in 1848 for $50,000 and $25,000 respectively, and in 1849 the remaining indebtedness of the stockholders was extinguished by a special dividend of $50,000. It should not be overlooked, however, that to reap these rewards most of the stockholders had, in giving notes, risked their entire personal fortunes, and had contributed gratuitously to the Company much valuable and active service in various capacities.

In the late thirties and in the early forties there were some attempts of the fire insurance companies throughout the country to get together and to reach some understanding on the subject of standardizing rates. During a period of prosperity, when there were no big fires, with premiums accumulating, in the zest of getting business, competition grew fiercer and the good resolutions were forgotten or ignored by many of the short-sighted companies. A big fire is to a company, very often, what a great misfortune or tragedy is to an individual: it gives pause and brings realization of the lack of preparedness and the folly that permitted it.

It was such a fire that occurred in 1849 at St. Louis, which wrecked many companies and entailed on the Ætna a loss of $125,000, the largest in all the thirty years of its history. Had the Company not profited by the lesson of 1845, which revealed anew the necessity of a good reserve fund, there might have been another crisis in its affairs. Following the St. Louis fire a convention of many companies was called in New York, and uniform, sound rates were adopted; for a time serious attempts were made to maintain them.

In this same spirit and to discourage demoralizing competitive practices which endangered the companies and insurers alike, the Ætna, in 1849, sent notices to all of its agents in Michigan, Wisconsin, Iowa, Illinois, and other western states, that Mark Howard, General Agent of the Protection Insurance Company, would visit them for the purpose of effecting an understanding between the agents of the three Hartford companies, the Northwestern and Albany companies of New York and two or three western companies. The object of these visits, as explained in the notice, was "to effect a perfect understanding on the mode of operation and on uniformity of rates and actions on the part of agents."

At about this period in the Company's existence there appeared on the roll of Ætna Directors a name which was to loom large in the world of insurance for many years to come — the name of Bulkeley. It will be recalled that away back in its days of infancy, the Ætna had decided to enter the field of life insurance and had secured an amendment to its charter for that purpose, but that no further action had been taken.

At the annual meeting of the Ætna stockholders in June, 1846, Eliphalet A. Bulkeley was elected as one of the seventeen Directors. By this time the Ætna had won an enviable reputation as a strong and stable institution, and its name had become a household word throughout the United States and Canada. Realizing all this, Mr. Bulkeley saw no reason why the tremendous asset of a good name, and one so popular and widely known, should not be utilized in promoting and developing a life insurance business in addition to that of fire. Whether he was the sole leader in the movement to revive the long-slumbering project is not disclosed, but the old Ætna records show that a resolution was adopted by the Board to petition the Legislature for an amendment modifying the one granted in 1820 and again empowering the Company to write life policies.

On June 6, 1850, the charter was amended and a committee, composed of Eliphalet A. Bulkeley, E. G. Ripley, and Miles A. Tuttle, was appointed to formulate plans for the new department. Within a week the committee reported:

> That capital stock, to be denominated the "Annuity Fund," should be raised to the extent of $150,000 — 5% in cash and approved notes for the balance — and to establish a Life Department, to be entrusted to seven members of the Board, namely, Robert Buell, Miles A. Tuttle, John L. Boswell, Eliphalet A. Bulkeley, Roland Mather, E. G. Ripley and Henry Z. Pratt, who shall be called Managing Directors; also a Vice-President of the Ætna Company to be Chairman of the Managing Directors and preside at their meetings; the Annuity Fund to be at all times kept separate from other funds of the Company.

By common consent Mr. Bulkeley was chosen for the dual position of Vice-President of the Ætna Company and Chairman of the Managing Directors of the "Life Department." Separate quarters were provided on the second floor of the Ætna building.

Realization soon came, however, that the business of fire underwriting and of life insurance differed widely at almost every point; that each was a profession in itself; and that for the same organization to supervise and direct the multitudinous details of both might tend to weaken one at the expense of the other. Whatever the controlling reason, the Ætna Directors in 1853 obtained from the Legislature another amendment to the charter, separating the Life Department from the parent company and constituting the stockholders of the "Annuity Fund" a separate corporation under the name of The Ætna Life Insurance Company, with Eliphalet A. Bulkeley President.

Thus was born — an offspring of "Old Ætna" — an institution which, in the years to come, was to win its place to the front ranks of life insurance. Mr. Bulkeley continued to serve as a Director of the older Company and as President of the Ætna Life until his sudden and lamented death in February, 1872. His son, Hon. Morgan G. Bulkeley, later to serve his state and country with distinction as United States Senator from Connecticut, became chief executive of the life insurance organization in 1879, succeeding Thomas O. Enders, and in 1880 was also made a Director of the Ætna Insurance Company, in both of which positions he has served continuously to this writing.

In the early 50's the Ætna was beginning to think in bigger terms and, financially, to rest calmly in the sense of security given to it by a safe and solid surplus that was accumulating. Two fires of real seriousness in a single year — 1852 — one at Montreal for $105,000 and another at Chillicothe, Ohio, to the amount of $114,000, seemed to produce no riffle in the meetings of the Board, and two years later the capital was increased by $200,000.

It was in 1852 that the name of Morgan reappeared on the Directorate of the Ætna, for five years after the death of his father, Junius S. Morgan was elected, and he in turn was followed in the years to come by his son and later by his grandson. Junius Morgan was born in 1813 at West Springfield (now Holyoke), Massachusetts. He began his business career at the age of sixteen with Alfred Welles, dry-goods merchant, in Boston. During the next twenty years he divided his time between dry-goods and banking in New York, Hartford and Boston, and in 1854 began his future great career as a banker when he entered and became a partner in the firm of George Peabody & Company of London, England. Ten years later Mr. Peabody resigned, and the firm, which rendered tremendous assistance in England to the Union during the Civil War, became J. S. Morgan & Co. Mr. Morgan was married in 1836 to Julia Pierpont, daughter of Rev. John Pierpont of Boston, and died at Nice, France, in April, 1890, at the age of seventy-seven. Although his departure for England in 1854 necessitated his retirement as a Director of the Ætna, he was ever deeply interested in its progress and continued until his death to give the Company the benefit of his wise advice and co-operation.

The Ætna was now to lose another valued worker.

Secretary Loomis, whose inimitable letters fill many pages in the old copy books and in themselves tell much of the history of the Company for nearly a quarter of a century, had his ambition appealed to in 1853 by an offer of the Presidency of the newly organized Home Insurance Company of New York City. He accepted the offer and resigned from the Ætna, after twenty years of efficient and loyal service, and entered upon his new duties. This new position not proving congenial, Loomis returned to Hartford one year later to become President of the Phœnix Insurance Company, organized in 1854.

In choosing a man to succeed Secretary Loomis, the Board made a happy choice in the selection of Edwin G. Ripley, who, as a Director, had been active in the affairs of the Company since 1847. Born in New Hampshire, Mr. Ripley came to Hartford as a young man and received his early business training in the wholesale grocery firm of Thomas K. Brace & Co. Here he came in close association with Mr. Brace, the President of the Ætna, and through him learned many of the problems of the insurance Company. Leaving the grocery firm, he later became a partner of his uncle, Philip Ripley, in the iron trade, which led eventually to the large and successful firm of E. G. Ripley & Co. Unlike Loomis, Mr. Ripley had no experience as an underwriter. He was quick to learn, however, and speedily proved his value to the Company, for in 1854, after a year of service as Secretary, he was promoted to the position of Vice-President, the failing health of President Brace making

it necessary to have some one share the extra burdens created by the Company's growth and expansion. Thomas A. Alexander, New York City agent of the Company, was called to the home office to succeed Mr. Ripley as Secretary, and here had new training for the higher positions he was to hold in the future.

The 50's were live, intense years in the history of the Ætna, years of expansion and bigger, broader adjustment to new needs. Business was growing and spreading at such a rate that the home office was taxed beyond the limits of its early organization. The offices of Assistant Secretary and Vice-President were created to lessen to a degree the pressure of two positions that had outgrown any mere part-time service. The Directors were no longer able to go on missions to different parts of the country and discharge the varied duties which they had been called upon to perform in the earlier years. Experts in these lines were now essential; special agents were named to appoint and supervise large corps of agents far from the central office; and through the new Western Branch, established at Cincinnati in 1853, hundreds of new agents were placed in the field.

Among these special agents appointed about this time particular mention might here be made of A. F. Willmarth. Although his duties were those of "traveling agent," his official title was Assistant Secretary — a position which in later years was to become increasingly important. He held the position for two years — 1851 to 1853 — when he resigned to re-enter field work. He eventually became

Vice-President of the Home Insurance Company of New York and one of the recognized leaders in the insurance world. The position of Assistant Secretary of the Ætna remained unfilled from 1853 to 1863, when Jonathan Goodwin, Jr., later Chicago agent, was named. He also served as Assistant Secretary but two years; and the position was not again revived until 1867, when, as our later story will disclose, it was re-created for a man who was to exert a tremendous influence in the affairs of the Company for over half a century to come.

The Ætna organization was doing big things that count. In 1853 the Company introduced the first blank Proof of Loss, and in the next few years inaugurated many other improvements in policy forms and methods and practices in underwriting. An important step in the progress of scientific and intelligent underwriting was the invention by Ætna employees of the system of manuscript charts of cities and towns, known later as the Sanborn system. For many years this system of maps, enabling the home office to determine the character of risks, was in use in most of the large fire insurance offices, and paved the way for other systems. Ætna surveyors in the South at the outbreak of the Civil War, while at work on diagrams for these maps, were arrested as suspected spies, their field notes confiscated, and they themselves turned over to vigilance committees and held until they proved the innocence of their activities. The Ætna is now one of the pioneers in a movement by a group of strong companies looking to the co-operative publication of a card-system of mapping, believed to be superior to the maps published under private management.

Another increase in the capital of the Company was made in 1857, when it was raised to the half-million mark, and two years later to a full million.

Thomas K. Brace, through whose inspiration, influence and initiative the Ætna was brought into existence, and who had done such valiant service in its interest, feeling the weight of years and failing health, resigned from the Presidency of the Company in 1857, to the sincere regret of his associates, though he consented to remain as a Director. He died June 14, 1860, in his eighty-first year. The boast of Augustus Cæsar, "I found Rome brick; I leave it marble," might, in its spirit, have been applied to Brace in relation to the Ætna. But he had not found it already made; he was one of those who had founded it; he had seen it slowly and surely rise from a small struggling organization, during the thirty-nine years of his devoted service, into a mighty national institution, known and honored in every section of the country. The foundation had not only been well and faithfully laid, but many stories had been built in the great edifice it was to become. No history of the Ætna would be just or complete without giving to Brace full credit for the splendid part he took in making that history what it is. In their resolutions of appreciation and regret adopted by the Directors on his death, they fittingly referred to him as "the projector and principal founder of this Institution."

The resignation of President Brace in 1857 made a number of changes and promotions necessary. Mr. Ripley succeeded to the Presidency, Mr. Alexander became Vice-President, and Thomas K. Brace, Jr., was elected Secretary. The duties of the position proved too great a drain on the health of the latter, and he resigned four years later, at which time he succeeded his father as a Director, a post he retained until 1870, the year of his death.

By 1858 the Ætna had extended its business across the entire continent to the Pacific coast. The Company was now enjoying rare prosperity, money was coming in freely, and there were years of comparative immunity from heavy losses. This stream of prosperity seemed to excite unduly a large and influential element among the stockholders. They felt that a premium received was a premium earned, and in their zeal for profits forgot the liability that stood behind every dollar paid in by policy-holders.

This brings us to one of the strong features of President Ripley's administration. He was enthusiastic for a large reserve fund, and worked loyally to maintain one. Reserves for insurance were not then made mandatory by law; but President Ripley knew, and the Board of Directors knew, the danger of paying dividends that left no reserve. They insisted that, independent of its capital and in addition to it, an insurance company should at all times have a fund sufficient to reinsure its outstanding risks, a policy now generally recognized as of fundamental importance and enforced by law. The Ripley forces won

"OLD ÆTNA'S" GROWING PAINS

the victory, to the great credit and prestige of the Ætna, to that of Hartford as an insurance center, and to the general cause of fire insurance in America.

President Ripley did much to lift fire insurance into something like scientific underwriting. A chance question as to whether the Company made money on the insurance of paper mills startled him because he could not answer it. But it started a train of thought that led to definite results. In a general way the Company knew that carpenter shops, cotton mills and certain other lines were specially hazardous, but the knowledge was based on vague and indefinite information. Why not classify all risks in the light of the past experience of his own and other companies? He began the careful collection of statistics on related risks, thus helping to lay the foundation of a work, since then infinitely extended, which has resulted in greater security of fire insurance as a business and has made the determination of rates more accurate.

In 1860 the country stood trembling on the verge of war. The presidential campaign was feverishly intense and bitter, particularly in the South. Feeling abated to a degree in the North after the election of President Lincoln, but in the South it became more bitter, more intense, more final; it was not a mere wave of excitement; it was deep, terrible earnestness. It was a critical time for the Ætna and for all institutions doing a national business. To the natural patriotic emotion that burned so pure in the hearts of millions that the Union might be saved, and the dark shadow of fear of all the horrors of Civil War, was added the natural anxiety for the safeguarding of great business and industrial interests.

The correspondence of the Company at this critical period was largely devoted to letters urging the Northern agents to be calm and courageous and to face bravely whatever the future might bring, and to the agents in the South, words of deep solicitude and the hope that a final break might be averted. Among many letters written by the Company officials at this time was one, characteristic of the others, by Vice-President Alexander to a Virginia agent, in which he wrote:

> We concur with you sincerely in the hope that some recourse of reconciliation will be found available for the preservation of the Union.

From this time forward, there was a flood of letters from Southern agents, asking for advice. The Ætna wrote them to discontinue writing new business until conditions had become more stable, and instructing them to inform existing policy-holders that "the Ætna would pay losses in full even if the South became a foreign country." On April 15, 1861 — the day after the fall of Fort Sumter and the very day of President Lincoln's first call for 75,000 volunteers, President Ripley again reiterated that the Ætna would stand behind all its promises. In a letter to Richard Curd, agent at Macon, Georgia, he wrote:

> All honest claims under our policies will be recognized by this Company, no matter where the claimant may be located. The spirit of war seems to be aroused in all parts of the country. May the end of all wars — Peace — be speedily brought about.

THOMAS A. ALEXANDER
1862 · PRESIDENT · 1866

 "OLD ÆTNA'S" GROWING PAINS

Three days later the Southern agents were notified to insert this "War Clause" in all outstanding policies:

Warranted by the assured free from claims for loss or damage arising from civil commotion or from piracy, seizure, sequestration or detention or the consequences of any other hostile act of the government or people, person or persons of any state of the United States of America or of any state or states claiming to have seceded therefrom.

But conditions were too bad, from the standpoint of difficulties of communication, sectional bitterness and other reasons, to continue any further southern business, and in May all Ætna agencies in the South were discontinued.

In July, 1861, Secretary Brace, whose health was breaking down under the growing and exacting needs of the Secretaryship, resigned, and Lucius J. Hendee, agent of the Ætna at Hebron, Connecticut, was elected to succeed him.

In August, 1862, there was deep sorrow and regret when the news was brought to the Ætna office that President Ripley had just died. He had been for nine years an active official of the Company, and had, in his short term of five years as President, made a splendid record, not only in carrying on but in advancing the traditions and prestige of his office.

During the century of the Ætna's existence the policy of promotion for merit has been a dominating principle, from which there have been few departures. When Secretary Perkins retired in 1828 he was succeeded by his assistant, James M. Goodwin; when he resigned in 1837 his assistant, Simeon L. Loomis, was promoted; when he left the Company in 1853

 ONE HUNDRED YEARS OF FIRE INSURANCE

he was succeeded by Edwin G. Ripley, whose active service as Director and personal assistant to President Brace since 1847 made him the logical successor; on his promotion to Vice-President in 1854, Thomas A. Alexander was advanced from his post of New York City agent to the position thus made vacant; likewise, when Ripley was elected President in 1857, Alexander succeeded him as Vice-President.

It was therefore in keeping with the policy of rewarding faithful and meritorious service that Vice-President Alexander was now chosen by unanimous vote of the Directors for the post of honor and responsibility made vacant by the death of President Ripley. For nearly twenty years he had labored loyally and efficiently in the Company's interests, and thus brought to his new and greater duties the accumulated wisdom of long experience, ripened judgment and expert knowledge of every phase of the business. In many ways President Alexander found larger and graver responsibilities than those of any of his predecessors, for the future of every American institution was now darkened by the clouds and storms of civil war which threatened the life of the very nation itself. He was succeeded as Vice-President by Henry Z. Pratt, who for many years had been an active member of the Board of Directors. Mr. Pratt's death in 1863 ended his service as Vice-President in less than a year, and the position was abolished, not to be revived for more than twenty-five years.

The Ætna was now realizing how big a company it was. Despite the war it was enjoying the pleasurable pangs of growing pains. In January, 1864, it was granted an amendment to its charter authorizing a half-million dollar increase in its capital, to be paid for out of surplus earnings. Other increases followed, and in June, 1865, the capital was raised to $3,000,000.

This prosperity of the Company during the trying years of war, with a large part of its regular field of operations debarred from occupation, reveals eloquently its solidity and the prudence and soundness of its management. It was now ready for the new era of national peace, which, strangely enough, brought the Company face to face with graver perils than it had been compelled to meet during the war or during the preceding half century of its existence.

Chapter VIII

NEW TIMES AND NEW FACES

AFTER the close of the war came a new era, a period of readjustment and reconstruction; business, like the nation itself, was again free, with the hampering and burdening restrictions of four long years removed.

These were trying years in the history of the Company in the arduous duties devolving on the President. In October, 1865, Mr. Alexander broke down under the strain, and feeling unable to continue his labors, reluctantly sent in his resignation. Perhaps believing that the end was not far off and that it would ease his mind a little were he to feel he was still in the harness, the Directors took no action on his resignation, so he remained nominally as President, though relieved of all duties, until his death on April 29 of the year following.

Though Mr. Alexander enjoyed the honor of the Presidency for but the brief period of four years, they were vital years in its history, and, despite the Civil War then raging, were prosperous for the Company. Beginning his career with the Ætna in 1842 as a clerk in the New York City agency, he had advanced steadily from local agent in New York to the successive positions of Secretary, Director, Vice-President and President in his twenty-four years. He was an able underwriter, an official of rare efficiency, and of fine character as a man. The Company suffered a real loss in his death.

The Ætna was singularly fortunate in the selection of its Presidents. They were men trained in its principles and its ideals, who had proved ever equal to each new responsibility. Lucius J. Hendee, who had been Secretary for five years, was elected President, and Jotham Goodnow of New Haven, who was later to be President, became Secretary.

President Hendee entered on his new duties at the age of 48, the very prime of life. He was born at Andover, Connecticut, and took his first lessons in underwriting as assistant to his uncle, Abner Hendee, the Ætna agent at Hebron, Connecticut. In 1852 he succeeded him as agent. His faithfulness and his unusual ability in conducting the agency attracted the attention of the home office, which kept a sharp lookout for a special quality of brains among its men, and he was the choice for Secretary in 1861, on the resignation of Thomas K. Brace, Jr. His record in this position, his sound judgment, as well as his long experience in underwriting, gave assurance that he would make good as President, and he did.

The prosperity of the Company for the few years preceding 1866 was surprising. In the seventeen years from 1849 to 1866, carrying with them four years of war, the capital rose from $300,000 to

$3,000,000 — but even this capital did not seem sufficient, for in 1866 the Legislature was asked for a charter amendment to increase the capital to $5,000,000. No further action was taken on this, however, until 1877, when the desired authorization was granted. Meanwhile, stirring events were to occur.

The rapid growth of the Company demanded not only more capital but a larger building. The working force in the home office, which for some years had been steadily increasing in numbers, was chafing under the congestion and inconvenience of quarters that were now proving wholly inadequate. In November, 1867, the Building Committee, appointed two years before, to arrange for the erection of a new home for the Company, reported its work completed, and the cost of the new building as a little less than $125,000. It was a fine four-story, brown-stone house, thoroughly up-to-date in its appointments, located at No. 670 Main Street, and served from 1867 to 1903 as the headquarters of the Company.

With the entry into the new building, a new man, destined to be a vital factor in the future of the Ætna, became associated with the Company. It was on November 30, 1867, that William B. Clark was made Assistant Secretary and entered on the career that was to lead him to the Presidency of the Ætna and to a service that was to run well over fifty years.

It was in Hartford, on June 29, 1841, that Mr. Clark was born. His early education at one of the public schools in his native city was followed by a year in the high school at New Britain and later at a private

OFFICE OF THE ÆTNA INSURANCE COMPANY
1867-1903

school kept by one of his uncles. The young boy wanted to work — a habit which he never outgrew — although his father, Abel N. Clark, who was proprietor and manager of the Hartford *Courant*, desired him to continue his education. He was employed in the Mercantile Bank of Hartford for six weeks, and then he went into his father's office just to help out with the collecting "for a few days." He had been there a year, when one day Nicholas Harris, principal of a private school where young Clark was studying bookkeeping in spare hours, entered the *Courant* office with an advertisement for a bookkeeper which he desired inserted in the paper.

Mr. Clark, Sr., saw the advertisement, learned that the company desiring help was the Phœnix Insurance Company, and after an interview secured the position for his son. The advertisement thus served its purpose without ever appearing in print.

"So," said William B. Clark, President of the Ætna Insurance Company, as he related the incident more than sixty years later, "at eight o'clock on Monday morning, January 19, 1857, I stood at the foot of the stairs of the Phœnix office waiting for some one to come and unlock the door."

The President of the Phœnix was our friend of earlier years, Simeon L. Loomis, who had been the genial and successful Secretary of the Ætna from 1837 to 1853. Young Clark remained bookkeeper but a short time when he was promoted to cashier. His salary had risen from $300 a year to $500, when one January, while making up the salary list of the employees, he left blank the amount of his own. When asked by Mr. Kellogg, Secretary of the Company, the reason for this omission, he said:

"I have rather been in hopes that I could fill it in for a larger amount."

"What was the amount you had in mind?"

"Eight hundred dollars," was the prompt reply.

Kellogg saw the point; so did Loomis when the situation was explained by the Secretary; the raise went through without a murmur and Clark never again had to ask for an increase — it just came.

He had been only two or three years with the Phœnix, when he became assistant to the President. On Loomis' death in 1863, Clark was made Secretary, holding this position for four years, when the offer of a higher salary and greater prospects of advancement led him to go to the Ætna. President Loomis knew underwriting, knew it thoroughly from A to Z; he was full of his subject, enthusiastic and eloquent, and no one who wanted to learn all the complexities of underwriting could have had a better teacher, and Loomis could not have had a keener, quicker pupil than his young assistant. Many years later, when William B. Clark was an acknowledged leader in the world of fire insurance, he paid a graceful and affectionate tribute to his early mentor and friend, when he said: "No man ever did more for his own son than Simeon L. Loomis did for me."

When Clark went to the Ætna, though nominally only Assistant Secretary he was in reality the underwriting Secretary of the Company; for Secretary

Goodnow, though trained in the details of banking, had no experience in the business of insurance. So in all the long years that followed, waiting for promotion and fuller official recognition of what he was doing, his actual position was even higher than what might have been inferred from his title, important as that was and is to-day. He had been only four years with the Ætna when the Company faced its greatest crisis.

Chapter IX

THE ÆTNA'S COURAGEOUS STAND

A NEVER-TO-BE-FORGOTTEN year in the history of the Ætna, of the insurance world, and, in fact, of the whole country, was 1871—the year of the Chicago fire, the greatest conflagration the United States had ever known. On Sunday evening, October 8th, it began; whether from the misadventure of a cow kicking over a lighted lamp in a stable, or the carelessness of a party of card-players, is not definitely known. The fire raged all that night, all the next day and until well past noon on Tuesday.

The catastrophe, which was appalling, started near the lumber district of the West Side, and fanned by a high and veering wind, it seemed nothing could stay its course; the flames jumped the river to the South Side with the ease of a fine horse taking a hurdle, and spread rapidly to the North Side. Rain on Monday night helped a little to conquer the fire, but not sufficiently, for all that night the whole city was one raging furnace.

Mere figures, eloquent as they are, tell but a part of the awful story. Two-thirds of the city's buildings were of wood, and because of an excessively hot, dry

THE ÆTNA'S COURAGEOUS STAND

summer they were but tinder boxes. One-third of the roof surface of the entire city and two-thirds of the cubic contents of all the buildings were destroyed. The burnt area was 2,024 acres; 17,450 houses were reduced to ashes, 250 lives were lost and 100,000 people were rendered homeless. Thousands of the frantic people of the burning city sought refuge on the lake shore, and even in the waters of the lake itself.

There were grim tense faces in the Directors' Room of the Ætna at this time; there were practically all day sessions; the maps and charts were eagerly scanned and discussed as each new word came by telegraph from some town near the burning city. At this time the Company's Chicago agents were Jonathan Goodwin, Jr., former Assistant Secretary of the Company, Henry L. Pasco, a former special Agent for the home office, and James S. Gadsden, who had charge of the inland marine underwriting at Chicago. E. J. Bassett, General Agent of the Ætna, and Special Agent J. C. Hilliard hurried to Chicago to be on the spot and aid in the adjustment of losses. Assistant Secretary Clark was also rushed West from the home office to secure, for a special meeting of the stockholders, complete information as to losses of the Company.

Two dramatic scenes in Ætna history, vitally connected yet distinct, were now being enacted simultaneously a thousand miles apart. In Hartford, the Directors, as in their two earlier big fires, decided instantly that every dollar of loss must and should be paid; the only question to be determined was the manner in which it would be done, the sacrifices that would be made, and the amount of the exact loss. General Agent Bassett estimated this at $3,500,000; but it was little more than guessing, for he could find no trace of the agency books and papers and concluded they had all been burned. This happily proved later to be a mistake, for most of the records were saved; but there was an interim when they could not be found. This was specially trying in the case of policies issued shortly before the fire which had not been forwarded to the home office in Hartford. Many of these were discovered when people brought in their policies for settlement of their claims.

While President Hendee and the Directors were planning how to raise the funds, for "every dollar must be paid," was their slogan and their inspiration, a different scene was being enacted at the other end, in Chicago. General Agent Bassett could have no more inspiring message to deliver to the panic-stricken insurers in his Company than the one he was given to deliver: "Every dollar of loss shall be paid."

The people, homeless, hungry, hopeless, after the fire was finally extinguished, had one thought, supreme, persistent, dominating, "What will the insurance company do?" It soon became manifest that many of the companies would become bankrupt; and the people, learning of this, became almost one great angry, half-crazed mob. Ex-Governor Marshall Jewell of Connecticut, who was a large stockholder and a director of the Phœnix Company of Hartford, happened to be in Detroit when the great fire broke out, and hurried to Chicago to take care of the interests of his

 THE ÆTNA'S COURAGEOUS STAND

company. Soon after his arrival he met General Agent Bassett of the Ætna, and together they decided that their first imperative duty was to make known to the people the stand that their respective companies had taken in regard to the payment of losses.

On the morning of Friday the 13th of October they stood together on the banks of the Chicago River, facing ruins, ruins, ruins as far as the eye could see. In the picturesque language of Frederick Law Olmsted, "it was possible from the top of an omnibus to see men standing on the ground three miles away, across what was once the densest, loftiest and most substantial part of the city." Around Bassett and Jewell were gathered a great crowd of people, sullen, stunned, yet at times with the tense repression that portends an outburst. Both men were known; the crowd awaited with feverish interest the first words they were to speak.

Mounting a barrel, Bassett told his brief story, amid a hush that was tense and dramatic. The speech may not have been a masterpiece of eloquence, but the words, "The Ætna will pay every dollar of loss, and I will now pay in full the first claim to be presented," was eloquence enough for the audience, if cheers were needed as proof. Then Bassett signed, on his barrelhead desk, a check for $7,350 to the order of John B. Drake, in full settlement of all demands under policy No. 34,382.

A few feet away, Governor Jewell, standing on an up-ended dry-goods box, spoke similar words for the Phœnix and paid the first claim made to his company by giving a check for $10,000 to Isaac F. Day. Those fortunate enough to be insured in either of these companies went away, their faces wreathed in smiles and with the glad light of new hope in their eyes, while others wondered what their companies would do.

Back in Hartford the Directors were busy discussing, planning and preparing to meet the great loss. The amount to be paid was estimated to be $3,066,030, though it finally proved to be $3,750,000; and here the great value of the reserve fund vindicated itself, though, of course, inadequate to cover fully an appalling demand such as had never been even contemplated by any insurance company. The Finance Committee of the Ætna was authorized to sell stocks and bonds of the Company and to borrow $300,000 from the United States Trust Company. The further action required was to be presented to the stockholders at a meeting to be held on November 9th.

At this meeting, which was a crowded affair, a detailed statement of the condition of the Company, and estimating the Chicago losses, was given, of which the following is a synopsis:

Gross Assets		$6,226,703.48
Liabilities		
Branch Losses Outstanding	$115,000.00	
Home Office Outstanding	200,691.86	
Losses at Chicago	3,066,030.00	
	$3,381,721.86	
Net Assets		$2,844,981.62
Reinsurance Reserve		1,800,000.00

The plan then proposed and submitted to the meeting was to reduce the capital of the Company

 THE ÆTNA'S COURAGEOUS STAND

from $3,000,000 to $1,500,000, thus cutting the holdings of each stockholder squarely in half, and then to sell $1,500,000 of new stock, thus bringing the total capital back to normal. The new stock was to be sold on terms of 20 per cent. in cash, 40 per cent. in notes payable in six months and 40 per cent. in twelve months' notes. This was the plan proposed, and within five days $900,000 of the $1,500,000 of new stock had been subscribed for by old stockholders.

How the stockholders acted in this crisis, their fine spirit of trust and co-operation, cannot be better told than in the few lines of a letter written by President Hendee, the day following this meeting, to General Agent Bassett in Chicago:

> Our stockholders' meeting yesterday was all that could be desired. It was fully attended, not an unkind or fault-finding word was said, and the votes reducing and increasing stock were carried unanimously. The room over the office and the hall adjoining were well filled by a good looking company of men and women. It was a glorious meeting and its action cannot fail to establish the credit of the "Ætna" for all times.

The mortality among the two hundred and two fire insurance companies involved by the fire was great, as sixty-eight, or about one-third, were compelled to retire from business at once, eighty-one either suspended temporarily or withdrew from active operations outside their own states, and fifty-three paid their losses in full. In 1909, of the companies that paid losses at the Chicago fire, only thirty-five still remained in business.

History was repeating itself, as after the fires of New York in '35 and '45; there was a killing-off of the weak companies, a strengthening of the strong and the organization of new ones. Prudent corporations grew even more prudent, transformed their losses as far as possible into new wisdom, and moved forward with new courage and confidence because of their memories of crises bravely lived through and of having mastered conditions that were adverse instead of being mastered by them.

The public that had been buying "cheap" insurance now began again to realize that adequate rates were an essential to the furnishing, by the companies, of sound indemnity. Those who had been protesting loudly that the companies were making too much money, piped in a lower key or relapsed into silence as the gigantic insurance expense-bill of the Chicago fire was discussed in the newspapers of the country.

The National Board of Fire Underwriters, which had been organized in 1866, had done good work in its few years of existence before the fire. It was an organization whose members were insurance companies who got together at that time with four principal objects: one, to establish and maintain, so far as practicable, a system of uniform rates of premium; second, a similar work on a uniform rate of compensation to agents and brokers; third, to repress incendiarism and arson by combining to punish offenders; fourth, to work for the common needs and prosperity of its members. In this connection it should be noted that with the passing years, the National Board gradually discontinued all activities relating to the subject of premium rates, and more and more has turned its attention to

 THE ÆTNA'S COURAGEOUS STAND

the great problem of fire prevention. It now has nothing to do with rates.

After the fire, the National Board promptly took hold of the general situation, while rates were promptly advanced to a safe basis and there was no protest from the public. State boards and local boards in smaller towns were formed and a temporary reform followed, but within sixty days reports of rate-slashing came to the Board, and it was recognized that the Board must itself grow into a stronger position where it could command rather than merely recommend. Legislation, at this time, took up again the question of the need of a legally enforced demand for a reinsurance reserve fund, and many states enacted laws to that end.

Hardly had the Ætna begun to take a long breath, after closing up the infinite details in settling the losses incident to the Chicago fire, when in November, 1872, the Company was visited by a new conflagration. This time it was in Boston with an appalling loss. The terrible fire that swept the business part of the city destroyed seven hundred and seventy-six buildings, all but sixty-seven of which were of granite or brick. The flames raged over sixty-six acres and entailed a total loss of about $75,000,000. Thirty-two fire insurance companies were rendered insolvent, of which twenty-six were Massachusetts corporations. The Ætna loss was $1,634,000, a rather staggering sum to pay within a year after the Chicago fire.

There was another stockholders' meeting, which might well have discouraged a body of men and women who had so willingly and loyally stood by the Company so short a time before. But there were no signs of discouragement or dismay; they took their medicine bravely. They voted to again reduce the capital, this time from $3,000,000 to $2,000,000, and to increase to the $3,000,000 again by the issue of $1,000,000 of stock. This new capital was rapidly provided and the Company again moved serenely on its way.

The two great fires led the Ætna to watch even more carefully than before the character of its risks and to distribute them even more cautiously. In 1873 the Directors decided to reduce lines of insurance in cities and large towns; and though this action might seem one where the wisdom of the Directors would be final, yet the matter was brought up at a stockholders' meeting. The stockholders gave what was practically a vote of confidence when they officially endorsed the action of the Directors.

The question of insuring in large cities came up again in the year following, when the Board voted to close the agencies at New York, Chicago and Boston and to make new arrangements for a better control of the situation by establishing branch offices in these cities. For New York, James A. Alexander, who had succeeded his father as agent in 1853, was appointed Manager at a salary of $10,000 a year, and for the similar position in the Chicago branch Jonathan Goodwin, Jr., who had been agent there at the time of the great fire, was appointed at $7,500 a year. No action was taken in the matter of Boston.

At the beginning of 1877 the Legislature granted

THE ÆTNA'S COURAGEOUS STAND

an amendment to the charter permitting the Company to increase its capital to $5,000,000. This action was in continuation of an appeal to the Legislature eleven years before. The Company did not require any such increase at this time, but it was part of their wisdom to look ahead when it might be necessary in a crisis or when the needs of expansion made it good to have this financial resource waiting and instantly available. At any rate, no action was taken in the way of using this privilege until four years later when it was voted to increase the capital to $4,000,000, to be offered to stockholders at ten per cent. payable in cash and the balance in properly secured notes.

In 1882 the Board, in recognition of President Hendee's twenty years of service with the Company, voted him an honorarium of $7,500; a graceful and just tribute to his devoted and wise guidance of the Ætna through a critical period.

It was in 1883 that the Board of Directors was strengthened and enriched by the election of a new member, a man of national importance in the world of finance and one whose counsel was of great value. This new Director was J. Pierpont Morgan, who seemed naturally to follow, in the third generation, the footsteps of his father and his grandfather in the directorate of the Ætna. Though there have been periods in the hundred years of the history of the Company when the name of Morgan did not appear in the Ætna's list of Directors, there was never an hour in that century when the family was not interested as stockholders.

It was at the age of forty-six that Mr. Morgan thus became officially active in the Company. He had already done big things in finance, but he was to do bigger things in the remaining thirty useful years of his life, that were to make his name known the world over as one of the very greatest of financial geniuses of history. He had organizing power of the highest order, and was a strong believer in the combination of allied interests into a great new economic unit and force. He brought order out of chaos and harmony out of discord on a scale that at the time seemed staggering to the imagination. He organized the United States Steel Corporation, harmonized the coal and railway interests of Pennsylvania, made his banking house one of the most powerful in the world, floated a government bond issue of $62,000,000 when it was needed quickly in an emergency, reorganized feeble or broken-down railroad systems and gave them the breath of new life and vigor, and either personally or through his bank had a hand in every big financial movement in the country.

This rare, broad-minded man, an enthusiastic yachtsman, a notable collector of books, pictures and other objects of art, a generous giver, a public-spirited citizen, was surely a vital addition to the Ætna forces, and a golden memory in its history and tradition. He remained with the Company until 1913, the year of his death, when he was succeeded by his son, J. P. Morgan, Jr.

At this period there were two amendments to the

 THE ÆTNA'S COURAGEOUS STAND

Ætna charter, one, in 1881, permitting the Company to write insurance against damage by lightning and other elements of nature, and five years later, one changing the date of the annual meeting from June to January.

The administration of President Hendee was a prosperous one for the Company in every way; the agency system had spread as never before, the business of insurance was growing rapidly into something more nearly reduced to principles and laws, for underwriting was evolving through conference, statistics and classified experience into an approach to a real science. In the twenty-two years since Mr. Hendee assumed the presidency, the Company had many severe fires; besides the Chicago and Boston conflagrations, which together cost the Company nearly $5,500,000, there were the Portland fire in 1866 with a loss of $170,000, the severest blow the Ætna had up to that time, the Vicksburg fire the year following when $110,000 of the company's funds was swallowed up, and the St. John, New Brunswick, fire, which entailed a loss of $262,000 on the Company.

The post of president of a corporation with such responsibilities and with the possibility of a crisis or the shadow of financial disaster hanging like a suspended sword over every hour, is a most trying one; it exhausted men before their time, and in September, 1888, President Hendee, after suffering from heart disease for several months, died, at the age of seventy. Besides his guidance of the Ætna, Mr. Hendee was associated actively with the National Board of Fire Underwriters from its organization in 1866. He was for eight years its Vice-President and for many years served as a member of its Executive Council. His career in the profession was marked by wise conservatism, sterling integrity and strict adherence to sound business principles.

In the changes in the official personnel of the Company, following the death of Mr. Hendee, Jotham Goodnow, who had become Secretary of the Ætna a month after Mr. Hendee's accession to the presidency, was now elected to fill the vacant office. He was born in Western Massachusetts in the very year that the Ætna was organized. When a young man he was bookkeeper in a large mill; and one day, in looking over some insurance policies on the mill property, he came across a policy of the Ætna. He opened it carefully, read it through deliberately as though every word were vital, then holding the paper reverently in his hand as though it were the key to some kingdom of dreams, he remarked fervently: "If ever I could become Secretary of a grand old company like that, it would be the height of my ambition." What would he have felt if the hand of fate had brushed aside the curtains hiding the future and shown him himself seated in the chair of the President of the Ætna addressing the Directors? But he was to occupy merely the position of cashier in three banks successively until in 1866, at the age of forty-seven, he reached the "height of his ambition" in his election to the secretaryship of the Ætna.

Mr. Goodnow's duties as Secretary from 1866 to the year of his promotion to the presidency had

JOTHAM GOODNOW
1888 · PRESIDENT · 1892

materially differed from those of most of his predecessors. His early career, as we have seen, had been banking, and he was untrained in fire insurance. He was able, nevertheless, to perform service of exceptional value in the financial and investment details of the business.

During all of these years Assistant Secretary Clark was regarded as the underwriting expert of the organization. And it was in recognition of this quality that when Secretary Goodnow on September 26, 1888, was advanced to the presidency, Clark was promoted to the position of Vice-President — a post which had been unoccupied since the death of Henry Z. Pratt more than twenty-five years before. Four months later, on January 17, he was elected to the Board of Directors. When Mr. Clark entered upon his new and larger duties, President Goodnow was nearly seventy years of age, and it was only natural that the executive responsibilities should fall, as they did very largely, upon the younger shoulders of the new Vice-President.

In the reorganization necessitated by these changes, new figures now appeared in the official ranks of the Company. Captain A. C. Bayne, a veteran of the Civil War who had entered the service of the Ætna in January, 1885, as special agent for New York State after serving the Hanover Insurance Company of New York in various capacities for over thirteen years, was called to the Home Office and elected Secretary, while James F. Dudley, another experienced underwriter, was chosen Assistant Secretary.

Mr. Dudley had entered the fire insurance business

in 1867 as an agent for the Union Fire Insurance Company in Massachusetts. Six years later he was appointed special agent of the North British and Mercantile Insurance Company for Pennsylvania, and soon after entered the service of the Ætna in a similar capacity, his territory including New York State as well as Pennsylvania. He returned to the North British company in 1885 as Assistant Manager, and it was while serving in this capacity he was called back to the Ætna, where he was to remain until his death on March 19, 1897.

An additional Assistant Secretaryship was also created at this time and was filled by the promotion of William H. King, who had joined the office force of the Ætna on June 13, 1866. King was a man of quiet, modest and unassuming character, inclined to minimize or hide his talents and abilities. He had worked long, loyally and efficiently in the interests of the Company, and Vice-President Clark, upon whose recommendation he was made Assistant Secretary, was glad of the opportunity officially to recognize and reward by this promotion not only the many years of faithful service but the abilities and capacity for larger responsibilities which he knew King possessed. In this connection, mention should be made that King's father, Seth King, also served the Company for many years as bookkeeper. He had joined the Ætna forces in 1838, President Brace agreeing to give up one-third of his salary and apply it on the salary of the new office assistant. He remained with the company continuously for over thirty years.

 ## THE ÆTNA'S COURAGEOUS STAND

In November, 1892, the Directors were shocked and grieved to learn of the sudden death of President Goodnow, who fell dead in the arms of his wife as he entered his home on November 19th.

The four short years of President Goodnow's administration had been comparatively uneventful, although marked by steady growth and expansion in the affairs of the Company. In 1890 the Western Branch of the Ætna, which had been established in 1853, was divided, and a new department — the Northwestern Branch — with headquarters at Omaha was organized.

This period saw also the retirement from the working forces of the Ætna of two veterans, Erastus J. Bassett and J. C. Hilliard — who had rendered such valued service to the Company during the great Chicago and Boston fires. Mr. Bassett came with the Ætna in 1862 and Mr. Hilliard in 1866. Bassett was born at Stockbridge, Massachusetts, in 1819, the year of the Ætna's birth, and died on July 26, 1891.

On the death of President Goodnow, the vacancy was filled promptly and as a matter of course by the election of William B. Clark. He had served the Company ably and loyally for twenty-five years, surely a long period, but he was now facing a future that was to cover an even longer period — a future of prosperity, of progress and prestige, one of splendid promise and finer achievement that was to constitute a new and greater era in his own career and in the history of the great Company whose destinies he was to guide and to guard.

CHAPTER X

PRESIDENT CLARK'S ADMINISTRATION

WHEN President Clark sat down at his desk in 1892 as the official head of the "Leading Fire Insurance Company of America," there must have been a reminiscent smile as his mind flashed back thirty-five years to that early morning in 1857, when he waited at the door of the Phœnix office prepared to make his modest entry into the world of fire insurance. It was a long, long road he had traveled since then — from humble bookkeeper and glorified office boy to the head of one of the great insurance organizations of the world. To have thought that he would continue his journey and participate in the centenary celebration of the Ætna twenty-seven years later, with himself still active, alert and aggressive as president, would have seemed a wild hope.

But Mr. Clark was never a dreamer; his specialty was action. He lost no time in looking backward, but shouldered his new responsibilities and resumed his onward march. His election as President was followed on December 7, 1892, by the promotion of Captain Andrew C. Bayne from the position of

Secretary to Vice-President and of Assistant Secretary Dudley to Secretary.

There now appeared a new figure in the official ranks of the Ætna in the person of Egbert O. Weeks, who was elected Assistant Secretary. He was an able underwriter of long training and wide experience in fire insurance. He was at this time forty-five years of age. When only twenty-one he began his career with the Wyoming Insurance Company and subsequently acted as special agent and adjuster for the companies. When, in 1883, Secretary Dudley, who had served the Ætna as special agent in Pennsylvania, was transferred to the New York field, Mr. Weeks succeeded him. Six years later he moved to Philadelphia, with the supervision of Pennsylvania, Maryland, West Virginia and Delaware, where he continued until his election as Assistant Secretary. His further progress with the Company was rapid, for in 1897 he became Vice-President and a Director, doing splendid work in both capacities until his death in 1902.

Mr. Weeks was a member of the National Board of Fire Underwriters and a member of the rate committee of fifteen. As chairman of the important sub-committee on large cities he was part of the movement of the National Board, which, shortly before his death, put that portion of fire insurance relating to large cities on a sounder basis, by materially readjusting the premium rates. The National Board now takes no action whatever on rate-making, but concentrates on fire-prevention and the broader questions of fire insurance. As Vice-President of the Ætna, Mr. Weeks had for his special field the Middle States and also entire supervision and control of the marine department of the Company.

When Captain Bayne died in October, 1893, there was another move-up in the official personnel. Mr. Dudley succeeded him as Vice-President, leaving the vacated position of Secretary to fall to W. H. King, while F. W. Jenness, a native of New Hampshire, who had been for five years a special agent in New York, was made the second assistant secretary.

The affairs of the Company were now moving along with the precision, ease, efficiency and smoothness of a perfectly oiled and adjusted piece of mechanism. While the business was growing rapidly, the official staff had been so increased, its work so well systematized, and the scope of the different departments so clearly demarked from each other, that no volume of work seemed to ruffle the routine in the least. From President Clark down through the whole list of officers, there was manifest practical ability of the highest order, underwriting experience gained through long hard training and service, and a loyalty and devotion to the old Ætna as though it were a cause or a crusade rather than a mere business institution.

No further changes of importance occurred in the official personnel of the Ætna until 1897. On March 19th of this year, the death of Vice-President Dudley left a vacancy which was filled by the promotion of Egbert O. Weeks, then Assistant Secretary. The resignation of Assistant Secretary Jenness to return

to the New York field as special agent, and the advancement of Mr. Weeks, created two vacancies, which were filled by the election of Henry E. Rees and Alexander C. Adams as assistant secretaries.

Mr. Rees was born at Macon, Georgia, on April 29, 1857, and when twenty-four years of age entered the fire insurance business as local agent in his native city. Three years later he was appointed special agent for the South Eastern Tariff Association, with headquarters at Atlanta. In the following year he was made Southern special agent of the North British and Mercantile Insurance Company, of which, James F. Dudley, later Vice-President of the Ætna, was then assistant manager for the United States. In 1889, a year after Mr. Dudley was elected Assistant Secretary of the Ætna, Mr. Rees was made southern special agent for the Company, and so continued until 1897. He was then called to the home office as Assistant Secretary, in which position he served for ten years. On May 6, 1907, he was elected Secretary, and five years later he became Vice-President and Director, in which positions he has since continued to serve. In 1918 Mr. Rees was elected to the presidency of the Southeastern Underwriters' Association. Of his thirty-eight years in fire insurance, he has given thirty years of continuous service to the Ætna as the Company rounds out the first century of its existence.

Mr. Adams, who became Assistant Secretary at the same time as Mr. Rees, was born at Barnstable, Massachusetts, on April 9, 1847. After a country school education he early went to Boston and there soon found his real vocation in fire insurance. When only eighteen he entered the service of the Howard Insurance Company of Boston, where he remained for seven years; from 1872 to '77 he was assistant secretary of the Globe of Boston, leaving this position to become New England field representative of the Liverpool and London and Globe, serving in that capacity for fourteen years. His twenty-six years of such experience had made him an underwriter of unusual ability, and in 1891 he joined the Ætna forces as General Agent in Boston. After serving ten years as Assistant Secretary he resigned and returned to Boston, to there take charge of the local and metropolitan departments of the Ætna.

So smoothly were the affairs of the Company running during these years, so natural and easy its expansion, that there is little of detail to chronicle; fires that would have been critical events in its early history were met as mere matters of routine, thanks to its splendid financial management and its growing reserves. When the announcement of war with Spain thrilled the nation in 1898 and the call was made for volunteers, the Ætna faced the situation with the same patriotism and prompt action as distinguished its course in the Great War, two decades later. In April, 1898, the Board of Directors voted:

> That all persons now employed at the home or branch offices of this company who are members of military or naval organizations of their respective states or the United States, shall, in the event of entering the actual service of the United States in the war with Spain, have their salaries continued while in such service during the time of their present enlistment. They shall

PRESIDENT CLARK'S ADMINISTRATION

also, after honorable discharge, have opportunity to return to the employ of this company.

Under the guiding hand of President Clark, the Company had safely passed through two periods of storm and stress — the panic year of 1893 and the Spanish war. The cares and responsibilities of his position were now beginning to tell on his health, and in 1900 he was urged by the Directors to take a six months' rest, which was his first real vacation in over forty years. During this year the Ætna suffered two large fire losses, one at Jacksonville, Florida, to the amount of $168,000, and the other at Ottawa, Canada, which cost the Company $198,000; that they occasioned no flurry in the home office proved the soundness of its financial condition.

These were years of frequent changes and additions in the official personnel due to increasing volume of business. It was a far cry from the early days, when, aside from the President and Directors, Secretary Perkins was the whole office force, keeping the books, attending to correspondence, drumming up agents, traveling around adjusting losses and doing a host of other things, to the year 1902, when, in addition to its Secretary, the Company found it necessary to increase its number of assistant secretaries from two to four. The two new incumbents were Almeron N. Williams and Dr. C. J. Irvin, of Philadelphia.

Mr. Williams is a native of Connecticut, having been born at Hartford on January 19, 1862. When but a young man he made his advent into the insurance world, like President Clark, in the office of the Phœnix of Hartford. He left the home office of the Phœnix to represent the Company in western New York, with headquarters at Rochester, and his success there justified his being later given charge of the western New England field. It was from this position that he came with the Ætna and was appointed special agent for the same territory. His field work proved a stepping stone to the higher position of Assistant Secretary, to which he was soon called. After ten years of varied and valuable executive experience in this position, he was in 1912 elected Vice-President of the Company and later was made a Director. Here again we may find a parallel in the careers of President Clark and Vice-President Williams. Both began in the same office in clerical capacities, and each was promoted from Assistant Secretary to Vice-President of the Ætna without serving in the intermediate position of Secretary.

Dr. C. J. Irvin, who was elected Assistant Secretary on the same day as Mr. Williams, is a son of President E. C. Irvin of the Fire Association of Philadelphia. He was born in Perry County, Pennsylvania, on November 30, 1863, and when twenty-one, graduated from the University of Pennsylvania. He was appointed special agent of the Fire Association of Philadelphia in 1888, and from 1891 to '93 was special agent of the Continental Insurance Company for the middle department, which position he resigned to become special agent for the Ætna. In 1899 he was elected vice-president of the Underwriters' Association of the Middle Department and in the succeeding year was made president.

PRESIDENT CLARK'S ADMINISTRATION

It was in 1905, after three years of service as Assistant Secretary of the Ætna, that Dr. Irvin, to the regret of the Company, resigned and requested to be transferred to his old field and old associates in Philadelphia, where he again took up his work as special agent; a position in which he has since continued to serve.

The rapid development of the business of the Company now began to crowd departments beyond the point of comfort. The Directors realized that the home office building which they had occupied since 1867, the very year in which President Clark entered the service of the Ætna, was outgrown. It was not of fire-proof construction, nor was it adapted to modern methods of doing business. What the Company needed was a new fire-resistive, up-to-date building, planned on lines of adequate provision for natural expansion of business for years to come.

In April, 1902, President Clark appointed a committee composed of Directors James H. Knight, Francis Goodwin and Charles E. Gross, to consult with the executive officers concerning the need of a new building. The report of the Directors, which was made in the following June, stated:

We have made a careful examination of the present quarters and find them already full and in fact crowded. The growing business of the Company calls for additional room as soon as it can be furnished, and it is the recommendation of your committee that a new thoroughly fire-proof building be erected, covering the ground now occupied and the so-called Conklin property on the north. This will give the Company commodious quarters for half a century to come.

Prophecy is a rather risky business; but of course, the Directors could not anticipate the remarkable strides the Company was to take, which rendered quarters "adequate for half a century," inadequate and over-crowded in 1919, after only fourteen years of occupancy. In December, the Board approved the plans made by a committee appointed for that purpose and appropriated $425,000 for the new building and in the year following added $50,000 to this amount. Under the direction of a building committee consisting of President Clark, Directors Goodwin, Gross and Knight and Secretary King, the work was begun. The architect selected was Benjamin Wister Morris of New York City.

Temporary quarters had to be found to house the Company during the period of the demolition of the old building and the erection of the new. This problem was solved by a two years' lease of space in the Connecticut Mutual Life Insurance Company's building in May, 1903, when the razing of the old building was begun. When the concrete foundation for the cellar walls of the new structure was completed, the first two bricks were laid by President Clark in the presence of the full official force of the Ætna. When the work was completed in May, 1905, the Company moved into its new quarters. The report of the building committee, made shortly afterward, reported the cost of the completed structure as a little over $479,000. The building is five stories in height, with a frontage of 94½ feet, and a depth of 165 feet. Its construction of granite, limestone, brick and iron, and tile roof, makes it as nearly fire-proof as human ingenuity could devise.

While the new building was in process of erection,

HOME OFFICE OF THE ÆTNA INSURANCE COMPANY
SINCE 1905

and everything seemed moving along serenely, the Company in 1904 struck a bad fire year. There were three real conflagrations — at Baltimore, Toronto and Rochester — with combined losses to the Company of $966,000. There was a shock through the country, when in February 7, 1904, the telegraph instruments clicked out the news that the business centre of Baltimore was on fire. Fanned by high winds, the flames swept like a pestilence over 150 acres and left few buildings in their path undestroyed. It was not a town of wooden buildings, as was largely the case at Chicago in the conflagration there thirty-three years before. This section of Baltimore was substantially built of stone and brick, with many buildings of what was called, and believed to be, fire-proof construction, yet even they could not withstand the furnace heat of this thirty hours' siege of fire. The total loss was $50,000,000, of which amount $727,000 fell to the lot of the Ætna.

While the embers were still glowing red in the streets of the devastated city, President Clark, with characteristic energy, and in the spirit with which the Ætna had borne all its crises, wrote these words, addressed to the Company's agents:

We know you are all interested in the effect the Baltimore fire will have upon this Company. We have lived through many conflagrations, notably New York, 1845; St. Louis, 1849; Chillicothe, Ohio, 1852; Montreal, 1852; Portland, 1866; Vicksburg, 1867; Chicago, 1871; Boston, 1872; Chicago (No. 2), 1874; Oshkosh, 1875; Virginia City, 1875; Haverhill, 1882; Boston (No. 2), 1889; Ottawa and Hull, 1900; Jacksonville, 1901; Paterson and Waterbury, in 1902, with numerous others of smaller amounts, always paying one hundred cents on the dollar, which we think clearly demonstrates our ability and willingness to continue in the good work of furnishing absolute indemnity to the insuring public.

Our Baltimore losses will somewhat exceed a half million dollars, but we have the cash in bank to meet all drafts as the losses are adjusted, and also to meet payments on our new fireproof office building now in process of erection. A glance at our last Annual Statement, showing over $15,000,000 of Assets invested in the choicest of securities, with a Surplus of over $6,000,000, and a Surplus of over $10,000,000 to the policy holders, is all the evidence needed to demonstrate the solidity of the Ætna and its ability to meet all its liabilities.

But the fire at Baltimore was after all but a trifle compared with the tragedy that occurred two years later, on April 18, 1906 — the greatest disaster of modern times — the earthquake and the conflagration at San Francisco. The first "shock" came in the early morning a little after five o'clock. Instantly all was confusion, consternation and terror caused by the jar of the violent concussion, the swaying of lofty buildings, the crashing fall of brick walls, the avalanche of chimneys and plaster. The people hurriedly half-dressed, rushed through the streets, dazed, frantic or paralyzed with fear.

Before six o'clock the first ominous puff of smoke was seen in the lower section of the city and the terrifying cry of "Fire" came from the lips of thousands. In a brief half-hour, wherever the eyes turned, could could be seen distinct and isolated columns of smoke and angry, leaping tongues of flame. For three days and three nights the fire raged and exacted an appalling toll from the stricken city. Some 2,000 acres, or 514 blocks, equivalent to one-sixth of the city plan, were reduced to ruins. Of the 28,000 buildings destroyed only 5,000 were such as involved steel, stone or brick in their construction; the others were of redwood, deemed comparatively unburnable. These houses stood the earthquake shock fairly well but fell before the flames. As in Baltimore, the "fire-proof" buildings suffered severely, and though some remained standing they were "gutted" and their contents consumed. The loss to life was about 500, which was much less than might have been expected, while the property loss reached the colossal figure of $350,000,000.

The people were homeless, destitute in every sense of the word, and their lot would have been hopeless were it not for the relief sent from every part of the country. Over nine million dollars in money was contributed, beside food, clothing and other necessities gladly furnished by the hand of humanity. But after all, as at the fire in Chicago, it was to the insurance companies that the thoughts of the people turned as their one hope as they faced their future.

What this fire cost the insurance companies may be seen, to a degree, in the statement made by President Burchell, of the National Board of Fire Underwriters, in the year following. He said that this single conflagration had cost the fire insurance companies of America every dollar of profit made out of underwriting in 47 years — that is, back to 1860 — and in addition to this, nearly $80,000,000 more. Never was there such a proof of what fire insurance means to America, as a protection, a safeguard and a source of new strength and courage in a crisis to the individual or the community that sees its cherished possessions reduced to ashes in a few brief hours.

Three thousand miles away — at Hartford, in the office of the Ætna — these were serious days. As in the previous critical times in the history of the Company, when suddenly called upon to face a great loss, there was no hesitancy as to what it would do, but merely how much would it be required to pay, and how could the funds best be provided. A single sentence in the minutes of the Directors' meeting of May 1st tells the story: "Officers are authorized to borrow $2,000,000 to settle claims and to sell such securities as may be necessary." This action, with money taken from the reserve created for just such a need, was the way out. But it was hard to see the underwriting profits of more than half a lifetime of the company wiped out in a few days.

What the losses would be was for a time a matter of estimate and guessing; but they were certain to be disastrously large, for the Pacific Branch had been prospering and had written a great amount of local business. President Clark, who for nearly forty years had exercised personal supervision at the home office over Pacific Branch affairs, knew the city of San Francisco, from an underwriter's point of view, better even than he knew Hartford. When he received the reports showing the territory affected, he was able to estimate within a few thousands the total losses of the Company.

The gross loss was $3,383,019.47, but as the Ætna had re-insured part of its risk in other companies, the net amount actually paid to meet claims was $2,891,287.77. In September the Directors passed a special vote of appreciation of the prudence and successful service of President Clark in the matter of the San Francisco fire and his wise handling of the Company's affairs.

In its settlement of losses, great as they were, the Ætna made a splendid showing. There were many technical points that might have been invoked to lessen the amount of its payments, but these were brushed aside without question or cavil; every loss was paid in full — one hundred cents on the dollar, without discount.

What San Francisco thought of the Ætna is shown in the report of Professor A. W. Whitney, appointed by a Committee of the Chamber of Commerce of San Francisco, to investigate the fire insurance side of the great conflagration. His report, which contained a list of the companies involved, and a complete statement of their record in the adjustment of losses and payment of claims, gave the Ætna Insurance Company a marking of one hundred per cent.

In the year following the fire — 1907 — there was new blood brought into the Company by the election of three assistant secretaries: Edgar J. Sloan, Edwin S. Allen, and Guy E. Beardsley. They were all trained underwriters who had proved themselves in field work in the service of the Company.

Edgar J. Sloan was born in Hartford on November 4, 1870, and was educated in the public schools of his native city. When he was eighteen years of age, he entered the local agency of the Phœnix at Hartford, and four years later became examiner for the Company. In 1897 he went with the Home Insurance Company of New York, serving first as special agent, and later as state agent for Connecticut and Rhode Island. In 1903 he joined the Ætna forces as special agent for Connecticut, Western Massachusetts and Vermont. Two years later he was made General Agent, then Assistant Secretary, and in 1912 he was elected to his present position of Secretary of the Company.

Edwin S. Allen, the second of the new assistant secretaries, the son of Francis B. Allen, well known in insurance circles as Vice-President of the Hartford Steam Boiler Inspection and Insurance Company, was born in New York City on July 12, 1871. His early education in the public schools of his native city preceded a course at Trinity College, Hartford, from which he graduated in 1894. It was in this year that he joined the ranks of the Ætna. By successive advances from clerk to examiner, special agent and general agent, he reached his present position of Assistant Secretary. In the same year that the Ætna rounded out its first hundred years, Mr. Allen completed a quarter century in the service of the Company.

The third of the new assistant secretaries, Guy E. Beardsley, was born on December 14, 1874, at Coventry, New York, and received his early education in the public and high schools of Hartford. Then he went to Yale and in 1896 graduated from the Sheffield Scientific School. After a few months at banking, he entered the service of the Ætna as an examiner.

PRESIDENT CLARK'S ADMINISTRATION

Here he remained for several years and then went to the National Union Fire Insurance Company of Pittsburgh, as special agent in Western Pennsylvania for a year, later serving the Home Insurance Company of New York for three years as special agent in Connecticut and Rhode Island, and in 1905 returning to the Ætna as special agent in Connecticut, Western Massachusetts and Vermont. With the exception of the four years spent in the field for the National Union and the Home, Mr. Beardsley's business career has been spent with the Ætna.

In 1907, the year that brought in the three assistant secretaries, the Company took a new, long stride forward when it secured a charter amendment permitting it to engage in ocean marine insurance. Since 1843 the Ætna had been doing an inland marine business, but which had never assumed large proportions. How this branch has developed during the last several years into a vital and successful part of the Ætna is related in a subsequent chapter.

The Directors, in 1909, in a spirit of further expansion, secured a charter amendment enabling the Company to write various phases of automobile insurance, which, during the preceding three years, the Company had been writing in a limited way. In the same year the capital stock was increased, from four to five million dollars, and two years later, by the thirteenth and last amendment to the charter to date, authority was granted to increase the capital from five to ten million dollars. Under this amendment no action has yet been taken.

It was in 1912 that the promotion of Edgar J. Sloan to his present position as Secretary of the Company left a vacancy that was filled by the election of Ralph B. Ives, who had already served eight years with the Ætna. He entered the employment of the Company in 1904 as clerk in the home office, in which place he remained until 1907, when he was appointed special agent and adjuster for Connecticut, Vermont and Western Massachusetts, with headquarters in Hartford. In 1910 he was elected chairman of the executive committee of the New England Insurance Exchange, serving with marked ability for two years, when he was relieved from field duties by President Clark and elected Assistant Secretary of the Ætna, which office he still holds. In 1915 he was assigned to service at Chicago in the Western Branch of the Company, with headquarters at Chicago, in the management of which he has since been associated with General Agent Thomas E. Gallagher and Assistant General Agent Louis O. Kohtz.

While the Company was enjoying the sunshine of prosperity about this time it met with a serious loss that could not be measured by a row of figures and a dollar sign. It was the loss of a man, a member of the Board of Directors — J. Pierpont Morgan, the great American financier — who died in Rome on March 31, 1913.

What Mr. Morgan meant to the Ætna cannot better be told than by quoting the resolution adopted by his associates on the Board of Directors:

Being a resident of New York City, he attended only a few meetings of the Board (elected Director June, 1883), but he was

PRESIDENT CLARK'S ADMINISTRATION

always a ready and willing advisor in the Company's financial matters, which has repeatedly resulted to its great advantage.

The reputation of a Corporation is the reputation of its Directors and Officers, and no one recognized this more nor sustained it better than Mr. Morgan. His integrity was so well known that his name in the Directorate of any company was a veritable tower of strength.

The Ætna Insurance Company has been greatly indebted for careful and successful direction to three generations in the Morgan family — to Joseph Morgan, his grandfather — to Junius Spencer Morgan, his father — both of whom were for a time successively Directors in this Company, and especially to our late associate himself.

Mr. Morgan was a mighty man, knowing only good deeds, so that he established himself thereby in the confidence, in the respect and in the love of his fellow men. As associates with him, we have learned his standards, and as his successors we must sustain them.

Upon his son, J. P. Morgan, Jr., fell the responsibility and honor of carrying on the Morgan tradition of service and loyalty to the Ætna when he was elected in January, 1914, to succeed his father as a member of the Board of Directors.

When in August of this year, the rumblings of possible war in Europe became the actual conflict itself, ushering in a world war of unbelievable awfulness, involving twenty-seven nations, every form of insurance felt the shock as sensitively as a seismograph registers an earthquake. Ocean marine insurance was naturally first affected, though quickly followed by the menace of incendiarism in munition factories and shipyards, which brought new problems to fire insurance companies. How the Ætna carried itself in those four terrible years, making a new chapter in the administration of President Clark, is given in later pages of this chronicle.

What the service of Mr. Clark really meant to the Ætna was expressed most delightfully and convincingly at an informal dinner given in his honor by the Directors and Officers on December 1, 1917, the fiftieth anniversary of his joining the Company. The spirit of the meeting was voiced in a resolution proposed by Director Francis Goodwin, grandson of Joseph Morgan, in whose coffee house the Ætna was born. This resolution is worthy of being quoted in full, as recording the spirit of a most important occasion not only in the life of President Clark, but in the life of the Ætna:

RESOLVED, That we, the Directors and Officers of the Ætna Insurance Company, assembled today to celebrate the completion of fifty years of service which Mr. William B. Clark has rendered as an Officer of this Company, of which for twenty-five years he has been President, desire to place on record,

First: Our congratulations on the uniform and remarkable success which has distinguished his administration as shown in the results which have been achieved.

Second: Our appreciation of the ability, fidelity, and steadfast courage which, during the days of adversity as well as in times of prosperity, have, through all vicissitudes of half a century, preserved the high and honorable reputation of the Company and maintained its position among the greatest insurance corporations of the world.

Third: Our felicitations that in all of the personal relations which have existed between him and the Officers and Directors of the Company he has, by his unfailing courtesy and consideration, won not only in the highest degree, the respect and confidence of his associates, but their sincere and lasting affection.

It rarely falls to the lot of an individual to celebrate more than one fiftieth anniversary in his business career, but President Clark may lay claim to two. In 1907, ten years before the event just related, the leading fire insurance men of New York City joined in

PRESENTED AT PRESIDENT CLARK'S FIFTIETH BUSINESS ANNIVERSARY
Presentation Address was made by J. Montgomery Hare

PRESIDENT CLARK'S ADMINISTRATION

presenting to him a beautifully engraved loving-cup in token of their personal affection and high esteem, and in recognition of the fiftieth anniversary of his entry into the business of fire insurance. In point of continuous service President Clark may justly be regarded as the dean of insurance executives. In June, 1919, the same month that the Ætna observed its one hundredth anniversary, its veteran and still active President reached the ripe age of seventy-eight years, fifty-two of which had been devoted to the service of the Company and sixty-two in the business.

Since his election as President of the Ætna more than a quarter of a century ago, Mr. Clark has contributed largely not only to the growth and expansion of the Company itself, but to the cause of underwriting in general. He has always taken a deep interest in the work of the National Board of Fire Underwriters, serving two years as Vice-President and one year as President of that organization, from 1894 to 1896, inclusive.

In the twenty-seven years of President Clark's administration of Ætna affairs, there has been much that was vital which cannot be expressed in a phrase. It has been possible to mention only a few of the outstanding events. No individual, and President Clark least of all, would claim personal credit for the tremendous growth which the Company has enjoyed in these years. From the humblest agent in the field, up through all the grades to the highest official, each has contributed his share. Throughout the entire organization there has been a fine spirit of mutual loyalty and devotion. Immediately associated with President Clark, and co-operating with him in every phase of the work, are the executive officials of whom brief mention has been made. While each of these is charged with the supervision of some particular division of the business, the duties of all are so interwoven and so nicely adjusted, that perfect team-work is the result. Nor is this spirit of co-operation limited to the official force: it is in evidence among the agents in the field, in the branch offices and in all of the relations between the Company and its agents.

Too much emphasis cannot be given to the part which the local agent has played in the development of the Ætna during the last hundred years. No history of the Company would be complete which did not tell the stories of how its great agency system was built up, the organization of its Western and Pacific Branches, the development of its marine business, which now reaches into every part of the world, the effects of legislation, and of the Company's progress during the Great War. So vital and important are these in the whole story of the Company and in the history of American fire insurance in general, they have been reserved for later and separate chapters.

CHAPTER XI

THE ÆTNA AND ITS AGENTS

IN the history of any institution we shall always discover that many separate factors and influences have contributed to its growth and greatness. So it is in the story of "Old Ætna." No single factor has exerted a greater influence in the building of this great insurance organization than has the agent. It is true, of course, that other elements have been vitally important — the firm foundation laid by President Brace and the early Directors, the formulation of fundamental principles for their guidance and for the direction of agents, courage and fortitude in facing disaster, prompt payment of losses, fair dealing, and sound and conservative business management. Lacking any of these the Ætna probably would be only a memory, like hundreds of others strewn along the path of American fire insurance.

Without the agent, however, no growth would have been possible, and the Company to-day, if it had survived at all, would be but a small local organization unknown beyond the borders of its home State. In a letter written only a few weeks before the Ætna

 ONE HUNDRED YEARS OF FIRE INSURANCE

celebrated its One Hundredth Anniversary in June 1919, its veteran President, William B. Clark, said:

> The success of the Ætna is largely owing to the faithful and continuous service of a large corps of most satisfactory local agents throughout this country and Canada. We feel deeply indebted to them for the services which they have rendered.

When the Ætna made its modest beginning in Joseph Morgan's Coffee House at Hartford one hundred years ago, there were fewer than a hundred insurance agents in the whole country, and even these were not agents as we understand the term to-day. They were merely solicitors for applications; in most cases they were not even that — they were simply *receivers* of applications; they had no authority to write an insurance policy. Every application had to be forwarded to the home office to be considered cautiously by the Officers and Directors; each one had to be accompanied by a drawing or survey showing the location of the building on which insurance was sought, and all surrounding buildings. The old files of the Ætna are filled with these crude drawings. They disclose the fact that some of the early agents, while good solicitors, were not finished artists. Judging from these sketches, there must have been some curious buildings in those days. However, they served their purpose, enabling the Directors to pass more or less intelligently on the proposed risk.

In the evolution of the insurance agent we may read much of the story of insurance, from its crude and simple beginnings centuries ago to its highly organized state of the present day. Every new business,

profession or occupation is simply the outgrowth of some new need. When savagery gave way to civilization, laws were found to be necessary for the regulation and protection of society; as laws multiplied, there arose the need for interpreting them; and in response to this need the lawyer was evolved.

The seeds of the future business of insurance were planted in the need of some merchant for others to share with him the risk of shipping his goods to a foreign port. He sought those with money who were willing to share his possible losses in return for a share in his expected profits. As trading increased and this new field for speculation or investment grew larger, those having money began to seek the opportunities for sharing such risks; they no longer waited to be sought. And here we find the germ of the great insurance organizations of the Twentieth Century. As these early underwriters grew more numerous, they gradually divided and formed themselves into groups, and these groups, in turn, became companies.

Cause and effect are sometimes so closely related that it is impossible to distinguish between them. Whether the first insurance agent grew out of the need of the merchant for assistance in finding others to share his risks, or whether groups of individual underwriters selected some one to represent them, we are unable to judge. It is probable that the agent evolved out of the needs of both, and, paradoxical as it may appear, it is not improbable that out of *his* need was evolved the insurance corporation, for which he now is the agent. It may well be, if the first agent represented the insured, that his unpleasant duty of calling upon the numerous individual underwriters to collect from them their share of losses, prompted the idea that it would be much easier and less embarrassing for him if all the underwriters would deposit their funds in a common pool.

While the exact origin of the insurance agent is therefore a subject for interesting speculation, it is worthy of note that with the advent of the Ætna Insurance Company, his occupation for the first time attained to the dignity of a *profession*. That the Ætna had a definitely new conception of the functions of an agent is shown in the following extract from a letter written in July, 1820, to Stephen Tillinghast, the Company's first agent in Providence, Rhode Island:

> Agents of insurance companies have generally no other power and discretion than simply to deliver instruments as drawn by the officers of the company. The Ætna agents are quite differently intrusted and empowered, and the highest confidence is reposed in their integrity and intelligence. In most cases they determine the rate of premiums and fill up and countersign blank policies with which they are previously furnished, without reference to the office.

In the early days of the Nineteenth Century there were few fire insurance companies and only a small scattering of agents. The operating field of each company was extremely limited. As we have seen, the few agents had no authority to issue policies. They received no commissions for securing business, their compensation consisting merely of a small fee for their labor in making the survey, which was paid by the insured, another small fee of fifty cents for filling in the policy, and finally a fee for assisting in the adjustment of a loss.

It, therefore, was an epoch-making event in the evolution of the insurance agent when the newly organized Company decided to establish its business on a national or on even an international scale. This new and bold policy depended solely for its success upon the ability of the Company to select agents distant from its home office who could be trusted to transact business with the same judgment and discretion, and with the same consideration for the welfare of the institution, as would be exercised by the Officers and Directors themselves. Doleful prophecies of disaster greeted this move. Even after a decade of business, echoes of these predictions still could be heard, for in 1830 Secretary Goodwin wrote to one of the agents:

> It is the opinion of some persons of considerable observation that an insurance company cannot succeed that transacts a majority of its business by agents.
> We do not subscribe to that doctrine, but on the contrary think that an intelligent agent is as capable of transacting the business of his agency as a Board of Directors are the business of the office. Such will not be the case, however, of an agent who is governed by no other motive than gain.
> Insurance like all other business must be conducted with judgment and caution to render it successful. It becomes a gambling business when no attention is paid to amount, location and character, and like all gambling will end in ruin.

It was no easy undertaking upon which the young Company was about to embark. Not only must the agents be found — men of unquestionable character, spotless integrity and mature judgment — but when found they must be trained for the duties and responsibilities of their new profession. Many textbooks of exceeding value even to the experienced agent of to-day might be compiled from the letters which were written to the early recruits by Ætna officials, and from the pamphlets and booklets which were prepared for their guidance during the first few decades of the Company's existence. Among these was a little booklet prepared by Secretary Perkins in September, 1819, entitled "Instructions and Explanations for the use and direction of the Agents of the Ætna Insurance Company," the first of its kind ever issued by a fire insurance company. Revised in 1826, again in 1830 and at frequent intervals thereafter, this primer of underwriting, supplemented by the letters of Secretaries Perkins, Goodwin and Loomis and finally by the "Ætna Bible"—an honor title bestowed on the "Guide to Fire Insurance" issued by General Agent J. B. Bennett of the Ætna's Western Branch in 1857—contain all the elements of a complete educational course for the profession of an insurance agent.

Let us turn at random the pages of the "Ætna Bible." Here on page 149 we will find the following advice to an agent under the caption "Soliciting":

> There is, probably, no occupation in life, where it is so necessary to combat the caprices of mankind, and to deal with humanity in such various phases, as the solicitation of insurance; and no class of men, consequently, require in a greater degree, that peculiar *tact* which a close knowledge of human nature gives its possessor than insurance agents.
>
> An agent who talks to all men in the same strain, using the same arguments in every case, will hardly reach the maximum of success. The successful agent has to study his subject as a

physician does a patient — they do not all require the same treatment.

Most men have some *keynote* — some *chord* — by touching which you lay bare the *soul*. It may vibrate ever so slightly, but vibrate it will, according to the nature which animates it; and this is all that is necessary. Many men, keen judges of humanity, understand this principle thoroughly, and can touch these keys with a delicacy of *finesse* indicating genius, if not positive intuition. This judgment can be a science in which all, by study, practice and observation, can become more or less proficient.

In the selection of its first agents the Ætna moved with the greatest caution. Those chosen were, almost without exception, either former residents of Hartford or known personally by one or more of the Directors. While it is always interesting to know the "firsts" in any enterprise, to devote even a line to the "first" Ætna agent in each locality where one may now be found, would alone fill a volume much larger than this. As there are to-day over 10,000 Ætna agents in the hamlets, villages and cities of the United States and Canada, this would mean an equal number of "firsts." There are certain special sections and localities, however, which deserve special mention because of their relation to the whole story.

It would appear from the records that Franklin Ripley, of Greenfield, Massachusetts, was the first agent appointed by the Ætna, although that distinction may, with equal warrant, be claimed for several others, for it is probable that the first dozen agents were named simultaneously. For convenience in making entries in the journal and other books of account, Secretary Perkins designated each new agent by a number. If the sequence of those numbers indicates the order in which the agents were chosen, then the case is made for Franklin Ripley. His number was "22." All lower numbers were used to indicate accounts other than those of agents. William L. Perkins of Ashford, Connecticut, of whom we shall hear more, might rise and challenge this reasoning, for he was appointed about the same time as Ripley and his account number also was "22"; but this probably was a mistake in entry, for Ripley's first policy is No. 44 and Perkins' No. 64. Other agents appointed during the first few months were Hall & Green at Rockingham, Vermont; George W. Hall, Brattleboro, Vermont; Daniel Rand, Middletown, Connecticut; Gurdon Robins, Fayetteville, North Carolina; Orin Beckley, Berlin, Connecticut; Roger L. Skinner, New Haven, Connecticut; John Ely, Jr., Albany, New York; Roger Whittelsey, Southington, Connecticut; Thomas Beals, Canandaigua, New York; Joseph Wood, Stamford, Connecticut; Stephen Tillinghast, Providence, Rhode Island; Alexander B. Converse, Troy, New York; Everard Peck, Rochester, New York; Isaac C. Bates, Northampton, Massachusetts; Ezekiel R. Colt, Pittsfield, Massachusetts; and Griswold & Follett, Burlington, Vermont.

There is no doubt that Gurdon Robins, of Fayetteville, North Carolina, wrote the first Ætna policy outside of Connecticut, No. 40, for $2,000, on which the premium was $35. Before moving to the South, Robins had lived in Hartford, and in after years he returned to his old home. He was a brother of Ephraim Robins who, as founder of the

 THE ÆTNA AND ITS AGENTS

general agency at Cincinnati for the Protection Insurance Company in 1826, came to be known as the father of all General Agents. Although never connected with the Ætna, he helped, nevertheless, to lay the foundations for the great Western Branch of the Company, the history of which will be given in another chapter.

There is a story or incident of interest connected with nearly all of the early agents whose names we have given. On July 3, 1820, John Ely, Jr., of Albany, sent in to the home office a policy for $5,000 on property owned by Martin Van Buren, eighth President of the United States. It was through Daniel Rand, the first agent at Middletown, that the Ætna inaugurated the business of Reinsurance by re-insuring the risks of the Middletown Fire Insurance Company, to which we have referred in our general story. Rand was the secretary of the Middletown company. A distinction of a different kind can be credited to Isaac C. Bates, the agent at Northampton, for it was through him that the Ætna paid in 1821 its first loss by fire.

For many years during the early life of the Ætna, the work of supervising agencies, appointing new agents, adjusting losses and other similar duties, were, as we have seen, performed by the Officers and Directors of the Company. It was not until near the middle of the century that expanding business and growing needs evolved specialists to discharge these duties, and they were known as *Special* and *General* Agents. In the history of American Fire

Insurance there appears to be more or less confusion in the use of the terms Special Agent and General Agent; in many cases they have been used interchangeably, and are so used even to-day. In order to avoid confusion, however, we will describe the Special Agent as one employed by the Company to travel, supervise agencies and appoint or recommend the appointment of new agents, and the General Agent as one who has charge of a branch of the Company's business, with authority to appoint sub-agents, supervise their work, receive their reports and adjust losses and otherwise conduct the business of the Company in a certain specified territory.

Whatever dispute there may be over the question of whether Franklin Ripley or William L. Perkins was the first *local* agent for the Ætna, there is no doubt that Perkins was the first *special* agent of the Company, and so far as is known, the first of all special agents. Under date of October 27, 1825, this entry appears in the Ætna minutes of a Directors' meeting:

> Voted to authorize employment of suitable person to travel in Pennsylvania, Ohio, Indiana, Illinois, Missouri and Southern states and establish agencies.

William L. Perkins was chosen as the "suitable person," and on November 30 he turned over his local agency at Ashford to the care of Ichabod Bulkley and prepared for what in those days was a formidable journey, for the stage-coach was still the only mode of inland travel. When he returned six months later, the Ætna was known and agencies had been established in practically every state of the Union. Perkins had traveled as far south as Natchez, Mississippi, and as far west as Fort Dearborn, Illinois, the future site of Chicago. Among the many agents he appointed, special mention may be made of Thaddeus Sanford at Mobile, Alabama. He proved to be an industrious agent, for when in the fall of 1827 occurred the great fire which wiped out Mobile and precipitated the first financial crisis in the affairs of the Ætna, the policies written by Sanford during the preceding year cost the Company over $60,000. This calamity did not shake the faith of the Directors far away in Hartford, for Secretary Perkins immediately on receipt of the bad news sent the following message to Sanford: "Exercising the same prudence as heretofore, do not decline risks," although at the moment he might have been glad if he could have written, as Secretary Loomis did twenty years later to Andrew N. Williams, an agent at West Woodstock, Connecticut:

We have been in this office sixteen years and this is the first intimation that we have an agency at West Woodstock. Altho' you have made us no money, we can certify you have lost none for us.

While Special Agent Perkins was traveling through the West and South, the Ætna officials back in Hartford were not idle. They were rapidly increasing the number of agencies in Connecticut and nearby States. In fact, by this time, the Company had become not only national in scope, but also international, for it had agencies in every important American town and in Canada as well.

Here again we find that the Ætna was a pioneer,

for it was the first American Company to appoint agents and write fire insurance in Canada.

It was on December 22, 1821, that Abijah Bigelow, of Montreal, Quebec, was appointed as the first Canadian agent for the Ætna. On that date Secretary Perkins wrote to him enclosing the commission. His letter is worth giving in full, as it not only illustrates the difficulties of communication in those days, but it also contains in part the terms of the agent's employment, and caution as to acceptance of too much liability subject to a sweeping fire — which is one of the very basic principles of fire underwriting today.

Hartford Con.
Dec. 22nd, 1821.

Mr. Abijah Bigelow:

Sir, I address you in consequence of a letter re$^{\underline{d}}$ by Mr. Ward Woodbridge from Mr. Jacob DeWitt, presuming from its contents that Mr. DeWitt has conferred with you upon the subject of an agency for the Ætna Ins. Co. of this place, and upon the supposition that the appointment would be agreeable to you. I have pleasure herewith to send you a commission — the other necessary documents must be forwarded by private conveyance for which I suppose I shall have an opportunity via Boston next week & shall send one hundred Blank policies signed by our Pres. & Secy. & sealed with the seal of the office, a letter of instructions, copies of policies, and advertisements. Mr. DeWitt remarks that he thinks higher premiums are now paid in Montreal than our proposals demand, if so it may not be best to use the advertisements sent, but whether you do or do not use them you will if you think proper advertise your Agency in the News paper — By our printed letter of instructions you will perceive that you are limited not to take a risk exceeding five thousand dollars. By this you will consider yourself authorized to take risks of any amt. not exceeding $10,000. The printed letter also limits your commission to two and a half pr ct. instead of which 5 pr ct. will be allowed and p$^{\underline{d}}$ you. — However anxious the Directors are to do business there is one point of prudence they wish to keep constantly in view — to wit, never to endanger the existence of the Company by risking too much exposed to a sweeping fire. We know indeed a whole city may be conflagrated but such a contingency is too remote to be calculated upon, while whole streets and squares are so often destroyed, it might with propriety be deemed folly in us to risk our whole or a major part of our capital upon them. We wish returns by mail though the postage will be considerable unless a few days delay will afford a safe and convenient private conveyance.

I will thank you to remark to Mr. DeWitt that upon the recommendation of Mr. Woodbridge when he returned from Montreal last season the office concluded to appoint him the agent which would long since have been done had an opportunity to for^d the papers been known to me.

I am respectfully your ob^t Servant
                    Isaac Perkins, Secy.

To-day the Ætna Insurance Company is as well known in Canada as it is in the United States; in fact, many Canadians look upon it as a Canadian institution, for it began operations there nearly half a century before the Dominion of Canada was formed. The story of the development of the Company's business there would be only a repetition on a smaller scale of the growth of the Ætna in the United States. Abijah Bigelow continued to serve as the agent at Montreal until 1835.

The second agent in Canada was David R. Stewart of Quebec, appointed in 1827. In the previous year John Leander Starr was named as the first Ætna agent at Halifax, Nova Scotia, and in 1829 Elisha De W. Ratchford became the first Ætna agent at St. John, New Brunswick. No agent was appointed in Toronto until June, 1842, when Director Joseph Morgan, in the course of one of his many trips as special agent for the Ætna, appointed John Walton as the first agent there. Walton served only two years when he was succeeded by Edward George O'Brien.

Unlike the Western Branch of the Ætna, with its headquarters in Chicago, or the Pacific Branch at San Francisco, the main business of the Company in the Canadian field has always been directed from the Home Office at Hartford, and for several years past has been under the immediate supervision of Secretary Edgar J. Sloan. In accordance with a ruling of the Canadian Superintendent of Insurance, however, the Company on January 1, 1916, established a Canadian Branch Office at Toronto, Ontario, to which all loss reports, monthly accounts and remittances must be sent, and Chief Agent A. M. M. Kirkpatrick, who is also one of the local agents there, was placed in charge as Chief Canadian Agent. All agents in Canada, however, are appointed and controlled by the Home Office, thus bringing them in direct touch with the officials of the Company, to the great advantage of both.

The only companies writing insurance in Canada at the time of the Ætna's entrance in 1821, were the Phoenix of London, which began its Canadian business in 1804, and the Quebec Fire Assurance Company, which celebrated its one hundredth anniversary in 1918. It was not until 1869, two years after the formation of the Dominion, that Canada began to collect insurance statistics. Many serious fires have occurred which have wiped out the profits of years, notably at Montreal, Quebec, St. John, New Brunswick, Ottawa, Toronto and Halifax.

 THE ÆTNA AND ITS AGENTS

It was in 1828 that the Ætna made its first experiment in the General Agency field and appointed as its first General Agent Jeremiah Van Rensselaer of Canandaigua, New York. He had been the secretary of the Western Fire Insurance Company of New York, which had just failed. When he came with the Ætna he brought with him about twenty former agents of the Western Company, located principally in Western New York towns. His territory was not clearly defined, for he was authorized to appoint sub-agents at any point in Western New York or in the Western country, except in such places as Ætna agents were already operating. Among the Company's principal Western agents at this time were Samuel Cowles, a former Hartford resident who had moved to Cleveland, Ohio, to take up the practice of law in 1819; Henry S. Cole, appointed at Detroit in 1823; General Simon Perkins, first Ætna agent at Warren, Ohio; William Goodman, second Ætna agent at Cincinnati, having in 1826 succeeded his father, Timothy S. Goodman, appointed in December, 1823; Nathaniel Sawyer, Chillicothe, Ohio; and Isaac Thom, Louisville, Kentucky, both appointed as first agents in 1825; James Crosby at Zanesville, Ohio, John Sering at Washington, Indiana, and James Smith at Vincennes, Indiana—all appointed in 1826 as the first agents in their respective towns.

It was on February 4, 1828, that Jeremiah Van Rensselaer received his commission as General Agent with full authority to appoint sub-agents at his pleasure. Doubt must have come to the minds of the Ætna officials as to the wisdom of what they had felt in the beginning to be a somewhat radical extension of their original plan for conducting their business through agents, for in the following October Secretary Goodwin wrote to Van Rensselaer stating that thereafter the appointment of agents in his territory would be made directly by the Home Office, but that his recommendations as to such appointments would be followed. This arrangement continued until January, 1829, when occurred the death of General Agent Van Rensselaer. To an applicant for the vacant position Secretary Goodwin wrote: "After mature deliberation at a special meeting the Directors concluded that it was inexpedient to appoint another General Agent, but to transact the business in the ordinary way."

With one exception, Van Rensselaer was the last General Agent of the Ætna until the appointment of J. B. Bennett and the establishment of the Western Branch at Cincinnati in 1853. The exception occurred in 1840 when Herman Baldwin, Ætna agent at Richmond, Virginia, was appointed General Agent for Virginia. His claim to the title of General Agent was largely technical, however. He was named at the request of other Ætna agents in Virginia, who found that if they could serve as sub-agents of a General Agent, it would be unnecessary for them to pay a special state tax which had been levied against all direct-reporting agents of foreign insurance companies. He was therefore a General Agent in name only.

With expanding business and an increasing number of agents at distant points, it became less and less possible for the directors of the Company to devote their time to traveling about the country supervising the agency work, and the Special Agent became more and more a necessary and important figure in the growing organization. Until about 1840 the duties of Special Agent were largely performed by Director Joseph Morgan, when additional men were employed.

Among these special mention may be made of Col. A. A. Williams, who served the Ætna as Special Agent from 1840 until after the close of the Civil War; S. B. Hamilton, one of the Directors, who was a Special Agent from 1840 to 1848, and who was then made local agent at Albany, New York, for the three Hartford insurance companies; W. I. Pardee, whose title was General Agent with headquarters at Oswego, New York, but who was really special agent for much of the western territory and was appointed in 1848; A. F. Willmarth, who was elected traveling agent for the New England territory in 1850 and later became the first Assistant Secretary of the Ætna, and in 1856 Vice-President of the Home Insurance Company of New York; C. C. Hine, appointed in 1859 to supervise the work of agents in Alabama and Georgia, and later editor of *The Insurance Monitor* of New York; Henry L. Pasco, appointed as special agent in the late fifties and later local agent at Chicago as a partner of Jonathan Goodwin, Jr., under the firm name of Goodwin & Pasco, until after the great Chicago fire of 1871; E. J. Bassett, who served the Ætna continuously as special agent with the title of General Agent from 1862 until his death in 1891; J. C. Hilliard, special agent from 1866 to 1891. Many other names familiar in the history of American Fire Insurance might be enumerated in this list. The Ætna to-day has special agents in every State in the Union and for all the Provinces of Canada.

It may be of interest to many of the Ætna agents of to-day, if not to the general reader, to mention the names of the first of their predecessors in some of the states and principal cities of the country, and to trace, briefly, the progress of a few of the more important agencies such as those at Chicago, Cincinnati, New York, and possibly one or two others which were destined to figure largely in the future history of the Company. The list follows:

Alabama, Mobile, Thaddeus Sanford, 1825
California, San Francisco, Edward H. Parker, 1858
Connecticut, Ashford, William L. Perkins, 1819
              Hartford, General Leonard A. Dickinson, 1868
District of Columbia, Washington, Moses Poor, 1826.
Georgia, Augusta, Horatio Alden, 1821.
Illinois, Chicago, Gurdon S. Hubbard, 1843.
Indiana, Washington, John Sering, 1826.
Kentucky, Louisville, Isaac Thom, 1825.
Louisiana, New Orleans, Bowers, Osborne & Co., 1823
Maine, Saco, Lauriston Ward, 1822.
Maryland, Baltimore, Leonard Kimball, 1824.
Massachusetts, Greenfield, Franklin Ripley, 1819.
              Boston, Charles D. Coolidge, 1826.
Michigan, Detroit, Henry S. Cole, 1823.
Mississippi, Natchez, H. A. Daingerfield, 1826.
Missouri, St. Louis, Christian Saunders, 1830.
New Hampshire, Portsmouth, Samuel Lord, 1821.
New Jersey, Paterson, Philomen Dickerson, 1821.
New York, Albany, John Ely, Jr., 1819.
              New York City, Edward Dickenson, 1826.
North Carolina, Fayetteville, Gurdon Robins, 1819.
Ohio, Cleveland, Samuel Cowles, 1819.

THE ÆTNA AND ITS AGENTS

Pennsylvania, Pittsburgh, Edward Seldon, 1820.
              Philadelphia, Mark Richards, 1826.
Rhode Island, Providence, Stephen Tillinghast, 1820.
South Carolina, Cheraw, Augustin Averill, 1821.
Vermont, Rockingham, Hall & Green, 1819.
Virginia, Richmond, Thomas May, 1824.
West Virginia, Wheeling, Samuel H. Fitzhugh, 1826.

As may be noted in the foregoing list, it was not until 1868, when the Ætna was nearly half a century old, that a local agent for the city of Hartford was chosen. Up to this time all of the Company's local business had been conducted directly through the home office. On January 22 of this year General Leonard A. Dickinson was appointed Hartford agent. Prior to the war he had gained a working knowledge of insurance as a clerk in the offices of one of the Hartford insurance companies. He served during the Civil War as a captain of the Twelfth Regiment, Connecticut Volunteers. He was a loyal friend of the Ætna and served the Company continuously, first alone, and then as senior member of the agency firm of Dickinson, Beardsley & Beardsley, until his death at the age of seventy-four years, on January 27, 1901. This agency, now operating under the firm name of Beardsley & Beardsley, has since continued to represent the Ætna in its own home and maintains its offices in the Ætna home office building.

With the establishment by the Protection Insurance Company of the General Agency under Ephraim Robins in 1826 and the Western Branch of the Ætna under J. B. Bennett in 1853, Cincinnati, which early came to be known as the "Queen City of the West," was destined to win a unique position as a school for fire insurance underwriters. Many men who later became dominant figures in the insurance world, there received their early training. It was late in 1823 when the Ætna entered Cincinnati and appointed Timothy S. Goodman, a former Hartford resident, as its first agent. He served until 1826, when he was succeeded by his son William, who retired in 1837, when Nathaniel Sawyer, the Ætna's first agent at Chillicothe, Ohio, was placed in temporary charge of the Cincinnati agency. He returned to Chillicothe in 1841. During the next four years the Ætna and Protection were jointly represented by Henry Stagg and W. B. Robins, son of Ephraim, who succeeded his father as General Agent for the Protection in 1846. From 1845 to 1848 the Ætna agent was Henry Hayes, another former resident of Hartford. On his retirement James H. Carter was appointed, and he served as local agent at Cincinnati until the fall of 1853, when the Western Branch was established under General Agent J. B. Bennett.

Another city which looms large in the early history of fire insurance, is Chicago. In the early 40's Chicago was still an infant, though strong, lusty and growing rapidly. Long before the Ætna established its first agency there, it had received many applications for insurance through agents in other localities. It was not until 1842, however, after Director Joseph Morgan had visited the city and made a careful survey of the situation, that the Company decided to risk the perils of what they designated as a "wooden city." In November, 1841, and again in May, 1842, A. G. Hazard, the Ætna's agent in New York City, forwarded to the home office applications which he had received from New York owners of Chicago property, but Secretary Loomis wrote in reply: "We have had many applications from Chicago, but they have been uniformly declined."

While in Chicago, Director Morgan made tentative arrangements with Gurdon S. Hubbard to represent the Ætna in that city. This was in the early fall of 1842; but he was not actually commissioned by the Company to act as agent until June 3d of the following year. The first applications sent in by Hubbard were for Stephen F. Gale and the firm of Botsford & Bairs on November 4, 1842. An extract from the letter of Secretary Loomis, dated November 15, acknowledging these applications, is of interest as indicating the hesitancy with which the Company entered the new field, and as being prophetic, as well as expressive of a fear which the great Chicago fire of 1871 more than justified.

"We would be very careful," wrote Loomis, "what risks we take in Chicago and how we take them. It is a new place, and in all such there is generally a tendency of everything to the center — hence, houses, shops and shanties occupied for purposes indescribably varied, are wedged in together with ample material to cause the destruction of the whole, good, bad and indifferent. *Against such calamity it becomes our duty to protect ourselves.*"

Hubbard continued to represent the Ætna until

1866 — at first alone and then as a member of the agency firm of Hubbard & Hunt. On the retirement of Hubbard the agency was taken over by a new firm composed of Jonathan Goodwin, Jr., former assistant secretary of the Ætna, and Henry L. Pasco, for many years a special agent for the Home Office. As we have already noted, they were the Chicago agents at the time of the great fire. This arrangement continued until June 3, 1875, when the Ætna converted the agency into a Branch office with Goodwin in charge as General Agent. He served in this capacity until his retirement in 1885, when he was succeeded on June 4th by James S. Gadsden, who for many years had been connected with the inland marine division of the Chicago agency. At the same time Louis O. Kohtz was appointed as Assistant General Agent and placed in charge of the inland marine work. His service with the Ætna began shortly after the close of the Civil War, through which he served. It was in 1866 that he entered the office of the Ætna's Chicago agency, and his connection with the Company has been continuous to the present time. On the death of Mr. Gadsden, which occurred on September 17, 1911, Mr. Kohtz was promoted to the position of General Agent of the Marine Branch.

As the City of Chicago grew with mushroom-like rapidity and its population leaped from the thousands into the millions, the Chicago Branch of the Ætna under Gadsden and Kohtz enjoyed a corresponding growth until in 1907 it had become one of the important departments of the great national organization of

THE ÆTNA AND ITS AGENTS

the Company. In this year, as we will read in a succeeding chapter, the Chicago Branch was merged with the Western Branch, the headquarters of which were transferred from Cincinnati to Chicago.

In our general story mention has been made of the difficulties confronting the Ætna in the South at the outbreak of the Civil War. An examination of the correspondence between the home office and the southern agents at this time strikingly illustrates the loyal and friendly spirit which always has distinguished the relations between the Ætna and its agents.

Thomas Muldon of Mobile, Alabama, was one of the last Ætna agents in the South to close his agency before the war and he also was one of the first, if not actually the first, to be re-appointed after the war. His last letter to the Ætna, on May 31, 1861, breathes a spirit of sadness and regret, despite the generally prevailing bitterness:

> My business relations with the Ætna for the last twelve years have been too pleasant to forget you all so soon. I fear, however, it will be a long time before you will again be able to open agencies South.

In reply Vice-President Alexander wrote:

> Our relations with our Southern agencies have been so cordial and satisfactory that we cannot allow ourselves to despair of a more speedy reunion than you appear to anticipate.

On July 12, 1865, immediately after the close of the war, Secretary Lucius J. Hendee wrote as follows to an applicant for appointment as agent at Mobile:

> We had the pleasure of a short visit from our former agent, Mr. Muldon, while in this city. He is anxious to represent the Ætna at Mobile whenever we decide to resume business in your city, and we shall give him the preference.

And so, in compliance with this promise, Thomas Muldon, on September 17, 1865, was re-appointed.

Among the earliest Ætna agents in the South, in addition to Gurdon Robins, of Fayetteville, North Carolina, who was the first, were Horatio Alden, a Hartford resident who moved to Augusta, Georgia, in 1821, and who later returned to his old home and became a director of the Company; Anson Kimberley at Darien, Georgia, who served from 1821 to 1837 and was then succeeded by Ebenezer S. Rees, grandfather of Henry E. Rees, who is now Vice-President of the Ætna and in direct charge of the entire southern field for the Company; Augustine Averill at Cheraw, South Carolina, appointed in 1822; and Salma Manton at Savannah, Georgia, appointed in 1821 and succeeded in 1824 by Isaac Cohen, who, with his son, continued to represent the Ætna there until the beginning of the war.

We have traced, however briefly, the development of the Ætna agencies and business in the West, the South, in Canada, and in a few of the important cities in those sections. Let us now, for a moment, turn to the East. Reference already has been made to the Company's entrance into New York City in 1836 following the disastrous fire of '35. Edward Dickenson appears to have been the first Ætna agent there, having been appointed in 1826. He served but a few months and was succeeded by Humphrey Phelps. But practically no business was done until 1836 when A. G. Hazard was named. He retired on July 18, 1845, the day before the great fire of 1845, which, as we have seen, precipitated the second crisis in the affairs of the Ætna. Upon his retirement, Hazard founded the Hazard Powder Company at Enfield, Connecticut. He was succeeded in the Ætna agency by Thomas A. Alexander, who in 1853 became Secretary of the Ætna and later Vice-President and President. His son James A. then became agent and so continued until June 4, 1874, when the local agency was discontinued and he was appointed General Agent of the New York City Branch office which was opened by the Ætna on that date.

James A. Alexander continued as General Agent until the formation of the firm of Scott, Alexander & Talbot, in January, 1889; on the death of William A. Scott in 1907 the firm name was changed to John M. Talbot & Co. Mr. Alexander remained with the firm until his death in 1913 at the age of eighty-six years, after more than seventy years of continuous service with the Ætna. He was born July 29, 1827, and as a boy of fifteen had entered the Ætna agency under his father and A. G. Hazard in 1842. In 1915 there was a general reorganization of the New York business when a new firm — Russell, Scott & Ziegler — was formed to take over the fire agency representation. In February, four years later, the firm name was changed to the present one of Russell & Ziegler. Meanwhile the firm of John M. Talbot & Company was changed to Talbot, Bird & Co., who for many years have been General Agents of the Marine Department in New York City.

From 1840 to 1870 practically all of the Ætna's

business in New Jersey was handled by the New York City and Philadelphia agencies. Prior to that time there had been several local agencies. It was not until the early 70's, when William B. Clark, then Assistant Secretary, personally traveled through the state and appointed local agents in the various towns and cities, that local agency representation was revived. This move was immediately followed by a gratifying increase in the business, which has since continued.

One of the many evidences of the mutual good will and loyalty that have characterized the relations between the Ætna and its agents during the past century, is the length of service of so many of its representatives. Some have served continuously for more than half a century, while terms of thirty and forty years are so numerous as to be commonplace.

Limited space has prohibited the recording of many events and incidents that have featured the growth of the thousands of Ætna agencies throughout the United States and Canada. As far back as 1897, more than twenty years ago, in commenting on the Ætna and its agents, the *Insurance Magazine* said:

> Many a year has gone by, more than forty of them, since any agent has had to say to a property-holder, "I should like to insure you in the Ætna; the Ætna is an old Hartford Company, and I can safely say that it will pay any loss whatever that its policy contract says it will pay." The Ætna agent has no soliciting work to do. He must inspect men and risks, but he is not compelled to solicit business. If an agent has the Ætna in his agency his reputation as an insurance man is established.

No history of the great agency system which has been so wonderfully developed by the Ætna, would

 THE ÆTNA AND ITS AGENTS

be complete that did not tell of the Western, Northwestern and Pacific Branches. Their stories, however, we have reserved for later chapters.

As the chief pioneer and veteran of what has come to be known as the "American Agency System" the Ætna Insurance Company has inaugurated a business which has spread its network of protection over the United States and Canada, and which, in the marine field, is now reaching into every part of the world.

Chapter XII

THE WINNING OF THE WEST

> VOTED, To establish a Branch Office at Cincinnati, Ohio, and to appoint J. B. Bennett as General Agent with full powers to appoint new agents, remove them for cause, adjust losses and attend to the interests of the Company in all particulars; the territory to embrace the following States: Ohio, Indiana, Michigan, Illinois, Wisconsin, Iowa, Missouri, Kentucky, Tennessee, Arkansas, Mississippi, and portions of Pennsylvania, Georgia, Alabama, Virginia, and the Territory of Minnesota. Compensation of General Agent, $2,000 and traveling expenses, and a commission of 10% on the net profits of the business in his territory—arrangement to begin September 12, 1853.
>
> Signed, Ætna Insurance Company,
>
> Hartford, Sept. 2, 1853.   E. G. Ripley, Secretary.

THIS prosaic entry in one of the old official record books of the Ætna records the opening of an epoch-making event in the history of the Company, and introduces a character who was to make a lasting impress on the profession of fire insurance underwriting.

Before we begin to build the great structure of the Western Branch, let us for a moment glance back to the early days of the Company. We have seen how, in the very beginning, it became the pioneer in the field of real agency work; we have noted the slow planting of agencies in the South and West and

North, and we have traced the development of the local agency in Cincinnati from 1823 to the middle of the century.

During all these years the Ætna's chief competitor in the Western field was the Protection Insurance Company, organized at Hartford in 1825. It was in the year following that the Protection opened a General Agency in Cincinnati under Ephraim Robins. In the story of his career may be read one of the many romances of American business.

At the age of forty, Robins had won success and comparative wealth as a merchant and exporter in Boston. Two years later a calamity of navigation destroyed his entire fortune. Discouraged, but undaunted, he turned from this disaster to build his life anew. His attention was suddenly caught by an item in a Hartford newspaper which a relative had sent him, telling of the formation there of the Protection—a new fire and marine insurance company. The recent loss of his own fortune, through lack of insurance protection, and his own need for immediate occupation, combined to inspire a new idea. He felt that no one could more fervently preach the gospel of insurance than he, and he believed that his experience in business and knowledge of men would enable him to win success in the new field as he had in the old.

Within a few months General Agent Robins was in far-away Cincinnati, laying the foundations of the great agency system in the West for the Hartford company. During the next twenty years, with an organization of hundreds of agents covering the villages and cities of the South and West, he restored his own fortunes and brought prosperity to the company at home. His death in 1846, however, seemed to mark a turn in the tide of the company's progress, for in August, 1854, following a series of heavy losses at sea and on land, insolvency brought an end to its career. W. B. Robins, who succeeded his father as General Agent, moved to England soon after the company failed, and with his entire family, met a tragic end by drowning while on a yachting trip.

It was under Ephraim Robins that Joseph B. Bennett, the first General Agent of the Ætna's Western Branch, received his early training. Born in England August 11, 1825, he and his brother, F. C. Bennett, came to America in 1832 with their parents and settled in Cleveland, Ohio, then a small village of 3,000 inhabitants, on the banks of Lake Erie. In 1834 the Bennett family moved to Cincinnati, then the greatest city in the West. In 1841 young Joseph entered the office of Ephraim Robins. Keen of mind, quick to learn and ambitious to succeed, it was not long before he had mastered every detail of the business. His advancement was rapid. Within a few years he had become one of the trusted investigators and loss adjusters of the agency.

In the summer of 1852 the Ætna was concerned in a loss by fire which destroyed the business section of Brandon, Mississippi. J. B. Bennett was on the ground to adjust losses sustained by his company. He discovered mistakes in one of the claims against the Ætna and saved the Company seventy-five per cent. of the original demand. This incident led to a correspondence which resulted, one year later, in the founding of the Western Branch of the Ætna, with Joseph B. Bennett in control as General Agent, and with offices in a little cottage at what then was 297 Elm Street, in Cincinnati.

That Bennett had a great opportunity before him is indicated in the letter written to him by Secretary Ripley of the Ætna on October 4, 1853:

> You are now in a position to build up a reputation and a profitable business for this Company and yourself, such as few men have the opportunity of doing. You begin with a good business already secured, and if the Company has its deserts, with a high reputation for fairness, promptness and liberality, there is no reason why your efforts should not be crowned with success.

With characteristic energy Bennett turned to his new task. Every local agency which had been established by the Ætna within the limits of his territory, except those at Chicago, Cleveland and Mobile, was placed under his control, so he was able to begin with a ready-made organization of no mean proportions. Within a year great good fortune came to him, though it spelled calamity and ruin to others — the failure of the Protection Company. He was quick to seize the opportunity. He was personally acquainted with the hundreds of Protection agents throughout the South and West, and was able to pick and choose among them. They brought with them to Bennett and to the Ætna a material share of the business which they had developed and the benefit of the schooling which they had received under Ephraim and W. B. Robins. It was not long, therefore, before Bennett had an army of more than one thousand active and experienced agents under his command, and he soon came to be known among them as "General." Until the day of his death, more than thirty years later, he was known throughout the insurance world as General Bennett.

An avalanche of prosperity now descended upon the Ætna as the result of the sudden activity of hundreds of new agents. During the seventeen years of J. B. Bennett's management of the Western Branch the premiums averaged one million dollars a year.

The literature of American fire insurance teems with incidents and stories of Bennett's career. That he was a genius in the profession of fire underwriting is conceded by all; but like most geniuses, he was eccentric and intolerant of restraint. With the increasing prosperity of the Western Branch, he soon came to regard the home office as a mere adjunct. As stated in the Insurance Report in 1907, by Ross F. Stewart, an old insurance underwriter who had served under General Agent Bennett nearly half a century before:

> Let it be said in sorrow that it was through this very spirit of independence that the meteoric career of a character acknowledged by all to have been one of the greatest, if not the greatest, fire underwriting has ever known, came to an inglorious ending. Not content with the renown which he and his Company had achieved as the chief pioneers and veterans of the agency system, Mr. Bennett sought to develop the Cincinnati Branch on lines wholly apart from those established as fundamental principles by the home office in Hartford.

Having nothing to risk but his position, General Agent Bennett was unhampered by responsibilities and obligations which statute and unwritten law placed upon the shoulders of the Officers and Directors back in Hartford. While they recognized the genius and talents of their Cincinnati agent, they likewise feared his impulses and eccentricities. Many are the incidents recorded in the old correspondence between the home office and the Western Branch which describe this situation. One, for example, occurred in 1864, following a fire which destroyed Colt's great pistol factory at Hartford. Some weeks later, in looking over Bennett's reports for the preceding month, the home office found a receipted bill for $4,000, for a colored poster of Colt's fire. Inquiry developed that Bennett, without seeking authority for what, in those days, was regarded as a stupendous expenditure for such purpose, had ordered the poster for advertising purposes and had paid the bill out of the Company's funds.

This action was followed by other infractions of the rule that Company funds should be expended only with the sanction of the Officers and Directors. When he began, however, to assume the authority of investing the funds of the Western Branch, and even went so far as to make preliminary arrangements for the expenditure of many thousands of dollars for the erection of an office building for the Company in Cincinnati, without consultation with the home office, the Officers and Directors felt that the time had come for a final understanding. Therefore, in the late winter of 1870 President Hendee, accompanied by a committee of three Directors, visited Cincinnati, where a final shock awaited them. They entered the Ætna's offices in the Company's building at No. 171 Vine Street, where they found the "General" seated at his desk. He slowly surveyed his visitors, making no motion to greet them, then turned his back with the curt remark:

"Be seated, gentlemen. I'll see you when I am through."

This was the final straw. Bennett's commission was revoked, and his brother, Frederick C. Bennett, was named General Agent in his place.

With his retirement from the Ætna, J. B. Bennett immediately took steps to erect a competing organization. Before the end of the year he had launched the Andes Insurance Company with a capital of $1,000,000. He gave it a name as nearly like that of the Ætna as he could, and adopted a seal similar to that of the Ætna, with a mountain as its most characteristic feature. The Chicago fire in 1871 ended its brief career. Bennett later organized two more companies — the Amazon and the Triumph. He died at Indianapolis on November 10, 1889, and was buried in Cincinnati, where his last resting-place is now marked by a monument erected to his memory by the insurance men of the United States.

Frederick C. Bennett in many respects was the antithesis of his gifted and eccentric brother. Although an able executive, he was modest and shy almost to diffidence. Like his brother, he received his early insurance training in the old Protection agency, entering the office under W. B. Robins in 1847. Although offered a post in the new Ætna agency in 1853, he remained with the Protection up to the time of its failure in 1854, when he entered the employ

OLD CINCINNATI OFFICE BUILDING OF THE ÆTNA INSURANCE COMPANY
171 VINE STREET

of his brother, where he continued in various capacities until March 9, 1870, when the Ætna Directors elected him General Agent. On the same date they also elected as Assistant General Agent, William H. Wyman, who was to live to celebrate, in 1904, fifty years of continuous service with the Company.

Mr. Wyman was born at Canton, New York, July 21, 1831, and received his early schooling in the Beloit and Milton Academies. At the age of nineteen he entered the Cincinnati office of the Protection Company as a junior clerk. He remained there until the failure of the company in 1854, when, with F. C. Bennett, he joined the ranks of the Ætna under General Agent J. B. Bennett. Wyman spent his first year with the Company traveling through the South and West as Special Agent, and in 1856 was appointed State Agent for the Ætna in Wisconsin. It was while serving in this capacity that he was promoted to the position of Assistant General Agent at Cincinnati in 1870.

During the years which followed, the Western Branch of the Ætna continued to expand under the guiding hands of Bennett and Wyman, until 1890. By this time the territory covered by the Western Branch had become so populous, and the volume of business so great, that it was decided to divide the field. On September 24 of this year the Directors voted to divide the Western Branch and establish a new branch, to be known as the Northwestern, with headquarters at Omaha, with William H. Wyman as General Agent. The territory allotted to the new department was composed of North and South Dakota, Minnesota, Iowa, Nebraska, Wyoming, Colorado, Kansas, Missouri, New Mexico and Indian Territory; while the States remaining in the Western Branch were Wisconsin, Illinois, Indiana, Ohio, Kentucky, Tennessee, Arkansas, Louisiana and Texas. The Chicago office was still operating as an independent branch.

With the establishment of the Northwestern Branch, Charles W. Potter, another Ætna veteran, was elected as Assistant General Agent to serve with Wyman at Omaha. He had entered the service of the Ætna in 1867 under J. B. Bennett, and during the intervening years had served as local agent at Milwaukee and State Agent for Wisconsin. He continued as Assistant General Agent only two years, however, when he resigned to accept the management, at Denver, of the Mountain Division of the Northwestern Department, where he continued until his death in 1918. W. P. Harford, who had been identified with the Western Branch for many years, was chosen for the vacancy caused by Potter's resignation, and served as Assistant General Agent under Wyman until their joint retirement in 1910, to which further reference will be made.

Frederick C. Bennett continued in sole charge of the Western Branch during the two years following the transfer and promotion of William H. Wyman. On November 30, 1892, the day on which William B. Clark was elevated to the Presidency of the Company, and upon his recommendation, N. E. Keeler, who had been connected with the Western Branch since boyhood, was elected Assistant General Agent at Cincinnati, to succeed Wyman.

After fifty years of continuous service in the ranks of insurance underwriting, of which forty-three were spent with the Ætna, death closed the long career of F. C. Bennett on May 25, 1897. No truthful history of American fire insurance could be written that did not write large the names of the two Bennett brothers. Both, in their day, wrought mightily for the cause of insurance in general and for the Ætna in particular. F. C. Bennett was one of the founders and first president of the old Western Fire Insurance Managers' Association, from which was evolved the present Western Union, the great organization of fire insurance underwriters of the West.

With the termination of Bennett's long leadership of the Western Branch, there was now to appear, in the person of Thomas E. Gallagher, a new figure in the Western field of fire insurance. Born at Dansville, New York, on July 31, 1848, Gallagher first entered the insurance business as a local agent at Elmira. In 1886 he became Special Agent for the Washington Fire and Marine Insurance Company. In 1888 he was appointed Special Agent in New York State for the Continental Fire Insurance Company, and later General Agent, until in 1894 he joined the ranks of the Ætna as Special Agent in the same state.

In accordance with a plan formulated by President Clark, N. E. Keeler, Assistant General Agent of the Western Branch, and Thomas E. Gallagher, became associated under the firm name of Keeler & Gallagher; and on June 2, 1897, the members of this firm were named joint General Agents to succeed F. C. Bennett. This arrangement continued until October, 1907, when Keeler, after forty-two years of continuous service with the Ætna, resigned, to take effect at the end of the year. He was given a pension for the remaining years of his life. His death occurred on June 10, 1912.

For some years prior to this period the Ætna officials had considered plans for a complete reorganization of its Western business. Cincinnati had long since surrendered to Chicago its prestige as the metropolis of the West. And so, with the retirement of Mr. Keeler, the following announcement was issued by President Clark on November 12, 1907, to the Western agents of the Company:

> After a long and careful consideration of the subject, we have decided to remove the Western Branch from Cincinnati to Chicago, and now expect to be located in offices in the National Life Insurance Company's building, 159 La Salle Street, in May next.
>
> In due time the Chicago City and Cook County Agencies will report to the Western Branch instead of as now to the Home Office at Hartford, thus consolidating our entire interests in the Middle West.
>
> The Branch at Chicago will be under the management of General Agent Thos. E. Gallagher, and Mr. Jas. S. Gadsden will continue as General Agent of the Inland Marine department.
>
> Mr. Louis O. Kohtz, our present Assistant General Agent at Chicago, will continue as Assistant General Agent in both Fire and Marine Departments.

The foregoing announcement was only the forerunner of another important change a few years later; for on October 5, 1910, President Clark issued a notice

to the agents announcing the decision of the Company to consolidate the Western and Northwestern Branches with headquarters at Chicago, under the management of General Agent Gallagher and Assistant General Agent Louis O. Kohtz. The new arrangement was to become effective on December 1st. In his announcement President Clark paid a glowing tribute to the long and faithful services of General Agent William H. Wyman and Assistant General Agent W. P. Harford, the former having served the Ætna for fifty-six years, and the latter forty-five. In recognition of these services they were granted generous pensions on their retirement. Mr. Wyman's death occurred on October 7th of the following year, while Mr. Harford died on October 25, 1910.

These events marked the close of a memorable era in the life of the Western Branch and the beginning of a new period of growth and prosperity. In 1915, as noted in the preceding chapter, Assistant Secretary Ralph B. Ives was transferred from the home office to Chicago, and the team work with General Agent Gallagher and Assistant General Agent Kohtz has produced gratifying results. Just as the story of the Ætna as a whole encompasses much of the history of fire insurance in America during the last hundred years, so the various steps in the progress of the Company's Western Branch have been coincident with the important developments of underwriting throughout the West since the middle of the nineteenth century.

CHAPTER XIII

THE PACIFIC BRANCH

IN the fifties, California seemed a long, long way from Hartford; there were no railways reaching to what President Ripley called "the remote Pacific shores," no telegraph service, and no method of communication, except by mail, which was slow and expensive. California had hardly been acquired by the United States as a territory when the news of the discovery of gold at Coloma, on the Sacramento River, thrilled the country.

Almost as if by magic was the sleepy little Spanish village of San Francisco transformed into a live, hustling, American town. There was a feverish rush of gold-seekers from all parts of the world. Thousands tracked across the plains and mountains, with ox-teams and prairie-schooners; many came on horseback or trudged wearily along on foot. Many others swarmed across the Isthmus, and in a single year five hundred ships, filled with adventurous miners, came 'round the Horn to reach the new El Dorado. In 1850 California became a State, and two years later San Francisco was a city of 42,000 inhabitants. Such an influx of new settlers meant the erection of thousands of new buildings, and with this naturally came a demand for fire insurance.

For several years prior to 1858 the Ætna had been urged to establish an agency in San Francisco, but the difficulties and disadvantages seemed so great that no action was taken until December 8, 1858, when Edward H. Parker was made local agent there. Mr. Parker was so highly recommended, and the distance from the home office being too great for advice and authority in every instance, that with a few general suggestions and limitations, he was urged to conduct the business there as though it were his own.

This arrangement was unchanged until 1866, when on August 15th the Board of Directors voted to send General Agent Erastus J. Bassett to California, with full power to look over the business of the Company, and to arrange for extending its operations by opening a general agency or to close up the local agency and withdraw from the field, as his judgment might dictate. On reaching the Coast and after studying the situation from all sides, he advised the establishment of a branch office in San Francisco, which resulted in the appointment in December, 1866, of Robert H. Magill as General Agent.

Mr. Magill came from Cincinnati, where he had been a member of the firm of R. H. & H. M. Magill, general agents of the Western Branch of the Phœnix of Hartford. The Pacific Branch of the Ætna, thus begun under Magill, covered California, Arizona, Idaho, Montana, Nevada, Oregon, Utah, and Washington. He continued in charge for two years until

October, 1868, when George C. Boardman succeeded him.

Mr. Boardman was born in Hartford, Connecticut, on May 20, 1828, of English stock that settled in this country about the middle of the seventeenth century. He received his early education in the schools of his native city and entered upon a mercantile life in Hartford and later in New York City. In 1855 he began his insurance career as special agent for the Merchants' Insurance Company of Hartford, and in 1860 was sent to California. In the year following he became secretary of the San Francisco Insurance Company, which had just been organized, and in 1863 he became president. Under his administration the company had remarkable success, but shortly after his resignation in October, 1868, to become General Agent for the Ætna, the San Francisco company retired from business. Mr. Boardman was a sound, conservative, and experienced underwriter, the first Special Agent of an Eastern company to visit the Pacific Coast, planned and promoted the first Board of Fire Underwriters there, and had a part in every development of fire insurance on the Coast.

Under Mr. Boardman's able and aggressive management the Ætna's Pacific Branch prospered. The receipts for the first year were $70,000, and in his last year with the Company the premium income of the Branch had reached nearly $1,100,000; every year, except 1906, the year of the San Francisco fire, the business yielded handsome profits. When Mr. Boardman had been twenty-eight years in charge alone,

MEMBERS OF THE FIRM OF
BOARDMAN & SPENCER, GENERAL AGENTS, PACIFIC BRANCH, AT TIME OF
THE CONFLAGRATION IN SAN FRANCISCO, APRIL, 1906

THE PACIFIC BRANCH

the business had so increased and the duties of the agency had proved so onerous, that in 1896 he took in as partner George W. Spencer, and the firm became Boardman & Spencer, General Agents.

Mr. Spencer was born in Philadelphia on September 17, 1843, and his early youth was spent at New London, Connecticut, where he received his education. When he was sixteen he returned to Philadelphia and engaged in business, where he remained until 1862, when he entered the army, and at the close of the war went to New York as an accountant. In 1868 he took a long trip to Tahiti to enter into a partnership there; but conditions not seeming favorable, he went to San Francisco and began his insurance career as accountant and Special Agent of the Ætna under Mr. Boardman. After serving in this capacity for eleven years, he left in 1880 to accept the position of manager of the Marine Department of Balfour, Guthrie & Company, but resigned in 1896 to return to the Ætna as an associate of General Agent Boardman.

When Rudyard Kipling visited San Francisco, Mr. Spencer entertained him at his home, and when the distinguished author left he had such vivid memories of his host that he wrote "The Prince Among Merchants," based on the experiences of Spencer; in his "American Notes" Kipling also pictures him as the "Captain of American Horse," representing an old soldier of the Civil War. On April 2, 1908, Mr. Spencer died suddenly, and the Company lost an able underwriter and a loyal and valued agent.

On May 10, 1908, Edwin C. Morrison, who had

been connected with the Company for about twenty-two years as special agent, became Assistant General Agent. In the year following, the death of Mr. Boardman brought a new change in the election of Morrison to the position of General Agent. Mr. Boardman, who died on April 24, 1909, at the age of eighty-one, had served the Ætna with rare ability and devotion for forty-one years, his entire period of service being with the Pacific Branch. His death brought sincere sorrow not only to the officers of the Ætna but to the insurance circles of the Pacific Coast.

On July 12, 1909, Arthur G. Sanderson was elected Assistant General Agent. He had long been connected with the Ætna's Western Branch; and when sent to San Francisco in 1906, as one of the adjusters of the losses incident to the great fire, he had rendered such valued service and had won such personal popularity that his election again proved the care and wisdom of the Company in the selection of its agents.

While the business of the Pacific Branch all these years had been growing in strength and prosperity, invisible lines of control and guidance stretched across three thousand miles to the home office in Hartford into firm, sure hands. From almost the very beginning of its existence the affairs of this Branch had been under the charge of Mr. Clark, first as Assistant Secretary and later as Vice-President and President. It was in 1866 that the Branch was opened, and it had hardly completed its first year when Mr. Clark came with the Company, so that the history of the Pacific Branch and President Clark's life with the Ætna are

THE PACIFIC BRANCH

contemporaneous, and their stories are constantly interwoven. He has ever been in perfect touch with all of its activities, and knows San Francisco from an underwriter's point of view as thoroughly as though he were on the ground. He has made every audit of the accounts of the Branch except in one year, when Vice-President Rees visited the Coast.

In 1874 President Clark, then Assistant Secretary, made his first visit to San Francisco, and the story is best given in his own words:

> In April, 1874, Mr. Boardman having had some difficulty with one of his employees, President Hendee said to me: "It is about time that somebody from this office visited the Pacific Branch, and I advise that you pack your trunk and go at once;" so on the thirteenth day of April I left Hartford for San Francisco. Only one railroad was in operation at that time — the Union Pacific — and it was a seven days' trip, with rather crude sleepers and getting meals at stations en route. I well remember, on the morning of my arrival on the Coast, of leaving the train and going through an arch of ice and snow to the restaurant, and at twelve o'clock on the same day in the Sacramento Valley, picking poppies by the roadside.
>
> It was a surprise visit to Mr. Boardman, our General Agent, and I had intended to reach his office the next morning before him. I arrived in the city at ten o'clock at night, but omitted to "leave a call," and when I awoke the next morning the sun was shining bright in my room. I looked at my watch and saw that it was ten o'clock. I jumped out of bed and proceeded to dress hurriedly. All at once I heard the whistles blowing, and on looking out of the window, saw workmen going by with their dinner pails. Then it occurred to me that there was a difference of three hours and twenty minutes between their time and my Hartford time. So I reached the office in good time that morning and surprised Mr. Boardman, and received a very warm welcome from him. This visit was followed by eleven visits to the Branch, namely, in 1890, 1896, 1899, 1903, 1906, 1909, 1911, 1913, 1914, 1916, 1918, and 1919.

On President Clark's return from his sixth visit to the Coast in March, 1906, he had reached Hartford on the first of April. A little over two weeks later — April 18th — came the terrible news of the earthquake and the great fire. On two or three previous visits to San Francisco Mr. Clark had made a careful study of the Company's local business, visiting each section, street by street, going over the maps with the General Agent, and fixing the maximum lines, particularly in the congested districts. It was this close knowledge that enabled President Clark, seated in Hartford, and studying the reports from the stricken city, to advise the Board that the net loss of the Company, after deducting re-insurance and salvage, would be about three million dollars. This was a remarkably close estimate, for the amount actually paid was $2,983,000.

While the story of the great fire has been given in detail in another chapter, it may be worth noting, as illustrating the generous spirit of the Company, the public announcement which was made at the time by Boardman & Spencer, General Agents. The policy-holders were notified that the vaults of the Company had just been opened and the records were found uninjured, and that the adjustment and payment of losses would proceed at once. Requirement of giving "immediate notice" of losses was waived; time for filing proofs of loss was extended; loss papers would be prepared by the adjusters without expense to the assured, and no attorney would be necessary; if policies had been burned the assured would suffer no delay, and all policies would be paid in cash, without discount, immediately on adjustment.

THE PACIFIC BRANCH

In the years following the fire the Pacific Branch speedily regained strength and vitality and continued to prosper. On December 2, 1912, General Agent Morrison died, at the age of sixty-two. He had been for a quarter of a century in the service of the Company as special agent, superintendent of agencies, Assistant General Agent and General Agent, and had been most successful in the management of the Pacific Branch. Assistant General Agent Sanderson was elected as his successor on January 1, 1913.

On President Clark's visit to the Coast early in 1913 he found Mr. Sanderson dangerously ill, and it was decided to appoint William H. Breeding as Assistant General Agent. Mr. Clark telegraphed the facts to the Company on March 8th, and on March 10th Mr. Breeding was elected by the Board as Assistant. Between the time of the sending of the telegram and the action of the Board, however, Mr. Sanderson died suddenly. On Mr. Clark's return to Hartford Mr. Breeding was promoted to the position of General Agent.

Born in Texas on March 20, 1871, Mr. Breeding received his education in the public schools of the State and acquired his early insurance training in local and general agencies in Texas. He was accountant and later special agent of the Alamo Insurance Company of San Antonio, and then Texas agent for the Germania Fire Insurance Company of New York; later he traveled for that company throughout the Southern field, and in 1900 was appointed Manager of their Pacific Coast department, which he established.

In 1907 he came with the Ætna, serving for six years as special agent and as Superintendent of Agencies, prior to his election as General Agent of the Company, which position he still holds.

Mr. Breeding proved himself a most successful and satisfying manager of the Pacific Branch, and for the year 1918 the premiums from fire underwriting alone exceeded two million dollars. An Assistant General Agent, George E. Townsend, was elected in March, 1915, to relieve Mr. Breeding of some of the arduous duties of the Branch. For several years Mr. Townsend had been special agent and agency superintendent, and remained in his new position until October, 1918, when he resigned.

While the entire marine business of the Company is under the immediate charge of its Marine Vice-President, William F. Whittelsey, at the Home Office; on the Pacific Coast, General Agent Breeding has supervision of the marine risks in his territory. The details of the work, however, are in the hands of a marine Assistant General Agent. From April 2, 1913, Ernest L. Livingston held this position until his death on March 6, 1918, when he was succeeded by the present incumbent, Harry Durbrow, who was chosen on May 13, 1918. Both proved exceptionally competent marine underwriters, and the premiums in 1918 amounted to over a million and a quarter of dollars, with a moderate profit, considering the war hazards.

The present territory of the Pacific Branch covers California, Nevada, Oregon, Idaho, Montana, Utah,

W. H. BREEDING
GENERAL AGENT
PACIFIC BRANCH
SAN FRANCISCO, CALIF.

 **THE PACIFIC BRANCH**

Washington, Arizona, Alaska, and the Hawaiian Islands. The history of this Branch extends over more than half the entire life of the Ætna. It seemed rather a bold move to establish a general agency away out on the Pacific Coast in 1866, when what are now flourishing States within its field were but mere territories, so sparsely settled that they were really little more than names and a boundary line. But the Directors never made any important move without studying the subject so thoroughly that success was assured. They elected good men as General Agents, men that had proved themselves of special fitness, and these men when chosen were given the largest possible freedom of discretion and the fullest sympathetic co-operation of the Home Office at Hartford.

The story of the Pacific Branch makes a bright and memorable chapter in the life of the Company and in the administration of President Clark, who, in the Ætna's centennial year, at the age of seventy-eight, made his latest trip to the Coast to inspect the affairs of the Branch. Under his fostering care it has developed to its present success and importance.

Chapter XIV

THE LAW MAKERS AND INSURANCE

IT is a comparatively simple and easy matter for a company confining its business within the borders of its own State to carry on all its activities. When it crosses the State line it enters a new jurisdiction and is subject to different laws. If the company seeks to do a national business, with branches, offices or agents in all the States, it has to face the somewhat puzzling problem of adjusting itself to laws and regulations of forty-eight separate commonwealths.

The Ætna had not been long in existence, with its plan of business development by means of local agency representation, before it began to feel the pressure and limitation of adverse legislation. It had early ventured into New York State and established agencies; but in 1823, when the State passed a law taxing the business of the agents of out-of-State fire insurance companies ten per cent., profitable underwriting became difficult. In 1825 the Ætna asked its agents at Troy and Albany to petition the Legislature to repeal or modify this obnoxious tax; but nothing came of this until after the great fire of 1835 in New York City, which wiped out so many local companies, and made foreign concerns necessary for the protection of the people, when the tax was reduced to two per cent.

Massachusetts proved a troublesome factor to the Ætna when the Legislature in 1827 passed a law relating to foreign fire insurance companies, and providing for a fine of $500 on any agent writing a policy in any company having a paid-up capital of less than $200,000. As the Ætna did not reach this amount until the late forties, the Company was barred.

A loophole was discovered in the Massachusetts situation in the early forties, when the scheme of "agent for the people" was introduced. As the plan was neatly expressed by Secretary Loomis, in a letter of November 18, 1843, to J. N. Stoddard, an agent for the people at Plymouth, Massachusetts, which read:

> Although we cannot make you an agent, you have the right to offer your services to your fellow citizens as an "insurance broker." You can become *their* agent for procuring insurance.

This plan did not escape the keen vision of the Legislature, assisted by the jealousy of local companies, for in 1847 a law was passed making the $500 fine applicable to any person who directly or indirectly represented foreign insurance companies. Meanwhile, in 1846, after the Ætna had attained a paid-up capital of $200,000, it re-entered Massachusetts, and in 1852 filed its first report under the laws of the State.

Had it been in but two or three States that pressure was brought to bear to keep out foreign companies, the situation would have been fairly easy. But the truth is that most local companies felt that foreign corporations entering their territory were interlopers, and in the early days they used every form of tactics they could devise to keep "foreigners" out. That this was a serious problem to the Ætna is manifest in a letter written in May, 1829, by Secretary Goodwin:

> Our doing business in other States where they have insurance companies has caused some heart-burning with stockholders and agents of local offices. The Legislatures in most of the States have been induced to pass laws intended to drive out agents of foreign offices, considering it an encroachment upon them. Where law has not had the desired effect, slander has been resorted to, and it has been maliciously reported of us that we were insolvent.

Sometimes this spirit of antagonism to foreign corporations had its good side, as events turned out; for in 1835 the Ætna was probably saved from losses that might have proved disastrous in the big fires in New York City and Pittsburgh by reason of the laws of New York and Pennsylvania having reduced the activities of the Ætna Insurance Company to a minimum in these two States.

Out in Ohio where the Company was vigorously extending its agency business, it met a setback in 1830 when the Legislature passed a law requiring foreign agents to pay a license fee of $50, and in addition four per cent. on premiums. The Company then promptly decided to discontinue its agencies at Chillicothe, Painesville, Cleveland, Ashtabula, Zanesville, and other places, retaining only its agency at Cincinnati. In the year following, the Legislature having repealed the $50 tax law and substituted a reasonable tax on premiums, the Ætna reopened its agencies and resumed business.

THE LAW MAKERS AND INSURANCE

At this time agents of foreign companies in Vermont were taxed eight per cent. on receipts; in New York ten per cent.; in New Jersey eight per cent.; in Pennsylvania twenty; in South Carolina eight; in Ohio four, in addition to the $50 license fee; and in Rhode Island the license fee was $200. Massachusetts and Maine made such severe restrictions that Connecticut companies were practically excluded from these States.

In the South, Tennessee joined in the movement to bar foreign companies, or to make their stay so oppressive and uncomfortable that they would shut up shop and go home. This the Ætna did when it closed up its Memphis agency in 1845 after a brief trial. The failure of local companies, which threatened to leave the State unprotected against fire, led in 1851 to the repeal of the obnoxious statutes.

In Virginia, so strong grew the opposition to all companies not bearing the Virginia brand of incorporation that the fire companies refused to put out fires in buildings insured in foreign companies; in other words, they would attend only "union" fires. Such a situation put bitterness and indignant protest into the ink with which Secretary Loomis wrote in November, 1841, to Robert Ritchie, agent at Petersburg, Virginia:

> There is something rather horrifying in the Fourth Resolution of the fire companies. Will they utterly disregard the claims of Society and not make an effort to save the property of one of their citizens because he may be insured by an office out of Virginia? Will they stand by and without manning their brakes see the property of one of their fellow citizens pass to destruction? Humanity would forbid it. No son of the Old Dominion would be such a bankrupt in chivalry as to permit it. If the insurance companies were to partake of a tithe of the feverish excitement

that seized your firemen, they would stop their agencies and abandon the place to its fate. But, Sir, we always aim to keep cool — the world will never wag right for all of us — but we must make the best of it, go on steadily, do our whole duty — make others, as far as we can, and be content. We hope good will come of the Resolutions, that all may be benefited and satisfied.

This general opposition continued for many years, for in April, 1865, President Alexander in a letter to J. B. Bennett, General Agent at Cincinnati, wrote:

Notice your troubles with State Legislature; they seem to crop up everywhere just now under the pressure of State institutions, which appear to attribute their absence of success to the fact that if competition did not exist brains would not be necessary to success.

During all this time the insurance business was progressive and reaching safer and saner lines of underwriting and administration. Soon after the war, those who prepared taxation schemes for the separate States realized that insurance companies were easy prey; and beside taxing premiums, imposed fees for filing statements and other ingenious devices for enriching the State. Fire insurance companies have had three serious problems: fires, legislation, and taxes.

In the earliest decades of fire insurance legislation, the greater part of the law-making seemed to be concerned with protecting the local companies against foreign competition and with increasing the revenues of the State. Fifty years or so ago it took a new turn in seeking to protect the people and to safeguard the companies in one way or another. Some of this legislation was good, some bad, and some dubious.

It was in 1874 that the much-discussed "valued policy" legislation was begun by the passage of a law by the State of Wisconsin, under the title: "An Act to Prevent Over-Insurance." The valued policy was a contract in which, in case of a total loss of the property, the full face of the policy would be paid irrespective of the value of the property at the time of the fire. The Ætna and other strong companies were opposed to it. Almost from the beginning of business, insurance companies expressly forbade agents writing such policies, because it was believed that they encouraged over-insurance and fraud. The companies claimed that it violated the essential principle of fire insurance, which is indemnity, restoring the insured to exactly the position held before the loss. If the insured were to profit by the fire, the policy would prove an inducement to carelessness, fraud and crime. The practical experience of the insurance company said one thing, the theory of legislators said another.

Then began an epidemic of valued-policy laws, which, by the year 1915, had been passed in twenty-two States. In that year, Wisconsin, the State that had started it all, after having given it forty years of trial repealed its law of 1874, and substituted for it an act forbidding insuring or paying losses in excess of the cash value of property.

Another form of legislation that has interfered with and modified the natural development of the business of fire insurance, is the excessive and unwise State supervision manifested in anti-compact laws. Early in the nineteenth century it was recognized that a just rate of premium was the only one that was safe and sound for insurer and insured. It should be a rate that would permit the insurance companies to pay ordinary losses and to leave a profit for stockholders, while permitting the laying aside of a reserve fund to meet extraordinary losses such as might come with a great fire.

Where the rate was put too low, it encouraged a volume of business that was unsafe, because it did not secure sufficient funds to meet losses, and led to the failures of companies. If the rate were excessively high, it left an extra margin for rate-cutting, which grew more vigorous and reckless in the fierce competition between companies, bringing them too often into the low rates, unsafe to them and to their customers. Every big fire proved this by wiping out weak companies; then a period of sanity and reform came in, with adherence to a fair rate for a little time, until, in the fervor of business-getting, rate-slashing commenced. The tendency seemed as natural as the recurrence of the ebb and flow of the tides.

The early conferences of the Ætna with the other Hartford companies were in recognition of this situation and of an earnest desire to end it in the interests of all companies. There were other conferences and meetings of local boards in different parts of the country seeking the solution of the same problem. There were two elements to be considered — the determination of a fair rate and the agreement to maintain it. The mastery of these two factors demanded co-operation, conferences, and compacts. To find out what was a fair rate required the classifying of statistics and experience, not of one company, but of many. It meant making underwriting a scientific process based on adequate data.

In 1885 an unwise campaign against this getting together of the companies was begun by an anti-compact law passed in Ohio, later followed by similar legislation in other States. The plea has been that insurance co-operation is monopolistic in character, and therefore this co-operation has been forbidden. Companies and their agents have been barred from fixing rates. Not only this, but companies have often been indicted, fined, and deprived of authority to issue policies because of membership in associations organized for the purely scientific purpose of ascertaining their average experience.

In the history of the Ætna are seen frequent disturbances in its Southern business, because of legislation that made its agency work there impossible or unprofitable. In January, 1889, the Ætna announced its re-entrance into Georgia after being out about ten years; and appointed Henry E. Rees, later Vice-President of the Company, as Special Agent for Georgia, North and South Carolina, and Florida.

In 1916 practically every foreign fire insurance comany, including the Ætna and all the other Hartford companies, withdrew from South Carolina because of the anti-compact and anti-discriminating laws. Companies were prevented from employing a common rating agent, which naturally put the South-Eastern Underwriters' Association out of the State. One provision of the law required that all risks of similar hazard must be rated alike, and gave the commissioner of insurance absolute power to raise or reduce any rate.

Connecticut has been most liberal and fair in its insurance legislation, and to this is partially due the high position it occupies in the insurance world. In 1907 the Legislature passed the "Reciprocal Obligations Act," which accorded to foreign insurance companies from another State doing business in Connecticut the same general treatment as Connecticut agents received in the other State.

There have been some who have urged fire insurance as a new avenue of government business. As has been repeatedly shown in these pages, one constant element in successful fire insurance is distribution of risks. State fire insurance means essentially concentration of risks, with appalling losses in a great conflagration. Had the San Francisco fire fallen on the State of California, the loss of $350,000,000 would have been one that would have paralyzed the state for a generation.

The greater part of the legislation now on the statute books of the States that has really advanced fire insurance, making it safer and more just for insurer and insured, has come from making mandatory on all companies the wise principles and policies evolved by a few leading companies in their natural growth and evolution.

Chapter XV

MARINE UNDERWRITING

MARINE insurance is the father of all the many phases of insurance known in the world today. Many centuries before marine underwriting, as we know it now, had been in existence, there was in operation a form of protection on vessels and their cargoes among the commercial nations of the ancient world.

This early form of insurance was called a "loss on bottomry"; it was a loan on the security of a vessel and its cargo at a high rate of interest; if the ship completed its voyage in safety, the loan and interest were to be paid by the ship-owner, but in case of the loss of the vessel the lender forfeited the principal and the interest. It was the reverse of the present system, the indemnity being paid in advance and returned plus interest or premium if the trip proved safe, while today the indemnity is paid only after loss and the premium is paid in advance.

It is said that the Rhodians had some form of meeting losses by sea during the period of their commercial activity from 916 to 893 B. C., though we have no details as to the method employed. The next development is found in the operations of the Hanseatic League, which dominated the commerce of Northern Europe for nearly four hundred years, from 1239 to 1630 A. D.

It is generally believed that marine insurance, as it now exists, originated in Italy. Giovanni Villani, a 14th century Florentine historian, speaks of marine insurance as having first appeared in Lombardy in 1182. At that time the whole banking and overseas trade of Europe was in the hands of the Lombard Jews. One family, at least, went to England and settled in London, in what is today known as Lombard Street, the center of the banking section. They entered into a banking and pawnbroking business, using the Lombard arms of the three golden balls as their sign, and also issued marine insurance policies. The earliest policies issued in England, in 1547 and 1548, were written in Italian, but the names of the subscribers or underwriters were in English.

Following its introduction into England, marine underwriting spread rapidly to the various commercial centers of Europe. The Lloyd's policy now used in England is very like that prevailing in the early part of the 17th century, and many features of the English policy have been incorporated in the policies used in America.

Coffee houses and insurance companies seem closely associated in the history of underwriting. It was in coffee houses that many of the great companies were born. This is natural, too, when we realize that in the earlier days these were the places where men assembled for business discussion as well as for social entertainment.

As with the Ætna, it was in a coffee house that "Lloyd's," the world-renowned shipping and insurance exchange, was organized. Its beginnings were humble in the coffee house established by Edward Lloyd in the middle of the 17th century. His little place was largely patronized by seamen and merchants; and to make it more popular, he started a system of correspondence at home and abroad to keep him informed of the movement and character of vessels for the information of his patrons. It was successful; it filled a real need, and was extended on a larger scale. Lloyd's soon became the meeting place of underwriters, and the foundation of a future great business was laid.

In America, prior to the end of the 18th century the only form of marine insurance was by individual underwriters, and these were for the most part British; early colonial correspondence has frequent reference to London indemnity for American shipping. It proved a slow and irksome process, and in 1759 the first marine insurance office was opened in New York. Others soon followed.

It was natural, and to be expected, that the Ætna in the city of Hartford, with its associations with West Indian trade and other shipping, would early look to marine underwriting as an adjunct or branch of its fire insurance business, and that there would be calls and suggestions for it to enter this field. It was in 1826, when the Company was seven years old, that the first application to the Legislature for a charter amendment authorizing it to underwrite inland marine risks was made. Because of the active opposition of certain marine insurance companies, this was refused; later trials were equally unsuccessful; and it was not until 1839 that the long-denied permission was finally granted.

But even with the authority to act, the Company did not actually begin to write inland marine insurance until four years later. The general attitude of the Board of Directors at this time may be seen in a letter written by Secretary Loomis in June, 1843, in which he said:

> We have procured an amendment to our charter authorizing the Company to insure against the hazards of Internal Navigation — but we have no power to go outside. Directors, however, are not yet prepared to enter upon this branch, and they will never do so at many points. As factories are becoming, nay, have already become, bad subjects for our protection, the Board will be more likely to go into Navigation as a substitute for this description of business. Our charter does not give us power of insuring money by mail or by steam boats.

In all the correspondence on the subject at this time there was an atmosphere of characteristic caution, and evidences of hesitancy about engaging in the new business. Marine risks seem to have been considered as a side-line, as taking a flyer in a new field where the flight would be low, cautious and tentative. This is clearly evident in Secretary Loomis' letter to W. S. Vernon, agent at Louisville:

> As more reflection on the subject of restrictions has been given by our Board, they agree, on the whole, that we might as well go into the business (Inland Marine) as other prudent corporations would, and do. And with your wise judgment and experience we feel safe in committing our interests to your charge.

There is one feature in this business that there is not in fire — the risks terminate in a few days, and if we get sick of our business in that line we can wind it up. If the business should prove fair, it may induce our Board to make your powers more general.

This was written in October, 1843, at the time of the appointment of the first agents. They were selected for river towns in the South, such as Appalachicola, Macon, Savannah and Columbus, Georgia, Mobile, New Orleans, Natchez and Louisville, and were authorized to take risks on cargoes of steamers and pole-boats, but not on the boats themselves. There was a strict limitation, too, to the area to be covered by the policies, which was up the Mississippi as far as St. Louis and on the Ohio to Pittsburgh. The cargoes of that species of river craft known as boxes, arks or broadhorns, because extra-hazardous, were declared non-insurable by the Company.

The first policies were issued in December, 1843. A few lines in the same month from Loomis to W. B. Robins, Ætna fire agent at Cincinnati, throw an interesting side-light on the difficulties of correspondence at this time:

The Board have this evening made you their Marine Agent. The documents will be forwarded by Mr. Junius S. Morgan, who leaves for the West on Monday morning next.

The primitive method of sending letters by hand still persisted, and a coming leader in the financial world did not scorn to act as the messenger.

With the marine insurance underwriting well begun in the South, the next step in the development of this branch of the Ætna's business was a reaching out to the larger field of the Great Lakes. In 1847 Capt.

E. P. Dorr was appointed General Agent at Buffalo, where an office was opened devoted to inland marine insurance. On the death of Capt. Dorr, O. T. Flint, who had been employed and trained in Capt. Dorr's office, succeeded him, and served until February 4, 1891; when the Board of Directors voted to discontinue the office at Buffalo, and to establish a separate branch for marine insurance in New York City, with H. J. Parmalee as Superintendent, and a branch in Chicago under the superintendence of James S. Gadsden, an expert underwriter and adjuster, who had done good work as one of the adjusters in settling the losses at the Chicago fire. Associated with Gadsden was Louis O. Kohtz, who was Assistant General Agent. In 1907, when the Western Branch was moved from Cincinnati to Chicago, Thomas E. Gallagher was appointed General Agent, and Gadsden continued as General Agent of the Marine Department; and on his death in 1911, Kohtz became General Agent of the marine business at Chicago.

The opening of the New York Branch marked the expansion of the inland marine business into the broader field of coastwise marine insurance, and prepared the Company for its ultimate entrance into the business of ocean marine underwriting. In the year following, Egbert O. Weeks was called from his field work in Pennsylvania, and made Assistant Secretary at the Home Office. In addition to other duties he was placed in charge of the inland marine business. Under his more direct fostering care this department thrived, and in 1896 the Directors voted to appoint a committee to investigate the general question of the advisability of the Company's going into the larger field of ocean marine underwriting. It was not until 1907, more than ten years later, however, that a charter amendment was secured permitting the Company to write ocean marine policies. Meanwhile, in 1897, Weeks was promoted to fill the vacancy caused by the death of Vice-President Dudley. Mr. Weeks continued to devote his energies to the development of the marine business until the close of his life on October 31, 1902. The department was then placed in the hands of President Clark, with William F. Whittelsey in active charge.

With the ocean marine amendment to its charter, the Ætna was no longer limited to risks on mere inland navigation; the broad oceans and the waters of the globe were open to its underwriting. Though it is now eighty years since the Ætna was authorized to take up inland marine insurance, the major part of the real history of its marine business really dates from March, 1907.

In January, 1908, the office of Marine Assistant Secretary was created, and William F. Whittelsey was the logical choice for the new position. He had practical experience and training in the inland and coastwise marine field. He had entered the employ of the Ætna in the re-insurance department at the home office, on February 2, 1891. For five years prior to this time he had been connected with the local Ætna agency in Hartford. Soon after coming with the Company he was appointed as examiner of fire risks for the suburban business of New York City. When Vice-President Weeks took control of the marine department in 1897, Mr. Whittelsey became his assistant, and so continued until the death of the former in 1902, when he practically assumed full charge of the department under the direction of President Clark. In 1905 he was appointed to the position of marine special agent at the home office, and served in that capacity until his election as Marine Assistant Secretary. Four years later, on January 25th, he was promoted to the new position of Marine Secretary. It was on January 31, 1917, that he won his final promotion to the post of Marine Vice-President, the position which he still retains. When he became Marine Assistant Secretary in 1908, the annual premiums of the Marine Department were over $422,000 (net). In 1918 the receipts of this department, including automobile insurance premiums, were $3,382,549 (net).

The present Marine Secretary is Raymond E. Stronach, who, after serving twelve years with the Company as chief clerk of the marine department and as assistant to Mr. Whittelsey, was made Marine Special Agent of the Ætna, and two years later was advanced to his present position when Mr. Whittelsey became Marine Vice-President.

The principal agencies of the Marine Department are located at Boston, New York, Philadelphia, Baltimore, Cincinnati, Jacksonville, Chicago and San Francisco. Prior to the establishment of the marine department, inland marine insurance was handled

largely by the regular fire insurance agents throughout the country, except in some of the larger ports like Buffalo and Chicago; but now the agents employed specialize in marine insurance.

There is a tang of romance of the very sea itself in marine insurance. There is a thrill of mystery in the fate of some fine, strong vessel that went serenely out of port one day and was never sighted nor heard of again; a tingle of fresh delight in the wondrous treasures recovered from some sunken ship buried for long under the waters; a dash of adventure and peril in the narrative of the captain of some vessel, marked off as lost and the insurance money paid, a prodigal of the sea, finally limping unexpectedly back into its harbor home. They seem the work of ingenious writers of fiction rather than the actual facts from the prosaic, musty, business records of an insurance company. The files of the Ætna archives tell many such stories.

There was the *Empress of Ireland*, which, on May 29, 1914, sank near the mouth of the St. Lawrence. She settled gently in the soft mud at the bottom of the river, which is 138 feet deep at low tide, and then decided to keel over at a sharp angle. Beside the bodies of those lost in the wreck, she contained 251 bars of silver and many valuable pouches of mail. To secure these by divers was difficult, and the successful attempt made was one of the most remarkable feats of deep-sea salvaging on record. Much of the work had to be done 108 feet below the surface of the water, an unusual depth. It was in 1915 that the attempt was made. To familiarize the divers with the arrangement of the ship and the location of the strong box, pasteboard models were made, and the divers were thoroughly schooled and drilled before the great day of the trial. They secured entrance to the ship through openings in her side, made by cutting through the plates of the vessel. One diver lost his life, but all the silver was recovered. The Ætna had paid the owners $82,000, and the Company's share in the salvage was $67,000, thus reducing the Ætna's net loss to about $15,000.

Most readers will recall the furor created in shipping circles when the *Thomas W. Lawson* was launched. She was one of the first steel schooners ever built, and the first with seven masts, and was fully equipped with machinery for hoisting the sails. After several coal-carrying trips along the coast between Boston and Norfolk, she was finally sent to Europe; but on this first trip went ashore on the Scilly Islands, and became a total loss. For the Ætna's share in this loss there was no salvage.

It sounds like a Stevenson story to read of the steamer *Pewabic* colliding with the steamer *Meteor* near Thunder Bay, Michigan, and then dropping down into the waters of Lake Huron, in August, 1865, with one hundred and fifty of crew and passengers, and a rich cargo of copper ore, on which the Ætna had paid over $45,000 of insurance to the owners. Then unromantic insurance companies sent down treasure seekers, called divers, who brought up little, though several attempts were made and nine lives were lost.

But fifty-two years after the wreck, in 1917, the invention of a new diving suit made another attempt feasible. Then divers, seemingly like ghouls of fiction, walked in an uncanny way through the rich saloons and cabins, now tenanted by skeleton guests, removing from them their diamonds and other jewels, much gold coin and other relics of value.

There is always something that makes the blood tingle in the thought of buried treasure, that makes even the mere catalogue of it seem thrilling and inspiring. The *Pewabic* divers brought up several watches, revolvers of ancient make, coins of dates prior to the Civil War, a black silk gown which dried out as good as new, cotton garments whose brilliant crimson and blue were undimmed by the long soakage, gentlemen's boots with the leather still soft, hand-made silk laces and dainty slippers. The slow work of recovering the lost cargo of copper is still in progress; and while the cost of salvage is great, the Ætna and other insurance companies interested have already reduced their original losses of more than half a century ago by several thousand dollars.

In its marine department the Ætna has claim agents all over the world who are daily settling claims, in connection with which documents in Spanish, Italian, Norwegian, French, Japanese and many other tongues must be carefully translated before the losses can be paid. The term "marine department" of the Company covers more than mere inland navigation and ocean risks; it also includes the automobile branch of the business.

 ONE HUNDRED YEARS OF FIRE INSURANCE

In 1906 the Company began writing automobile risks and sent out its first letter to agents. The inland marine amendment to its charter, in 1839, was sufficiently broad in the words "against the hazards of inland navigation and transportation" to cover fire insurance on automobiles; but the Company wanted larger powers, so in 1907 it secured a new amendment authorizing it to insure automobiles against damage by fire, theft or collision.

In its earliest years of automobile insurance, the fire losses were greater than the losses by theft; but in later years the position has been reversed, and fire losses have decreased, while losses by theft have increased, as stealing automobiles has become an organized business by ingenious, reckless and unscrupulous gangs throughout the country.

The Ætna also writes collision insurance, and covers the loss from fire, sinking, or collision when the car is on a ferry, steamboat, or railroad train. Under another form of policy, registered mail is insured for banks, brokers and financial corporations against all risks of loss by fire, transportation, theft or otherwise, from the time the package is deposited in the post-office for registration until delivered to the consignee at destination, anywhere in the United States, Canada or Mexico. The Tourist Baggage Policy covers baggage and personal effects of the insured or of his family while traveling in any part of the world.

Under a marine policy the Ætna has covered, at one time or other, about every imaginable risk. The main features, of course, are the insuring of hulls,

 MARINE UNDERWRITING

cargoes and freight; but it has insured merchandise on mule-back in Venezuela, rubber in rafts down the Amazon, ivory from the Sudan, cotton from Egypt, furs from Russia, gold from Alaska, copra from the East Indies, coffee from Brazil, cotton from the South (even covering it on the old bark *Pass of Balmaha*, later converted into the raider *Seeadler*, recently sold by salvors in the East Indies). Besides covering munitions and war materials for Europe, the Company has insured horses being shipped there for the cavalry and guns, wheat and flour down the Great Lakes to Buffalo, iron from the Lake Superior mines to Cleveland, and coal from the Eastern mining centers to points on Lake Superior, hides from Iceland and Archangel, automobiles to Mozambique, and codfish from the Grand Banks.

Now firmly established, the ocean marine part of the Company's business has grown like a green bay-tree from the start and today its agents may be found in every important shipping center of the world.

Chapter XVI

DURING THE GREAT WAR

THE assassination of Archduke Francis Ferdinand, heir to the throne of Austria-Hungary, and of his wife, on June 28, 1914, was made the excuse to plunge the whole world into such a war that even imagination could not have conceived it as possible. Three years later America was drawn into the titanic conflict.

It was not long before the great war made shipping on the ocean an extra-hazardous risk, and affected every company doing ocean marine underwriting; and this was quickly followed by the stealthy bomb or torch applied by alien enemies in the United States to depositories of war material, to factories and to arsenals and shipyards. In speaking of war conditions in 1916, President Clark of the Ætna Insurance Company said:

> Perhaps the biggest year the fire insurance companies ever had was the fiscal year of 1914-15. While every indication pointed toward even greater success this year, and the insurance men were expecting a record-breaking season, events have occurred which materially change the aspect of the situation. In the munition factories of the East, explosions and fires have occurred in great numbers. Factories manufacturing clothing and other supplies which were reported to be war orders suffered similar

"accidents" every few weeks. The insurance companies have paid out huge indemnities as a result. Only additional precautions taken by manufacturers at the instruction of the fire insurance companies have prevented even greater losses.

There was a spirit of incipient panic among marine insurance companies in the fall of 1914, regarding ocean risks; but the prompt decision of the Ætna and other companies to protect their customers and to continue marine underwriting despite the war aided greatly in restoring confidence, and a serious financial disaster in marine circles was thus prevented. There was quick action on the part of the Company, for it was on September 14, 1914, that Marine Secretary Whittelsey appeared before the Board of Directors and reported his views on marine conditions as affected by the war.

Among the large marine insurance losses of the war was that of the Cunard steamship *Lusitania*, torpedoed and sunk without warning on May 7, 1915, by a German submarine off Old Head of Kinsale on the Irish coast. The Ætna came off fortunately with but a slight loss, about $16,000 on the cargo.

The loss of the *Arabic*, a White Star line steamer, on August 19, 1915, was one of the historic events of the marine warfare of the period. The vessel was sunk without warning off the southern coast of Ireland while on her way to New York; over fifty passengers, including two Americans, and a number of the crew, were drowned. The usual line of diplomatic correspondence followed, and the German Ambassador in Washington formally assured our Government that Germany would give "complete satisfaction if it developed that the submarine commander exceeded his instructions." Later the German Government put in an explanation that the *Arabic* was torpedoed in self-defense, refused to pay an indemnity, and then suggested that the matter be arbitrated. This seems to have closed the incident, which cost the Ætna about $5,270.

The *Gulflight* was another vessel that figured prominently in the diplomatic interchange of letters preceding by over two years America's entry into the war. The *Gulflight* was an American tank steamer carrying 50,000 barrels of gasoline, *en route* from Port Arthur, Texas, to Rouen, France, and torpedoed by a German submarine off the Scilly Islands on May 1, 1915. Three or four weeks later the German Admiralty admitted the torpedoing, but said that the submarine commander mistook the vessel for a belligerent. The cost to the Ætna was about $5,000.

These are but typical of the dozens of vessels insured in part by the Ætna that were the victims of submarines or mines.

At every change of conditions, with their presentation of new problems and policies, the Ætna was ready to meet them in a fearless spirit of patriotic service. Resolutions were adopted by the Board of Directors that salaries of Company employees entering the military or naval service of the United States Government would be continued, and their places held for them.

The demand for men to serve in the army and navy of the nation depleted the clerical staff; and as

Ætna Insurance Company
HARTFORD, CONNECTICUT

The following is an extract from the Minutes of the Meeting of the Board of Directors of the Ætna Insurance Company, November Eleventh, Nineteen Hundred and Eighteen:

Voted: That on this day made memorable by the signing of the Armistice Terms by Germany, thus preparing the way for World-Wide Peace and Democracy, we the President and Directors of the Ætna Insurance Company in gratitude to those men who have left the employ of this Company to join the Colors and so heroically do their part to serve our Country, spread upon the records the following names to perpetuate the honor and esteem in which we hold them as true Americans:

HONOR ROLL

 DURING THE GREAT WAR

was common in all business institutions, the vacant places were filled by girls. When the armistice treaty was signed the Directors adopted this resolution:

VOTED: That on this day, made memorable by the signing of the Armistice Terms by Germany, thus preparing the way for world-wide peace and Democracy, we, the President and Directors of the Ætna Insurance Company, in gratitude to those men who have left the employ of this Company to join the Colors and to heroically do their part to serve our Country, spread upon the records the following names, to perpetuate the honor and esteem in which we hold them as true Americans.

Then follows the list of names. A handsomely engraved copy of this resolution, containing the names of all on the Honor Roll, has been presented to each member and is reproduced herewith.

In all the calls for contributions to Red Cross work and to other war needs the Company responded loyally, and subscribed several million dollars for the Liberty Loan Bonds of our Government and for the Victory Loan Bonds of Canada.

A significant aftermath of the great upheaval caused by the war may be found in the announcement by the Ætna, in January, 1919, that the Company was prepared to accept risks against the hazards of riot and civil commotion. This decision was the reflection of a feeling existing in many quarters that the world-wide anarchistic propaganda launched by the Bolsheviki leaders in Russia might lead to the destruction of property in America.

When the Ætna began its first century America was slowly recuperating from a great war; as it began its second century the world was emerging from the grim shadow of the greatest war in history.

Chapter XVII

THE PAST AND THE PRESENT

GREATER than the success of any individual are the mental and moral qualities behind that success. True greatness is never an accident; it is but the final flowering of characteristics working through the years toward that greatness and making it inevitable. What is true of an individual is equally true of a corporation.

In looking back over the hundred years of the Ætna, we find, breathing through its manifold acts and activities, the same clearly defined principles and policies. These are insistent, constant and dominating. They have inspired and guided the Company alike in its dark hours of struggle and crisis and in the sunlit days of prosperity. Presidents, vice-presidents, secretaries and directors changed with the years, the old dropped out and the new came in, and the ranks closed up into what seemed the same advancing body, inspired by the same traditions, the same ideals, the same purpose, and the same unswerving loyalty and devotion.

When President Brace made his brief address to the stockholders gathered together in that first meeting at Morgan's Exchange Coffee House on June 15, 1819,

THE PAST AND THE PRESENT

his clear, forceful words could not have been wiser had he the prophetic vision to see through the long years of the century. He spoke with fervor of the supreme importance of the character of its officers. He realized that no company could rise higher than the men that made it; and he urged, in the selection of the Board of Directors, the necessity of "character, energy, enterprise and tireless devotion." The men constituting that first Board were men measuring up to that high standard, and the same standard has been maintained in every year of the Company's history.

The story of the Company's Presidents, Secretaries and other officers has already been told in these pages; but of the men who have sat around the Directors' table and determined what the Ætna should be and what it should do, there has been no space to give details except with a special few who were somehow thrown into unusual prominence. How loyal the service of all, and how safe and sound their decisions, needs no proof other than that evident in the splendid achievements and prestige of the Company, whose fire business now covers an entire continent and its marine underwriting the whole world. It is only occasionally, in facing some real crisis, like the fire at Mobile or at New York, that the curtain is drawn aside for a moment and we see the united spirit of devotion that inspired them at all times.

The Company has been remarkable in the length of service of its Directors; and this may explain, to a degree, the continuity of loyalty to the Ætna's early ideals and traditions. The period of service of some of these Directors is worthy of special mention. Drayton Hillyer served for fifty-five years, Roland Mather fifty, Walter Keney forty-five, Gustavus F. Davis forty-four, Samuel Tudor, Jr., and Joseph Church forty-three, Thomas K. Brace and Robert Buell forty-two, A. C. Dunham forty, Francis B. Cooley thirty-eight, William F. Tuttle thirty-seven, Samuel S. Ward thirty-three, Charles H. Brainard thirty-two, J. Pierpont Morgan, Nathaniel Shipman and Joseph L. Pratt thirty-one, Joseph Morgan and Griffin Stedman twenty-eight, Austin Dunham twenty-seven, and Eliphalet A. Bulkeley twenty-six. Of the Board serving in 1919, the One Hundredth Anniversary year of the Company, the terms of five had exceeded the quarter-century mark — Hon. Morgan G. Bulkeley thirty-nine years, Atwood Collins thirty-five, William B. Clark thirty, Rev. Dr. Francis Goodwin twenty-nine, and Charles E. Gross twenty-six years.

The personnel of the first Board of Directors as elected at Morgan's Coffee House was noted as a detail of that meeting, and those serving the Company in the same capacity one hundred years later are seen to be men of similar character, men of prominence and leaders in their community. They are:

William B. Clark, President of the Ætna Insurance Company.

Hon. Morgan G. Bulkeley, President of the Ætna Life Insurance Company.

Atwood Collins, President of the Security Trust Company of Hartford.

Rev. Dr. Francis Goodwin, grandson of Joseph Morgan.

Charles E. Gross, General Counsel of the Ætna since 1891, and senior member of the law firm of Gross, Hyde and Shipman of Hartford, which has acted as counsel for the Ætna for nearly half a century.

James H. Knight, President of the First National Bank of Hartford.

Charles P. Cooley, Vice-President of the Fidelity Trust Company of Hartford.

Arthur L. Shipman, member of the law firm of Gross, Hyde and Shipman.

Charles L. Spencer, President of the Connecticut River Banking Company of Hartford.

Charles A. Goodwin, lawyer, and great-grandson of Joseph Morgan.

Henry E. Rees, Vice-President of the Ætna.

Almeron N. Williams, Vice-President of the Ætna.

J. P. Morgan, of New York City, financier, great-grandson of Joseph Morgan.

H. B. Cheney, of the firm of Cheney Bros., silk manufacturers at South Manchester, Connecticut.

John L. Way, Vice-President of the Travelers Insurance Company of Hartford.

In analyzing the elements contributing to the growth and greatness of the Ætna, emphasis has been placed on the high character of the Officers and Directors who have managed its affairs during the first century of its existence, and to the loyalty and devotion of its agents. To the latter the Company owes a large measure of its success. As we have noted, the Ætna did not invent the agent, but it did transform him by raising his work to the dignity of a profession. The Ætna agent has been made to feel that he is not a mere cog in a machine, but a real member of a great family, contributing his share to the welfare and prosperity of all.

The same spirit of fairness, consideration and liberality that has characterized the relations between the Company and its agents has also featured the Ætna's relations with the insuring public. From the very beginning losses were paid fully and promptly. The Company faced many severe fires, and while it was sometimes difficult to provide the great sums needed to pay the claims, they were always met without delay. The perfect faith and certainty that the Company would always "make good" was not based on a study of the latest Ætna balance-sheet, but on the character of the men behind it.

President Brace's words, written in 1822, that "he would never consent that any honest insurer in the Ætna should be choused out of a just claim by a mere subterfuge or mere legal lack," could have been written by every other President of the Company with equal force and truth. The avoidance of litigation and technical quibbling has ever been a dominating policy of the Company.

The business of fire insurance is really two-fold, as its sources of profit are two. Its profits come from the excess of premiums over losses and expenses, and from the interest on invested funds. It thus becomes dual in its nature — underwriting and investment banking. It is a question whether the business of fire underwriting as a whole in America during the last century can be termed profitable. In this connection there is peculiar significance in the statement made by the National Board of Fire Underwriters following the San Francisco fire, that in that disaster the American fire underwriting profits of more than forty years had been wiped out in a few hours. The same note was sounded a few years ago by Henry H. Hall, in "One Hundred Years of American Commerce," in which he stated: "The business of fire underwriting in the United States for the past century has been done at a loss; and the most successful companies, as a whole, have not retained more than simple interest upon their capital and invested funds."

In the presence of such statements one may faintly realize how rare was the underwriting ability, and how wise and far-seeing the banking and investing management, that transformed the Ætna infant of 1819, with its paid-in capital of $15,000, into the Ætna giant of 1919, with assets well over $30,000,000, and the payment of over $178,000,000 for losses during the last hundred years. It is a record of which all its officers, from the days of 1819, with President Brace and his directors, to the days of 1919, with President Clark and his official staff, may well be proud.

As the biography of a great statesman must naturally overflow into larger relations of which it forms an inseparable part, and becomes, to a degree, a history of his country, so the story of the origin, life and progress of the Ætna must carry with it concurrently the history of fire insurance in America for the same period.

 ONE HUNDRED YEARS OF FIRE INSURANCE

When the Ætna was organized in 1819, fire insurance as a real business was still in its infancy. It was then little more than prudence and shrewd guessing; there were few statistics of value, and little in the way of classified experience. It was somewhat like venturing into a new country, but slightly explored and sparsely settled. There was pioneer work to be done, and this pioneering and the progress that came from it made history. Much of this history the Ætna made; of all of it the Ætna was a part.

The real, vital history of fire insurance in America is contemporaneous with the life of the Ætna. The great development came from ideas, suggestions, innovations and experience that gave fire insurance new impetus, and progressively raised it to higher planes of safety, surety and scientific underwriting: many of these the Ætna originated; in many others it co-operated; in none was it a factor without influence. It is in this spirit of recognition of its splendid record as an individual institution, and of the vital part it has played in the evolution of fire insurance as a business, that this story of "The Leading Fire Insurance Company of America"— to quote President Clark's slogan — has been written.

APPENDIX I

ORIGINAL CHARTER OF THE ÆTNA INSURANCE COMPANY WITH AMENDMENTS

The Charter of the Ætna Insurance Company was granted at the May Session of the Legislature of the State of Connecticut, 1819, and the Governor's signature of approval was attached June 5, 1819.

During the one hundred years from 1819 to 1919 there were thirteen amendments made to the original charter and two general laws which have the effect of amendments. The original charter and amendments are here given:

ORIGINAL CHARTER

SECTION 1. *Be it enacted by the Senate and House of Representatives, in General Assembly convened,* That the subscribers to the petition praying for an act of incorporation, with powers and privileges necessary and convenient to the business of insurance against losses by fire, &c., be and they hereby are incorporated, and made a body politic, by the name, style and title of the *Ætna Insurance Company,* and by that name, style and title, shall be, and hereby are empowered to purchase, receive, have, hold, possess and enjoy to themselves, and their successors, lands, tenements, rents, hereditaments, goods, chattels, and effects of every kind and nature; as also United States stocks, and bank stock of the United States Bank, or any Bank in the United States, and the estate and stocks aforesaid to alien, grant, sell and dispose of; to sue and be sued, plead and be impleaded, in all courts of justice; also, to have and use a common seal, and the same to change at pleasure; also to ordain and execute all by-laws, and regulations, by them deemed necessary, for the well-ordering and governing said corporation; provided said by-laws and regulations are not repugnant to the constitution and laws of this state, and of the constitution and laws of the United States.

SEC. 2. The capital stock of said corporation shall not be less than one hundred and fifty thousand dollars, and may, at the pleasure of said corporation, be increased to any further sum, not exceeding five hundred thousand dollars, and shall be divided into shares of one hundred dollars each, and on the said capital stock of one hundred and fifty thousand dollars, in part of said stock, shall be paid into the treasury of said corporation, for the use of said corporation, within thirty days after the first meeting of said corporation, five per centum; and within sixty days next after said first meeting of said corporation, the further sum of five per centum on said stock, shall, in like manner, for like purposes, be paid into said treasury; and the remainder of said stock shall be secured to be paid by mortgage on real estate, or endorsed promissory notes, approved by the president and directors of said corporation, and shall be payable in thirty days after demand; and such endorsers shall have a lien on the stock for which such note or notes are given.

SEC. 3. There shall be seventeen directors for the well-ordering the affairs of said corporation, chosen by one or more ballots from among and by the stockholders of said corporation, which said directors shall hold their office at pleasure for one year, and until others are chosen in their room; and the annual meeting for the choice of said directors, shall, after the first election, be holden in the city of Hartford, on the first Thursday of June, or on such day in the month of June as shall be appointed by said board of directors.

SEC. 4. The said directors shall choose one of their number to be president of said corporation, and in case of his absence from business, may, so often as necessity shall require, elect from among themselves a president for the time being; and in case any vacancy shall occur in said direction, said directors may elect a director or directors, from among the stockholders, to fill such vacancy, who shall hold their office at pleasure, until others are chosen in their room; and said directors shall have power to appoint for the time being, such officers, secretaries, agents and servants as they shall judge necessary, and shall be capable of performing such other acts, and exercising such other powers, as shall be by them deemed for the best interest of the company. And no director shall be entitled to any emolument unless by vote of the stockholders in general meeting.

SEC. 5. The directors shall determine what number of their own body shall constitute a quorum for the transaction of business, and when such quorum is formed, if the president is not present, the electors present shall appoint a president pro tempore.

SEC. 6. The number of votes each stockholder shall be entitled to in the choice of directors, or any other concern or business of the company, shall be equal to the number of shares he shall be the owner of; provided, no stockholder shall, by virtue of the number of shares he may be the owner of, in any case, be entitled to more than fifty votes.

SEC. 7. The stockholders shall be entitled to vote in person, or by proxy duly appointed; and none but stockholders shall be eligible as directors.

SEC. 8. Public notice shall be given, by order of the directors, at least ten days previous to any meeting of the stockholders, in a newspaper printed in the city of Hartford, and in such other manner as they may judge expedient.

SEC. 9. Said corporation may ensure on dwelling houses, and all other buildings, on ships and vessels of every description, while in port or on the stocks, on goods, chattels, wares, merchandise, and on all kinds of mixed and personal estate of every description, and shall be liable to make good and pay to the several persons who shall be assured by the said corporation, for all losses they may sustain by fire in the subject matter insured agreeable to the contract of assurance, and of their policy, effected with said corporation. *Provided always*, that no stockholder shall be liable to said corporation, for any amount beyond the amount of stock by him holden, and unpaid to said corporation, and neither the members of nor said corporation shall, in any event, be liable beyond the amount of their said capital, for any loss, or losses, whatever; but for misconduct or fraud, the person guilty thereof, shall be personally liable to said corporation, or to the insured, as the case may be.

SEC. 10. The capital stock of said corporation shall be transferable according to the rules and regulations prescribed by the directors; and every subscriber of any share, or shares in said stock, who shall neglect to pay the installments aforesaid, or to secure the residue of the said share or shares as aforesaid, shall forfeit to the said corporation, such share or shares, and all payments made thereon, and all profits which may have arisen thereon.

SEC. 11. All notes or policies of insurance, signed by the president, and countersigned by the secretary, shall bind and oblige said corporation according to the terms and tenor thereof.

SEC. 12. In case any insured, named in any policy or contract of insurance, made by the said corporation, shall sell and convey, or assign the subject matter

 APPENDIX I

insured, during the period of time for which it is insured, it shall be lawful for such insured, to assign and deliver to the purchaser such policy, or contract of insurance, and the same shall enure to his benefit, and in every respect as effectual as though the same had been delivered by said corporation to said assignee. *Provided always*, that before any loss happens, such assignee shall obtain the consent of the assignor to such assignment, and shall obtain said assent to be endorsed on or annexed to the said policy or contract of assurance, executed and signed as a new policy or contract ought to be according to such rules as shall be prescribed by the directors, and not otherwise.

SEC. 13. Thomas K. Brace is authorized to call a meeting of the subscribers to said petition, to be holden in the city of Hartford, in the month of June, 1819, which meeting may be organized, by a moderator and such committees as shall be deemed proper, and said meeting may be adjourned from time to time, until said corporation shall be organized agreeable to the charter; and the stock shall be taken up to the amount of one hundred and fifty thousand dollars, before said directors shall be chosen, and before said corporation make any assurance.

SEC. 14. As soon as the installments aforesaid shall have been paid or secured by endorsed notes, and the remainder of the stock secured agreeable to the provisions aforesaid, and the whole to be done to the satisfaction of said directors——and no part of said stock shall be assignable, or transferable until both of said installments shall have been paid, anything in this act to the contrary notwithstanding.

Provided, this act may at any time be altered, amended, or revoked by the General Assembly.

General Assembly, May Session, 1819.
DAVID PLANT, *Speaker of the House of Representatives*.
JONATHAN INGERSOLL, *President of the Senate*.
Approved June 5, 1819.   OLIVER WOLCOTT.

AMENDMENT NO. 1

Life Insurance

Be it enacted by the Senate and House of Representatives, in General Assembly convened, That it shall and may be lawful to and for the said corporation to add to their present actual capital the sum of fifty thousand dollars, and at the pleasure of the company, may increase said addition to any sum not exceeding one hundred and fifty thousand dollars; and the whole of said capital stock, created by, and raised under this act, shall be denominated the annuity fund, and shall be secured and paid into the treasury of said corporation, and vested in the same proportion and manner as is authorized and required by the act to which this is an addition, in relation to the fire insurance stock thereby created. And the stock created by this act shall be exclusively held and pledged as a fund for the payment of annuities which shall be granted by said company, and of losses upon insurance for a life or lives, or in any way dependent upon life or lives, and shall in no case be liable for the other debts, contracts, liabilities or engagements of the said company. And said annuity fund shall alone be liable to pay, bear and satisfy all losses, expenses, payments and charges in respect to insurance on life or lives, or in any manner dependent on life or lives, and annuities which may be granted by said company; and said Ætna Insurance Company are authorized and empowered to grant annuities, and make insurance dependent on life or lives; to establish a form of policy, create officers for the corporation, prescribe the mode of authentication of policies, and all other instruments lawful for said company to execute, by seal or the signature of officers, or an officer, appointed by the corporation for such purpose.

Provided always, that this act may be repealed, altered, or amended by the Legislature. General Assembly, May Session, 1820.

DAVID PLANT, *Speaker of the House of Representatives.*
JONATHAN INGERSOLL, *President of the Senate.*

Approved May 26, 1820.   OLIVER WOLCOTT.

AMENDMENT NO. 2
Inland Marine and Transportation

Upon the petition of the Ætna Insurance Company, shewing to this Assembly, that in the year 1819 they were incorporated by the Legislature of this State, for the purpose of insuring against loss or damage by fire, which business they have ever since conducted; that their capital is ample and abundantly secured; that the business of inland navigation, and of insurance against the hazards incident thereto, have of late years greatly increased, while the number of offices empowered to issue such policies is limited; that the petitioners have frequent applications from their present customers and others, to take this description of risks, which, under their present charter, they are obliged to decline; that it would be for the mutual advantage of themselves and the public, to extend their powers to this department of insurance; and praying the Legislature to make the necessary amendment to their charter, as by petition on file dated the 11th day of April, 1839, may more fully appear.

And now this Assembly, having inquired into the allegations of said petition, do find the same to be true; therefore,

Resolved by this Assembly, That the Ætna Insurance Company be, and they are hereby fully authorized and empowered to issue policies against the hazards of inland navigation and transportation; and said policies, when duly executed by the proper officers of said company, shall be to all intents and purposes, binding upon said company, in the same manner as though the power to issue the same, had been granted by their original charter.

Approved May 8, 1839.   WILLIAM W. ELLSWORTH.

AMENDMENT NO. 3
Life Insurance

Upon the petition of the Ætna Insurance Company, praying for an amendment of that portion of their charter authorizing insurances upon life.

Resolved by this Assembly, That policies of Insurance issued by said company on the life of any person, expressed to be for the benefit of a married woman, whether the same be effected by herself or her husband, or by any other person on her behalf, shall enure to her separate use and benefit, and that of her or her husband's children, if any, as may be expressed in said policies, independently of her husband and his creditors and representatives, and also independently of any other persons effecting the same in her behalf, his creditors and representatives; *always provided* that this section shall not apply to insurances where the annual premium on the policy shall exceed the sum of one hundred and fifty dollars, unless paid from the private property of the wife.

Approved June 6, 1850.   THOMAS H. SEYMOUR.

APPENDIX I

AMENDMENT NO. 4
Incorporating the Shareholders of the Annuity Fund of the Ætna Insurance Company as a Life Insurance Company

Upon the petition of the Ætna Insurance Company, praying for such an alteration of its charter as will constitute the shareholders of the annuity fund of said company, their successors and assigns, a distinct corporation for the purpose of life insurance, and the assumption of life risks, as per memorial on file, dated May 9, A. D. 1853, will more fully appear.

Resolved by this Assembly, That the shareholders of the "Annuity Fund" of the said "Ætna Insurance Company," their successors and assigns, forever, be and they are hereby made and constituted a body corporate and politic for the purpose of life insurance, and for the assumption of all or any hazards connected with life risks, by the name of the "Ætna Life Insurance Company" and with and by that name shall have and possess all the powers and privileges and be subject to all the duties imposed upon the shareholders of said "Annuity Fund" under their present charter and the amendments thereof, and shall also have all the powers and privileges incident to a distinct corporation; *provided*, that all the liabilities and obligations of said Ætna Insurance Company for and on account of its "Annuity Fund" shall continue and exist against said company hereby incorporated, under the said name of the Ætna Life Insurance Company, and that all debts, liabilities or obligations due to said Ætna Insurance Company for and on account of its "Annuity Fund," may be collected and enforced by said company in the name of the Ætna Life Insurance Company, and that all suits in favor of or against said Ætna Insurance Company, for and on account of its "Annuity Fund," may be continued in force and prosecuted to final judgment by or against said company, in the same manner as if this resolution had not been passed.

SEC. 2. That the stock, property, affairs and business of said corporation shall be managed and conducted by not less than seven nor more than ten directors, a majority of whom shall reside in this state, who shall be chosen by ballot from and by the stockholders of said company, and the present managing directors and officers of said company shall be the officers of said corporation until the first Monday of July next, when and in each successive year thereafter, on the day aforesaid, an election shall be held for the choice of directors of said company, ten days previous notice thereof, having been given in some newspaper printed in said Hartford; each stockholder shall be allowed one vote for each and every share of stock held by him, and the directors of said company shall choose a president and secretary of the said corporation, who shall hold their offices for one year, and may appoint such other officers and agents as shall by them be deemed expedient for conducting the business of the company.

Approved May 28, 1853.   THOMAS H. SEYMOUR.

AMENDMENT NO. 5
Authorizing Increase of Capital

Upon the petition of the Ætna Insurance Company, praying for an increase of capital.

Resolved by this Assembly, That the Ætna Insurance Company be, and they are hereby authorized and empowered to add to the capital stock of said company, from time to time, any number of shares, not exceeding in the aggregate, ten thousand shares, of the par value of one hundred dollars each at such time or times, as the directors of said company may deem proper, which said additions to said capital shall be made from the surplus earnings of said company and shall be divided pro rata, among the persons who may be stockholders at the time or times when such additions shall be made.

Approved May 16, 1857.   ALEXANDER H. HOLLEY.

AMENDMENT NO. 6
Authorizing Increase of Capital

Resolved by this Assembly, That the Ætna Insurance Company be and they are hereby authorized and empowered to add to the capital stock of said company, from time to time, any number of shares, not exceeding in the aggregate, fifteen thousand shares, of the par value of one hundred dollars each, at such time or times, as the directors of said company may deem proper, which said additions to said capital shall be made from the surplus earnings of said company and shall be divided pro rata, among the persons who may be stockholders at the time or times when such additions shall be made.

Approved January 15, 1864. WILLIAM A. BUCKINGHAM.

AMENDMENT NO. 7
Authorizing Increase of Capital

Resolved by this Assembly,— SECTION 1. That the Ætna Insurance Company be and they are hereby authorized and empowered to add to the present capital stock of said company, any number of shares not exceeding in the aggregate twenty thousand shares, of the par value of one hundred dollars each, at such time or times and upon such terms and conditions as the directors of said company may deem proper, which said additions to said capital shall be divided pro rata among the persons who may be stockholders at the time or times when such additions shall be made.

SEC. 2. That so much of Sec. 6 of the original charter of the Ætna Insurance Company, approved June 5, 1819, as provides that no stockholder shall by virtue of the number of shares he may be the owner of, in any case be entitled to more than fifty votes, be and the same is hereby repealed.

Approved February 14, 1877. RICHARD D. HUBBARD.

AMENDMENT NO. 8
Hazards of Lightning and Other Elements.

Resolved by this Assembly, That the Ætna Insurance Company may insure against any loss or damage to all kinds of property by the elements including damage by lightning.

Approved March 1, 1881. HOBART B. BIGELOW.

AMENDMENT NO. 9
Changing Date of Annual Meeting

Resolved by this Assembly, — SECTION 1. That the annual meeting of the Ætna Insurance Company for the choice of directors of said company, and for the transaction of other proper business, shall, after the year 1886, be holden on the third Thursday of January in each year, or on such other day in the month of January in each year as shall be appointed by the board of directors of said company.

SEC. 2. The directors of said company who may be chosen at the annual meeting to be held in June, 1886, shall hold their office until the next annual meeting and until others are chosen in their room.

SEC. 3. So much of the charter of said company as is inconsistent herewith is hereby repealed.

Approved February 24, 1886. HENRY B. HARRISON.

 APPENDIX I

AMENDMENT NO. 10
Number of Directors

Resolved by this Assembly,—SECTION 1. That the stockholders of the Ætna Insurance Company may hereafter at the annual meetings of said company choose by ballot from among their number a board consisting of not less than nine nor more than seventeen directors, who shall respectively hold their offices until the succeeding annual meeting and until others are chosen in their places.

SEC. 2. So much of the charter of said company as is inconsistent herewith is hereby repealed.

Approved March 1, 1897.   LORRIN A. COOKE.

AMENDMENT NO. 11
Ocean Marine Insurance

Resolved by this Assembly, That the Ætna Insurance Company may issue policies of insurance against marine disasters upon all kinds of vessels and personal property of every description.

Approved March 26, 1907.   ROLLIN S. WOODRUFF.

AMENDMENT NO. 12
Automobile Insurance

Resolved by this Assembly, That the Ætna Insurance Company may issue policies of insurance against damage to automobiles resulting from fire, from the hazards of transportation and marine navigation, from theft of any of their parts or equipment, and from collision with a stationary or moving object.

Approved March 30, 1909.   FRANK B. WEEKS, *Lieutenant Governor*
And Acting Governor.

AMENDMENT NO. 13
Authorizing Increase of Capital
AMENDING THE CHARTER OF THE ÆTNA INSURANCE COMPANY

Resolved by this Assembly,—SECTION 1. That the Ætna Insurance Company is hereby authorized to increase its capital stock, from time to time, from the present amount of five million dollars to any amount or amounts not exceeding, in the aggregate, the sum of ten million dollars.

SEC. 2. The shares of each increase of said capital stock as hereby authorized shall be of the par value of one hundred dollars each, and may be issued to the stockholders of the company upon such terms and conditions as the directors, at the time of the respective increases, may deem proper; provided, however, that no such shares shall be issued at less than par.

Approved March 21, 1911.   SIMEON E. BALDWIN.

GENERAL LAWS

In addition to the foregoing charter rights of the Ætna Insurance Company, the following authorizations have been assumed by the company, under the laws of the State of Connecticut, namely:

Insurance Against Wind Storms, Hail, Lightning, Tornadoes, Leakage of Sprinklers and Explosions

CHAPTER 53, SECTION 3510 (LAWS OF 1909)
AN ACT AMENDING AN ACT RELATING TO INSURANCE

Be it enacted by the Senate and House of Representatives in General Assembly convened:

SECTION 1. Section 3510 of the General Statutes as amended by Chapter 23 of the Public Acts of 1903 is hereby amended by adding after the words "wind storms" in the fourth line thereof, the word "hail," so that said section as amended shall read as follows: *Insurance companies organized under the laws of this state* having power to insure against loss by fire, may make insurance against loss by wind storms, hail, lightning, tornadoes, cyclones, leakage of sprinklers and sprinkler systems installed or maintained for the purpose of protecting against fire, and by explosions whether fire ensues or not; provided the same shall be clearly expressed in the policy, but nothing herein shall be construed to empower such companies to insure against loss or damage to person or property resulting from explosions of steam boilers.

SEC. 2. This act shall take effect from its passage.

Approved May 13, 1909.   FRANK B. WEEKS, *Lieutenant Governor And Acting Governor.*

CHAPTER 13 (LAWS OF 1915)
An Act Concerning Marine Insurance

Be it enacted by the Senate and House of Representatives in General Assembly convened:

SECTION 1. Any corporation authorized by law in this state to issue any contracts relating to inland marine and transportation insurance or relating to ocean marine insurance may, as a part of such contracts, make insurance upon vessels, freights, goods, wares, merchandise, specie, bullion, jewelry, profits, commissions, bank notes, bills of exchange, and other evidences of debt, bottomry and respondentia interests, and every insurance pertaining to marine risks of transportation and navigation.

SEC. 2. This act shall take effect from its passage.

Approved March 10, 1915.   MARCUS H. HOLCOMB, *Governor.*

APPENDIX II

CHRONOLOGICAL HISTORY OF THE ÆTNA INSURANCE COMPANY

1819

April 19. Petition filed with General Assembly of Connecticut for Company's charter.
June 5. Charter of Company granted by Legislature and approved by Governor Oliver Wolcott.
June 15. First meeting of stockholders at Morgan's Exchange Coffee House, Hartford, and election of directors.
First meeting of Directors and election of Thomas K. Brace, President, and Isaac Perkins, Secretary.
Offices of Company opened in law office of Isaac Perkins in Morgan's Exchange Coffee House.
June 25. Rules and by-laws adopted.
July 15. First investment of Company — twenty shares of stock of the United States Bank.
First installment of five per cent. cash paid on Company stock.
August 14. Theodore Pease, Director, died.
August 15. Second installment of five per cent. in cash paid on stock.
August 17. First fire insurance policy written by the Ætna — for $6,000 for Joseph Morgan, a Director, on his Exchange Coffee House, the premium being $45.
August 19. Date which the Company had advertised that it would be ready to do business.
September 2. Adopted "Book of Instructions" for agents.
September 27. Thomas K. Brace resigned as President.
Henry L. Ellsworth elected President.
October 12. Re-insured risks of Middletown Insurance Company (First known case of re-insurance).
December 15. Voted first dividend — six per cent. on $15,000 of capital paid in.

1820

February 16. Voted to limit single risks to $10,000 except by unanimous vote of the Directors.
May 26. Charter amended to permit Company to write life insurance.

1821

March 6. Henry L. Ellsworth resigned as President.
Thomas K. Brace, first President, again elected.
May 29. First individual risk over $10,000 ($17,000) accepted by Company and written by Stephen Tillinghast, agent at Providence, Rhode Island.

June 28. First fire loss of Company, amounting to $4,000 on building of Shepherd & Co., at Northampton, Massachusetts.
December 22. Established first agency in Canada by appointing Abijah Bigelow agent at Montreal. The Ætna was the first American fire insurance company to do business in Canada, and was preceded only by one English company and one Canadian company.

1822

March 11. First trip of Company official to adjust losses, when Secretary Perkins visited Norfolk, Virginia, to adjust losses on woolen factory there.
June 10. First trip of Company official to appoint agents, when Secretary Perkins made tour of New England states.
December 16. Increased capital of Company from $150,000 to $200,000.

1823

First contested claim for insurance. Company won verdict on ground of fraud.

1825

January 10. Agents of Company in New York state petitioned Legislature to repeal or modify law taxing foreign companies ten per cent. on their business in the state.
October 27. William L. Perkins, local agent at Ashford, Connecticut, was appointed first Special Agent of Company and was employed to travel through the southern and central states and establish agencies.
December 8. Adopted new rules and schedules of rates prepared by Secretary Perkins.

1826

February 23. Voted to ask Legislature for amendment to charter to permit writing of Inland Marine Insurance.

1827

January 22. Joseph Morgan appointed as Special Agent to investigate business of Company in Canada and settle losses at Quebec.
November 19. Appointed committee to devise ways and means to meet losses from big fire at Mobile, Alabama, amounting to over $50,000.
November 26. Appointed committee to confer with officials of two other Hartford companies with reference to combating legislation in various states excluding foreign insurance companies and also on the subject of rates.
December 13. Adopted new schedule of premium rates.

1828

January 2. Established first General Agency by appointing Jeremiah Van Rensselaer of Canandaigua, New York, as General Agent for Western country and Western New York.
June 9. James M. Goodwin elected Secretary to succeed Isaac Perkins.

1829

Elected William W. Ellsworth, later Governor of Connecticut, as first General Counsel for the Company.

1830

Adopted new schedule of premium rates.

1835

April 15. Authorized purchase of lot and buildings west of Treat's (formerly Morgan's) Exchange Coffee House, for new offices for the Company.
August 3. Subscribed for three hundred shares of stock in proposed Hartford & New Haven Railroad.

APPENDIX II

December 16. Great fire in New York City. Ætna's loss only $10,000.
Company moved from its offices in Coffee House to new offices at No. 53 State Street.

1836
April 25. Voted to purchase Exchange Coffee House property.

1837
January 30. Voted $50,000 to settle losses at St. John, New Brunswick.
April 24. James M. Goodwin resigned as Secretary.
June 8. Simeon L. Loomis elected Secretary.
November 6. Director Joseph Morgan authorized to visit St. John, New Brunswick, and adjust losses.

1838
June 7. President Brace authorized to make inspection tour of agencies in New York, New England and Canada.

1839
April 8. Voted to ask Legislature for amendment to charter to permit writing of inland marine and transportation insurance.
May 8. Charter of Company amended as above requested.
December 23. Voted to join with other Hartford companies in agreeing upon new schedule of regulations and rates.
Principal fire losses of Company during this year were the following: Richmond, Virginia, $15,000; Stonington, Connecticut, $24,000; St. John, New Brunswick, $33,500; New York City (Oct.), $45,000, (Dec.), $12,000.

1840
Director Joseph Morgan made several trips for the Company as Special Agent.
Principal fire losses of company during the year were as follows: Wilmington, N. C., $28,000; New York City, $12,000; Ithaca, N. Y., $11,000; Paterson, N. J., $13,000.

1841
July 20. Voted to refuse risks on distilleries and theaters.
November 12. Subscribed to one hundred shares of stock in contemplated railroad between Hartford and New Haven.

1842
April 19. Director Joseph Morgan authorized to make extensive trip through south and west and appoint agents.
Gurdon S. Hubbard appointed as first agent at Chicago.

1843
September 5. Voted to begin writing of inland marine and transportation insurance.

1844
June 21. Director Joseph Morgan authorized to make tour of inspection of Western country and Canada, and appoint agents.
April 16. Subscribed to $2,000 of stock in contemplated railroad between Northampton and Springfield, Massachusetts.

1845
July 19. Big New York City fire which threatened life of the Company. Ætna's loss $120,000.
Thomas A. Alexander, later President of the Ætna, appointed New York City agent to succeed A. G. Hazard.

ONE HUNDRED YEARS OF FIRE INSURANCE

December 30. Voted to increase capital stock of Company from $200,000 to $250,000.

1846
February 25. Voted to reinsure risks of Memphis Insurance Company of Memphis, Tennessee.
Fire at St. Johns, Newfoundland. Ætna's loss, $77,000.

1847
July 23. Joseph Morgan, Director since 1819, died.

1849
June 7. Voted to increase capital stock of Company from $250,000 to $300,000.
St. Louis fire in this year cost Ætna $125,000.

1850
June 6. Legislature granted new amendment to charter to permit Company to engage in the business of life insurance.
June 25. New life insurance department organized, although no policies were written until the following year.

1851
Company began writing life insurance.
June 5. Eliphalet A. Bulkeley elected Vice-President, and also chairman of Managing Directors of Life Annuity Fund.
September 10. A. F. Willmarth elected first Assistant Secretary of the Ætna. He later became Vice-President of the Home Insurance Company. He retired as Assistant Secretary on June 13, 1853.

1852
June 3. Junius Spencer Morgan, son of Joseph Morgan, elected Director of the Ætna. He later went to England and became a partner in the great London banking firm of George S. Peabody & Company, which afterwards was changed to J. S. Morgan & Company.
Fire at Montreal, Canada. Ætna loss $105,000.
Fire at Chillicothe, Ohio. Ætna loss $114,000.

1853
May 28. Company's charter amended separating the Life and Fire Departments of the Ætna and incorporating the life department as a separate corporation under the name of The Ætna Life Insurance Company, with Eliphalet A. Bulkeley as President.
June 13. E. A. Bulkeley retired as Vice-President.
Edwin G. Ripley was elected Secretary to succeed Simeon L. Loomis.
A. F. Willmarth retired as Assistant Secretary.
September 2. Joseph B. Bennett appointed General Agent of the Ætna and head of new Western Branch of the Company with headquarters at Cincinnati, Ohio.

1854
June 8. Edwin G. Ripley promoted from Secretary to Vice-President.
Thomas A. Alexander, New York City agent, elected Secretary.
December 1. Voted to increase capital stock from $300,000 to $500,000.

1857
May 16. Charter amended authorizing increase of capital from $500,000 to $1,500,000, to be paid for out of surplus of Company.

APPENDIX II

June 23. Stock dividend of $500,000 declared, thus increasing capital from $500,000 to $1,000,000.
August 4. Thomas K. Brace resigned as President.
Edwin G. Ripley elected President.
Thomas A. Alexander elected Vice-President.
Thomas K. Brace, Jr., elected Secretary.

1858
Appointed Edward H. Parker of San Francisco as first Ætna agent on the Pacific Coast.
December 17. Henry L. Ellsworth, former President of Ætna, died at Fairhaven, Connecticut.

1859
December 27. Voted stock dividend of $500,000, thus increasing capital from $1,000,000 to $1,500,000.

1860
June 14. Thomas K. Brace, former President of the Ætna, died.

1861
Closed agencies in the South on account of the Civil War.
July 3. Thomas K. Brace, Jr., resigned as Secretary.
Lucius J. Hendee elected Secretary.

1862
August 26. President Edwin G. Ripley died.
Thomas A. Alexander elected President.
Henry Z. Pratt elected Vice-President.

1863
August 31. Vice-President Henry Z. Pratt died.
October 7. Jonathan Goodwin, Jr., elected Assistant Secretary.

1864
January 15. Charter of Company amended to permit increase of $500,000 in capital stock.
February 9. Stockholders voted to increase stock from $1,500,000 to $2,250,000 to be paid for out of surplus and distributed as a stock dividend.

1865
Close of Civil War and re-opening of agencies in the South.
October 12. President Thomas A. Alexander resigned on account of ill health, but no action was taken on his resignation.
December 15. Jonathan Goodwin, Jr., resigned as Assistant Secretary and later became local agent of the Company at Chicago.

1866
February 4. Voted stock dividend of $750,000, thus increasing capital of Company from $2,250,000 to $3,000,000.
March 29. President Thomas A. Alexander died.
Lucius J. Hendee elected President.
Jotham Goodnow of New Haven, elected Secretary.
June 7. Voted to ask Legislature to amend charter to permit increase in capital stock from $3,000,000 to $5,000,000 (no action taken by Legislature until 1877).
August 15. E. J. Bassett, special agent of Company, visited San Francisco and established Pacific branch of the Ætna.
Fire at Portland, Maine, cost Ætna $170,000.

ONE HUNDRED YEARS OF FIRE INSURANCE

1867
November 30. William B. Clark elected Assistant Secretary.
In this year the Ætna moved from its old offices at 53 State Street to new office building on Main Street.
Fire this year at Vicksburg, Mississippi, cost Ætna $110,000.

1871
October 8. Great Chicago fire. Ætna's loss $3,782,000.
November 9. To meet losses of Chicago fire the Ætna reduced its capital stock to $1,500,000 and then sold $1,500,000 new stock.

1872
November. Great Boston fire. Ætna's loss $1,604,000.
December 30. To meet losses at Boston the Company again reduced its capital — this time to the extent of $1,000,000 and issued new stock to that amount, thus again restoring the capital to $3,000,000.

1874
Fire at Chicago, Illinois. Ætna's loss $95,000.

1877
February 14. Charter amended authorizing increase of capital from $3,000,000 to $5,000,000 and repealing part of Section 6 of original charter limiting voting power of stockholders.

1878
Fire at St. John, New Brunswick. Ætna's loss $262,000.

1881
March 1. Charter amended authorizing Company to accept risks against loss or damage by fire caused by lightning and other elements of nature.
June 2. Voted to increase capital from $3,000,000 to $4,000,000.

1883
J. Pierpont Morgan, son of Junius Spencer Morgan and grandson of Joseph Morgan, elected Director. He continued to serve until his death in 1913.

1886
February 24. Amended charter to permit change in date of annual meeting from June to third Tuesday of January.

1888
September 4. President Lucius J. Hendee died.
September 26. Jotham Goodnow elected President.
William B. Clark elected Vice-President.
Andrew C. Bayne elected Secretary.
James F. Dudley and William H. King elected Assistant Secretaries.

1889
February 13. Rescinded resolution adopted in 1841 refusing risks on distilleries, theaters, etc.
Voted financial relief for Johnstown flood sufferers.
September 25. Voted to re-establish agencies in New Hampshire, from which state, the Company, with many others, had withdrawn four years before.

1890
Divided Western Branch of Company and opened Northwestern Branch with headquarters at Omaha, Nebraska.

APPENDIX II

1891
Closed Marine Branch at Buffalo and opened Marine Branch offices at Chicago and New York City.

1892
November 21. President Jotham Goodnow died.
November 30. William B. Clark elected President.
December 7. Andrew C. Bayne elected Vice-President.
James F. Dudley elected Secretary.
E. O. Weeks elected Assistant Secretary.
Voted to participate in insurance exhibition at World's Fair, Chicago.

1893
June 7. Voted to confine fire business of Company to America and Canada and British-American provinces.
September 6. Voted to enter into re-insurance treaty with Munich Re-insurance Company.
October 14. Vice-President Andrew C. Bayne died.
October 18. James F. Dudley elected Vice-President.
William H. King elected Secretary.
F. W. Jenness elected Assistant Secretary.

1896
February 19. Authorized purchase of Conklin property on Main Street to provide additional land for new office building.
July 1. Assistant Secretary F. W. Jenness resigned.

1897
March 19. Vice-President James F. Dudley died.
E. O. Weeks elected Vice-President.
April 7. Henry E. Rees and Alexander C. Adams elected Assistant Secretaries.

1898
April 25. Voted to guarantee salaries and positions of Ætna employees enlisting for service in the War with Spain.
Ottawa, Canada, fire. Ætna's loss $198,000.

1901
Fire at Jacksonville, Florida. Ætna's loss $168,000.

1902
June 18. Voted to erect new office building.
October 31. Vice-President E. O. Weeks died.
November 5. Voted to sell Ætna building at 413 Vine Street, Cincinnati.
December 3. Approved plans for new office building at Hartford.
Dr. C. J. Irvin and Almeron N. Williams elected Assistant Secretaries.

1903
April 24. Rented offices in Connecticut Mutual Life Insurance Building pending erection of new Ætna building.

1904
February 7. Great Baltimore fire. Ætna's loss $727,000.
Fire at Toronto, Canada. Ætna's loss $181,000.

1905
Moved into new office building on Main Street (still occupied).

[245]

1906
April 18. San Francisco earthquake and fire. Ætna's net loss $2,983,000.
September 10. Board of Directors adopted resolution commending President Clark for wise handling of affairs in connection with San Francisco disaster.

1907
March 26. Charter amended authorizing Company to enter the business of ocean marine insurance.
October 14. President Clark reported total losses of San Francisco fire and announced that all losses had been paid and all loans repaid.
May 6. William H. King elected Vice-President.
Henry E. Rees elected Secretary.
Edgar J. Sloan, Guy E. Beardsley and E. S. Allen elected Assistant Secretaries.

1908
April 12. Fire at Chelsea, Massachusetts. Ætna loss $165,640.

1909
January 13. William F. Whittelsey elected Marine Assistant Secretary.
January 14. Voted to embark in business of ocean marine insurance.
March 30. Charter amended to permit Company to write automobile insurance.
November 22. Voted to increase capital from $4,000,000 to $5,000,000.

1911
March 11. Charter amended to permit increase in capital from $5,000,000 to $10,000,000.

1912
January 25. William F. Whittelsey elected Marine Secretary.
February 16. Vice-President William H. King died.
April 24. Henry E. Rees and Almeron N. Williams elected Vice-Presidents.
Edgar J. Sloan elected Secretary.
Ralph B. Ives elected Assistant Secretary.

1913
March 31. Death of J. Pierpont Morgan, Director, at Rome.

1914
January 28. Election of J. P. Morgan, Jr., as Director, he being the fourth generation of Morgans to serve on the Ætna directorate.

1915
June 14. Rearranged treaty with Munich Reinsurance Company because of the Great War.

1916
January 1. President Clark announced beginning of the Ætna Fire Underwriters' Agency.
July 10. Voted to continue salaries and hold positions for Ætna employees who enlisted (account of threatened war with Mexico).

1917
January 31. William F. Whittelsey elected Marine Vice-President.
Raymond E. Stronach elected Marine Secretary.
April 16. Voted authority to officers to issue policies against hazards of war, such as explosions, etc.
June 20. Voted contribution to Red Cross.
December 1. Officers and Directors gave dinner in celebration of President Clark's fiftieth anniversary as an officer of the Ætna.

APPENDIX II

December 10. Adopted resolution notifying Ætna employees called to military or naval service of the United States that their salaries would be continued and places held for them.

1918

January 26. Voted to change Directors' meetings from Monday to Saturday on account of national "Coalless Mondays."

May 2. Voted contribution to Red Cross.

November 11. Voted contribution for United War Work campaign.

Vote of gratitude to Ætna employees who served in the military or naval forces of the United States or Canada during the Great War.

1919

June 5. One Hundredth Anniversary of signing of the Ætna Insurance Company's Charter.

June 15. One Hundredth Anniversary of the organization of the Ætna Insurance Company.

APPENDIX III

ORIGINAL STOCKHOLDERS OF THE ÆTNA INSURANCE COMPANY, 1819

Name	Number Shares	Name	Number Shares
Eliphalet Averill,	50	Heman Laflin,	10
Chester and W. Andross,	8	John Mather,	10
Thomas K. Brace,	69	Return S. Mather,	10
Judah Bliss,	50	Denison Morgan,	10
Horace Barber,	20	Joseph Morgan,	12
Horace Belden,	10	Nathan Morgan,	12
Frederick Bange,	43	Dwell Morgan,	20
Olmsted Bulkley,	7	Ralph R. Phelps,	5
Charles Babcock,	12	Caleb Pond,	56
Nathaniel Bunce,	12	Theodore Pease & Co.,	10
Thomas Belden,	50	Daniel Pitkin,	10
Elisha B. Cook,	5	Joseph Pratt,	50
Elisha Colt,	10	Isaac Perkins,	10
Merrit W. Chapin,	10	Wanton Ransom,	12
Jesse Charlton,	5	Riley and Brown,	50
H. and S. Chaffee,	12	Benjamin and M. Stebbins,	20
Elisha and William Dodd,	13	Jesse Savage,	20
David Deming,	5	Luther Savage,	12
Henry L. Ellsworth,	40	Asahel Saunders,	12
Timothy Ellsworth,	12	Henry Seymour,	10
Eli Ely,	12	Spencer and Gilman,	10
Asa Farwell,	8	Levi Stewart,	8
Edmund Fowler,	10	Griffin Stedman,	19
Edmund Freeman,	5	Henry Shepard,	12
James M. Goodwin,	20	Israel Shepard,	12
Alva Gilman,	12	Charles Sheldon,	10
Thomas D. Gordon,	12	Elisha Shepard,	12
Joseph B. Gilbert,	12	Christopher Saunders & Co.,	39
Daniel Gillett, Jr.,	10	George Smith,	12
Erastus Graves,	30	Normand Smith,	12
Hall and Green,	30	Samuel Tudor, Jr.,	50
Joel Holkins,	30	Deodat Woodbridge,	10
John Hall,	30	Lemuel White,	12
John Hempsted,	5	Thomas Williams,	10
Joseph Harris,	5	Ward Woodbridge,	50
Henry Kilbourn,	62	Elijah White,	20
John Kelsey,	10	Thomas S. Williams,	20
Sam and William Kellogg,	10	John Waburton,	6
Gaius Lyman,	50	Eunice White, Jr.,	9

APPENDIX IV

DIRECTORS OF THE ÆTNA INSURANCE COMPANY FROM 1819 TO 1919

It is a curious coincidence that the Ætna Insurance Company had had exactly one hundred Directors in the one hundred years of its life when it celebrated its Centennial Anniversary in June, 1919. Of these, twenty-five had served for twenty-five years or longer.

The following list contains the names and terms of service of all Directors of the Company from 1819 to 1919. The dates opposite their names indicate the years in which they were *first* and *last* elected, except in the case of those now serving.

Thomas K. Brace,	1819–1860
Thomas Belden,	1819–1841
Samuel Tudor, Jr.,	1819–1861
Henry Kilbourne,	1819–1841
Eliphalet Averill,	1819–1820
Henry Seymour,	1819–1821
Griffin Stedman,	1819–1846
Gaius Lyman,	1819–1821
Judah Bliss,	1819–1821
Caleb Pond	1819–1820
Nathaniel Bunce,	1819–1820
Joseph Morgan,	1819–1847
Jeremiah Brown,	1819–1820
Elisha Dodd,	1819–1840
Theodore Pease,	1819–
Charles Babcock,	1819–1828
Henry L. Ellsworth,	1819–1836
James M. Goodwin,	1819–1836
Christopher Saunders,	1820–1829
Isaac Perkins,	1820–1827
Jesse Savage,	1821–1843
Joseph B. Gilbert,	1821, 1827–1829
Joseph L. Pratt,	1821–1851
George Beach,	1821–1837
Nathan Morgan,	1821–1824
Thomas S. Williams,	1822–1825
Oliver D. Cook,	1825, 1828–1832
Stephen Spencer,	1826–1840
D. F. Mercer,	1826–1827
James Thomas,	1828–1849
Dennison Morgan,	1828–1835
Dudley Buck,	1830–
Haynes L. Porter,	1830–
Elisha Peck,	1831–1842
Daniel Burgess,	1831–1840

ONE HUNDRED YEARS OF FIRE INSURANCE

Ward Woodbridge,	1833–1856
Joseph Church,	1834–1875
Horatio Alden,	1837–1838
Ebenezer Seeley,	1838–1845
Silas B. Hamilton,	1839–1850
Frederick Tyler,	1841–1854
Robert Buell,	1841–1882
Samuel Boughton,	1841–1846
Whitehead I. Cornell,	1842–1844
Miles A. Tuttle,	1842–1858
Ezra White, Jr.,	1843–1847
John L. Boswell,	1844–1854
Ebenezer Flower,	1845–1866
Eliphalet A. Bulkeley,	1846–1871
Roland Mather,	1847–1896
Edwin G. Ripley,	1847–1862
Samuel S. Ward,	1847–1879
Henry Z. Pratt,	1848–1863
Austin Dunham,	1850–1876
John W. Seymour,	1851–1852
Junius S. Morgan,	1852–1853
Gustavus F. Davis,	1853–1896
Drayton Hillyer,	1854–1908
Thomas A. Alexander,	1854–1865
Walter Keney,	1855–1889
Charles H. Brainard,	1857–1888
William F. Tuttle,	1859–1895
George Roberts,	1861–1877
Thomas K. Brace, Jr.,	1861–1869
Erastus Collins,	1863–1879
Edwin G. Morgan,	1864–1882
Lucius J. Hendee,	1866–1888
Francis B Cooley	1867–1904
William R. Cone,	1870–1889
Henry E. Russell,	1872–1893
Nathaniel Shipman,	1876–1906
Asa S. Porter,	1877–1883
A. C. Dunham,	1878–1917
James A. Smith, Jr.,	1880–1896
Morgan G. Bulkeley,	1880–
Alva Oatman,	1883–1883
J. Pierpont Morgan,	1883–1913
Thomas O. Enders,	1884–1894
Atwood Collins,	1884–
Jotham Goodnow,	1889–1892
William B. Clark,	1889–
Francis Goodwin,	1890–
Nelson Hollister	1890–1897
Andrew C. Bayne,	1892–1893
Charles E. Gross,	1893–
James F. Dudley,	1894–1897
James H. Knight,	1895–
George H. Day,	1896–1907
E. O. Weeks,	1898–1902

APPENDIX IV

Charles P. Cooley,	1905-
Arthur L. Shipman,	1907-
William H. King,	1908-1912
Charles L. Spencer,	1909-
Lyman B. Brainerd,	1909-1916
Charles A. Goodwin,	1909-
Henry E. Rees,	1913-
A. N. Williams,	1913-
J. P. Morgan, Jr.,	1914-
Horace B. Cheney,	1917-
John L. Way,	1918-

APPENDIX V

OFFICERS OF THE ÆTNA INSURANCE COMPANY FROM 1819 TO 1919 AND THEIR TERMS OF SERVICE

PRESIDENTS

Thomas K. Brace, June 15, 1819, to September 27, 1819.
Henry L. Ellsworth, September 27, 1819, to March 6, 1821.
Thomas K. Brace, March 6, 1821, to August 4, 1857.
E. G. Ripley, August 4, 1857, to August 26, 1862.
Thomas A. Alexander, September 10, 1862, to April 29, 1866.
Lucius J. Hendee, March 4, 1866, to September 4, 1888.
Jotham Goodnow, September 26, 1888, to November 21, 1892.
William B. Clark, November 30, 1892, to date.

VICE-PRESIDENTS

E. A. Bulkeley, June 5, 1851, to June 13, 1853.
Edwin G. Ripley, June 8, 1854, to August 4, 1857.
Thomas A. Alexander, August 4, 1857, to September 10, 1862.
Henry Z. Pratt, September 10, 1862, to August 31, 1863.
William B. Clark, September 26, 1888, to November 30, 1892.
Andrew C. Bayne, December 7, 1892, to October 14, 1893.
James F. Dudley, October 18, 1893, to March 19, 1897.
E. O. Weeks, April 7, 1897, to October 31, 1902.
W. H. King, May 6, 1907, to February 16, 1912.
Henry E. Rees, April 24, 1912, to date.
A. N. Williams, April 24, 1912, to date.

MARINE VICE-PRESIDENT

William F. Whittelsey, January 31, 1917, to date.

SECRETARIES

Isaac Perkins, June 15, 1819, to June 9, 1828.
James M. Goodwin, June 9, 1828, to May 1, 1837.
Simeon L. Loomis, May 1, 1837, to June 13, 1853.
Edwin G. Ripley, June 13, 1853, to June 8, 1854.
Thomas A. Alexander, June 8, 1854, to August 4, 1857.
Thomas K. Brace, Jr., August 4, 1857, to July 3, 1861.
Lucius J. Hendee, July 3, 1861, to March 4, 1866.
Jotham Goodnow, April 18, 1866, to September 26, 1888.
Andrew C. Bayne, September 26, 1888, to December 7, 1892.
James F. Dudley, December 7, 1892, to October 18, 1893.
William H. King, October 18, 1893, to May 6, 1907.
Henry E. Rees, May 6, 1907, to April 24, 1912.
Edgar J. Sloan, April 24, 1912, to date.

APPENDIX V

MARINE SECRETARIES
William F. Whittelsey, January 25, 1912, to January 31, 1917.
R. E. Stronach, January 31, 1917, to date.

ASSISTANT SECRETARIES
A. F. Willmarth, June 5, 1851, to June 13, 1853.
Jonathan Goodwin, Jr., October 7, 1863, to December 15, 1865.
William B. Clark, November 30, 1867, to September 26, 1888.
James F. Dudley, September 26, 1888, to December 7, 1892.
William H. King, September 26, 1888, to October 18, 1893.
E. O. Weeks, December 7, 1892, to April 7, 1897.
F. W. Jenness, October 18, 1893, to July 1, 1896.
A. C. Adams, April 7, 1897, to April 7, 1907.
Henry E. Rees, April 17, 1897, to May 6, 1907.
C. J. Irvin, December 3, 1902, to June 12, 1905.
A. N. Williams, December 3, 1902, to April 24, 1912.
Edgar J. Sloan, May 6, 1907, to April 24, 1912.
E. S. Allen, May 6, 1907, to date.
Guy E. Beardsley, May 6, 1907, to date.
Ralph B. Ives, April 24, 1912, to date.

MARINE ASSISTANT SECRETARIES
William F. Whittelsey, January 13, 1908, to January 25, 1912.

APPENDIX VI

LOSSES PAID BY THE ÆTNA INSURANCE COMPANY IN ONE HUNDRED YEARS

During its first century of existence the Ætna Insurance Company has paid out over $178,000,000 in losses. Of this amount more than $156,000,000 represents payments for fire losses, the difference being for marine, automobile and other risks. There were no losses until 1821, two years after the Company was organized.

The following table shows the losses of the Ætna by years for the first ten years and for each decade thereafter:

LOSSES

Years	Fire	Marine, etc.
1819	0	0
1820	0	0
1821	$ 4,032	0
1822	5,333	0
1823	4,071	0
1824	21,843	0
1825	22,695	0
1826	41,639	0
1827	59,622	0
1828	104,349	0
1829–38	986,207	0
1839–48	2,608,598	$ 95,154
1849–58	7,196,408	745,096
1859–68	11,064,996	1,429,410
1869–78	23,817,791	1,598,718
1879–88	12,524,289	716,232
1889–98	19,046,981	1,104,285
1899–08	30,526,204	2,074,217
*1909–18	48,166,027	10,739,617
Totals	$156,201,085	$18,502,729

Grand Total, $174,703,814.

* To December 31, 1918. The total losses paid from December 31, 1918, to June 15, 1919, are in excess of $3,000,000, bringing the grand total of loss payments for the century to more than $178,000,000.

INDEX

Adams, Alexander C., assistant secretary, 131
Ætna Insurance Company, act to incorporate, 31, 32
  adds a Life Insurance department, 93
  applies for permission to do inland marine and navigation business, 63, 81
  at outbreak of the Rebellion, 101
  capital stock, how secured, 53
  capital stock, increased, 61, 89, 99, 105, 108, 121, 143
  capital stock, reduced, 117, 120
  Charter, with amendments, Appendix I, 231-238
  Directors of, 1819 to 1919, Appendix IV, 249
  first advertisement of, 34
  first agents, 46, 155, 166, 167
  first Canadian agent, 160
  first crisis in affairs, 65
  first Directors, 35, 36, 37, 38
  first disputed claim, 59, 60
  first insurance watch, 47
  first investment of capital, 41
  first loss, 55
  first manual for agents, 45
  first office of, 40
  first policy, 42
  first quarter-century, 83
  first reinsurance, 46
  first seal, 38
  first six months' business, 48
  first special agent, 158
  first stockholders, Appendix III, 248
  first subscriptions to its capital, 34
  in the Great War, 220-223
  limit of risk $10,000, 51
  losses paid, 1819 to 1919, Appendix VI, 254
  Marine Department, 210-217
  moves to 53 State Street, 76
    to 670 Main Street, 108
    to new building, 136
  Northwestern Branch, 183, 184, 187
  officials of, 1819 to 1919, Appendix V, 252
  Pacific Branch, 188-197
  past and present of the Company, 224-230
  policy on Yale College, 63
  reinsures Middletown Insurance Company, 46
  terms of subscription to the stock of, 33
  Western Branch, 176-187
Ætna Life Insurance Company, 93
African Colonization Society, 20
Agents established over wide territory, 58, 59
Agents, the Company's, 149-175
Alabama, first Ætna agent in, 166
Albany, New York, first Ætna agent, 156, 157, 166
Alden, Horatio, agent Augusta, Georgia, 166

Algiers, war with, 19
Alexander, James A., New York City Agent, 120
  Manager (1872), 173
Alexander, Thomas A., 107, 120, 171, 173, 202
  New York City Agent (1845), 87, 172
  Secretary (1854), 97
  Vice-President (1857), 100, 104
  President (1862), 104
  death (1866), 106
Allen, Edwin S., assistant secretary, 141, 142
America, first Savings Bank in, 19
American Agency System, 175
"Amicable Contributionship," London (1696), 8
Anthracite coal, first used, 22
Anti-compact laws, 203-205
Arabic, loss of the (1915), 221
Ashford, Connecticut, first Ætna agent, 156
Augusta, Georgia, first Ætna agent, 166
Averill, Augustin, agent Cheraw, S. C. (1821), 167, 172
Averill, Eliphalet, Director, 36, 37, 69

Babcock, Charles, Director, 36, 38
  on Lafayette Committee, 63
Baldwin, Herman, agent, Richmond, Va., 164
Baltimore, first Ætna agent, 166
  great fire of 1904, 137
Bang, Frederick, second policy-holder, 42
Bank, first savings bank in America, 19
Bank of the United States, 19, 21, 41, 65
Barbon, Nicholas, first insurer in England, 6
Bassett, E. J., 113, 114, 115, 116, 127, 189
  General Agent, 165, 188
Bates, Isaac C., Agent, Northampton, Mass., 156
Battle of Lake Erie, 21
Bayne, A. C., Secretary (1888), 125
  Vice-President (1892), 128
  death (1893), 130
Beals, Thomas, Agent, 156
Beardsley, Guy E., Assistant Secretary (1907), 141-143
Beardsley & Beardsley, agents, Hartford, 167
Beckley, Orin, Agent, 156
Belden, Thomas, Director, 37
Bennett, F. C., General Agent Western Branch, 178, 182, 185
Bennett, Joseph B., General Agent Western Branch, 154, 167, 168, 175, 176, 178, 179, 180, 181, 182, 202
Bigelow, Abijah, first Canadian Agent, 160
Bliss, Judah, Director, 37
Blount, Sir John, 11
Boardman, George C., General Agent Pacific Branch, 190, 191, 193, 194

[255]

INDEX

Boat building, 24
Boston, Massachusetts, first Ætna agent, 166
Boston fire (1872), 119
Boswell, John L., Director, 93
Botsford & Bairs, 169
Bowers, Osborne & Co., agents New Orleans (1823), 166
Brace, Jonathan, 29
Brace, Thomas K., 29, 30, 34, 35, 36, 43, 49, 54, 57, 59, 66, 67, 78, 79, 80, 81, 86, 87, 96, 99, 100, 104, 224, 226, 228, 229
  first President, 36
  resigns, 36
  signature, 50
  second President, 54, 66, 78
  death (1860), 99
Brace, Thomas K., Jr., Secretary (1857), 100, 103, 107
  death (1870), 100
Brainard, Charles H., Director, 226
Breeding, William H., General Agent Pacific Branch, 195, 196
Brown, Jeremiah, Director, 38
Buell, Robert, Director, 93, 226
Bulkeley, Eliphalet A., 92, 93, 94, 226
  Vice-President (1850), 93
  President Ætna Life Insurance Co., 94
Bulkeley, Hon. Morgan G., President Ætna Life Insurance Company, 94, 226
Bunce, Nathaniel, Director, 38

California, first Ætna agent in, 166
Canada, 159-162
  first Ætna agent in, 59, 160
  first American Company in, 160
Canandaigua, New York, first Ætna agent, 156, 163
Canned goods, first, 22
Capital stock,
  increased, 61, 89, 99, 105, 108, 121, 143
  reduced, 117, 120
  authorized, 143
Carter, James H., agent at Cincinnati, 168
Caution in proceeding, 57
Charter, the original with amendments, Appendix I, 231-238
  petition for, 31, 32
Cheney, H. B., Director, 227
Cheraw, South Carolina, first Ætna agent, 167
Chicago, Illinois, first Ætna agent, 166, 169
Chicago a "Wooden City" (1842), 168-169
Chicago Fire (1871), 112
  first claim paid, 115
  losses promptly paid, 194
Chillicothe fire (1852), 95
Chronological history of the Ætna, Appendix II, 239-248
Church, Joseph, Director, 226
Cincinnati, Ohio, first Ætna agent, 163
Clark, William B., 109, 126, 127, 130, 133, 134, 135, 136, 137, 140, 141, 144, 145, 146, 147, 148, 174, 184, 185, 186, 192, 193, 194, 195, 213, 220, 226, 229, 230
  Assistant Secretary (1867), 108, 113
  Secretary of Phœnix, 110
  Vice-President (1888), 125, 128
  President (1892), 128-148, 192-197
Clay, Henry, 18, 20

Cleveland, Ohio, first Ætna agent, 163, 166
Coast Survey begun, 22
Coffee House an institution, 26
Cohen, Isaac, agent Savannah, Georgia, 172
Cole, Henry S., agent Detroit, 163, 166
Collins, Atwood, Director, 226
Colt, Ezekiel R., agent, 156
Colt, Ezra, town clerk, 49
Columbian Insurance Co. of New York, 13
Company lived through many conflagrations, 137
Company's records, 57
Connecticut, early underwriting in, 14
  first Ætna agent, 156, 158, 166
  oldest insurance company in, 15
Connecticut legislation, first, 206
Converse, Alexander B., agent, 156
Cooley, Charles P., Director, 227
Cooley, Francis B., Director, 226
Coolidge, Charles D., agent Boston, 166
Cotton mill, erection of first, 22
Country produce marketed, 22
Courant, Hartford, 32
Cowles, Samuel, agent Cleveland, 163, 166
Crittenden, John J., 21
Crosby, James, agent Zanesville, Ohio, 163
Curd, Richard, agent Macon, Georgia, 102

Daingerfield, H. A., agent Natchez, Mississippi, 166
Davis, Gustavus F., Director, 226
Day, Isaac F., 116
Deaf and Dumb Asylum, Hartford, 30
Deaf mutes, first school for in U. S., 22
Detroit, Michigan, first Ætna agent, 163, 166
Development of the U. S., 22
Dickenson, Edward, agent New York City (1826), 166
Dickinson, Leonard A., agent Hartford, 166, 167
Dickerson, Philemon, agent Paterson, N. J., (1821) 166
Directors, 1819 to 1919, Appendix IV, 249
Directors' banquet, 73
Distilleries, prohibited risks in 1841, 82
District of Columbia, first Ætna agent, 166
Dividends, first, 49
  second and third, 52
  special, 77, 91
Dodd, Elisha, Director, 31
Dorr, Captain E. P., marine agent, Buffalo, 212
Drake, John B., first claim paid in Chicago fire, 115
Dudley, James F., Assistant Secretary (1888), 125
  Secretary (1892), 129
  Vice-President (1893), 130, 213
  death (1897), 130
Dunham, Austin, Director, 226
Dunham, A. C., Director, 226
Durbrow, Harry, Marine Assistant General Agent, Pacific Branch, 196

Eagle Bank of Providence, stock sold, 66
Eagle Fire Insurance Co. of New York, 13
Ellsworth, Henry L., 42, 44, 54, 63, 66
  second President, 44
  death, 45
  director, 66

[256]

INDEX

Ellsworth, Oliver, 44
Ellsworth, William W., 44, 45
Ely, John, Jr., agent Albany, 156, 166
Empress of Ireland, wreck of the (1914), 215
"Era of Good Feeling," 20

Fayetteville, N. C., first Ætna agent, 166
Firebricks first made, 56
Fire department equipments, 48
Fire Insurance, ancient, 3, 4
"Fire Office," London (1680), 6
Fireplaces and stoves, 57
Fitzhugh, Samuel H., agent Wheeling, W. Va., 167
Flint, O. T., Marine Agent, Buffalo, 212
"Foreign" Companies, taxed, 75
Franklin, Benjamin, 13
"Friendly Society," London, 7

Gadsden, James S., Chicago agent, 113, 170, 186, 212
Gale, Stephen F., 169
Gallagher, Thomas E., General Agent Western Branch, Chicago, 144, 184, 185, 186, 187, 212
Gas-lighting, first, 22
General Agents, first, 163, 175
Georgia, first Ætna agent, 166
Goodenough, Asa, 27
Goodman, Timothy S., agent Cincinnati, Ohio, 163, 167
Goodman, William, Cincinnati, Ohio, 163, 168
Goodnow, Jotham, Secretary (1866), 107, 111
   President (1888), 124, 125
   death (1892), 127
Goodwin, Charles A., Director, 71, 227
Goodwin, Rev. Dr. Francis, Director, 71, 135, 136, 146, 226, 227
Goodwin, James, 71, 90
Goodwin, James M., 38, 52, 63, 68, 71, 74, 76, 78, 103, 164, 200
   on Lafayette Committee, 63
   Secretary, 71
   resigns (1837), 78
Goodwin, Jonathan, Jr., Chicago agent (1871), 98, 113, 120, 165, 170
Great fires at
   Baltimore, 137
   Boston, 119
   Chillicothe, 95
   Chicago, 112
   Jacksonville, 133
   London, 5
   Montreal, 95
   Ottawa, 133
   Portland, 123
   Rochester, 137
   St. John, N. B., 123
   St. Johns, N. F., 89
   St. Louis, 91
   San Francisco, 138
   Toronto, 137
   Vicksburg, 123
Great Lakes, marine risks on, 212
Great War, during the, 220–223
Greenfield, Mass., first Ætna agent, 155, 166
Gregory, Attorney General, 21
Griswold & Follett, agents Burlington, Vermont, 156

Gross, Charles E., Director and General Counsel, 135, 136, 226, 227
Guide to Fire Insurance (Bennett), 154
Gulflight, loss of the (1915), 222
Günther, Count Anton, 5

Halifax, N. S., first Ætna agent, 161
Hall, George W., agent Brattleboro, Vermont, 156
Hall & Green, agents Rockingham, Vt., 156, 167
Hamilton, S. B., special agent, 165
"Hand-in-Hand Company," London, 8
Philadelphia, 13
Harford, W. B., Assistant General Agent, 184, 187
Hartford Convention of 1814, 18
Hartford Fire Insurance Company, 15, 47
Hartford newspapers, 25
Hartford population, 25
Hartford trade, 23–25
Hartford and New Haven Insurance Company, 15
Hayes, Henry, agent Cincinnati, Ohio, 168
Hazard, Augustus G., agent New York City, 87, 172
Hendee, Lucius J., 103, 107, 114, 117, 121, 123, 124, 171, 181
   Secretary (1861), 103
   President (1866), 107
   death (1888), 123
Hilliard, J. C., Special Agent, 113, 127, 165
Hillyer, Drayton, Director, 226
Hine, C. C., Special Agent, 165
Hubbard, Gurdon S., agent Chicago, Illinois, 166, 169
Hubbard & Hunt, agents Chicago, Illinois, 170

Illinois, first Ætna agent, 166
Imlay, William H., 76
Indiana, first Ætna agent, 166
Inland Marine, 211–213
Insane, Retreat for the, Hartford, 30
Insurance agent, his field, etc., 150–155
Insurance displaces pension system, 20
Insurance Magazine, 74
Insurance, primitive, 3
Irvin, Dr. C. J., Assistant Secretary, 133–135
Ives, Ralph B., Assistant Secretary, 144, 187

Jacksonville, great fire of 1900, 133
Jenness, F. W., Assistant Secretary, 130
Jewell, Marshall, 114

Keeler, N. E., General Agent Western Branch, 184–186
Kellogg, Samuel, Jr., third policy-holder, 42
Kellogg, Secretary, 110
Keney, Walter, Director, 226
Kentucky, first Ætna agent, 166
Kerosene oil, first used, 56
Key, Francis S., 18
Kilbourne, Henry, Director, 37
   on Lafayette Committee, 63
Kimball, Leonard, agent Baltimore, Maryland, 166

17   [257]

INDEX

Kimberley, Anson, agent Darien, Georgia, 172
King, Seth, 126
King, William H., Assistant Secretary, 126
  Secretary, 130, 136
Kirkpatrick, A. M. M., Chief Agent Canada, 162
Knickerbocker Fire Insurance Co., of New York, 13
Knight, James H., Director, 135, 136, 227
Kohtz, Louis O., Assistant General Agent, Western Branch, 144, 170, 186, 212

Lafayette's visit to Hartford in 1824, 62
Lake Erie, Battle of, 21
Law Makers and Insurance, 198-206
Letters of Secretary Perkins to agents, 51
Letter books, old, 49
Life insurance department, 92, 93, 94
Lightning Insurance, 123
Livingston, E. L., Marine Assistant General Agent, Pacific Branch, 196
"Lloyds," 209
"Lombard House," London, 9
London, great fire of, 5
Loomis, Simeon L., Secretary, 78, 80, 82, 84, 86, 96, 103, 109, 110, 154, 169, 199, 200, 210, 211
  letters, 79, 83, 88
Lord, Samuel, agent, Portsmouth, New Hampshire, 166
Losses, only two cents up to May 1821, 55
Losses, heavy in early years, 81
Losses paid, Appendix VI, 254
Louisiana, first Ætna agent, 166
Lusitania, loss of the (1915), 221
Lyman, Gaius, Director, 37
  on Lafayette Committee, 63

McAdoo, Secretary of the Treasury, 21
Magill, Robert H., General Agent Pacific Branch, 189
Maine, first Ætna agent, 166
Manton, Salma, agent Savannah, Georgia, 172
Maps, Sanborn System of, 98
Marine risks, great variety in, 219
Marine Underwriting, 207-219
  ancient instances of, 207, 209
Maryland, first Ætna agent, 166
Massachusetts, first Ætna agent, 166
  legislation, 199
Matches, first used, 56
Mather, Roland, Director, 226
May, Thomas, agent Richmond, Virginia, 167
Merchants Bank of New York, 65
Michigan, first Ætna agent, 166
Middletown Fire Insurance Company, 15
  reinsures in the Ætna, 46
Miscellaneous forms of Insurance, 218
Mississippi, first Ætna agent, 166
Missouri, first Ætna agent, 166
Mitchell, Donald G., 28
Mitchell, Walter, Secretary Hartford Fire Insurance Company, 28
Mobile, great fire at, 65
  losses at, 67
Monroe Doctrine, origin of, 19
Monroe, James, President, 19

Montreal fire, 95
Morgan, David, 27
Morgan, Isaac, 27
Morgan, John, 27
Morgan, Jonathan, 27
Morgan, Joseph, Director, 26, 27, 42, 64, 67, 70, 72, 73, 74, 77, 90, 95, 121, 146, 165, 226
  trips, 64, 70-72
  death, 90
Morgan, Junius S., Director, 26, 90, 95, 121
  J. Pierpont, 27, 121, 144, 145, 226
  J. P., Jr., 122, 145, 227
Morgan, Lucy, 71, 90
Morgan, Miles, 27
Morgan, Nathaniel, 27
Morgan's Exchange Coffee House, 26, 27
Morris, Benjamin W., architect, 136
Morrison, Edwin C., General Agent Pacific Branch, 191, 192, 195
Muldon, Thomas, agent Mobile, Alabama, 171
Mutual Assurance, Philadelphia, 13
  New Haven, 15
Mutual Insurance Company of New York, 13
Mutual Insurance Company of Norwich, Connecticut, 15

National Board of Fire Underwriters, 68, 118, 119
New building of the Ætna, 136
New England democracy, 24
New England in 1819, 22-25
New Hampshire, first Ætna agent, 166
New Haven, 22
New Haven Fire Insurance Company, 16
New Jersey, first Ætna agent, 166
New London, 22
New York, first Ætna agent, 166
New York City, first Ætna agent, 166, 172
  great fire of 1835, 75
  of 1839, 81
  of 1845, 85
  payment of losses, 87
New York Insurance Company, 13
New York, New Haven & Hartford R. R. Co., stock subscribed for, 77
Niles' Weekly Register, 43
North, John G., agent at New Haven, Connecticut, 63
North Carolina, first Ætna agent, 46, 136, 166
Northwestern Branch, 175, 183, 184, 187
Norwich Fire Insurance Company, 15

Ocean steamship, first, 22
O'Brien, E. G., agent Toronto, Canada, 162
Officers of the Ætna 1819 to 1919, Appendix V, 252
Ohio, first Ætna agent, 166
  legislation, 200
Ottawa, great fire of 1900, 133
Overall's Insurance Company, London, 12

Pacific Branch, 188-197
Pardee, W. I., special agent, 165
Parker, E. H., agent San Francisco, California, 166, 189

[258]

INDEX

Parmalee, H. J., superintendent marine insurance, N. Y., 212
Pasco, Henry L., agent Chicago, Illinois, 113
special agent, 165, 170
Past and Present, 224-230
Patent leather, first made, 22
Peace Society, the first, 22
Pease, Theodore, Director, 38, 42
Peasley, J. C., agent Burlington, Iowa, 83
Peck, Everard, agent at Rochester, New York, 156
Pennsylvania, first Ætna agent, 167
Pension system, 20
Perkins, Frederick, 59
Perkins, Isaac, 30, 34, 36, 40, 41, 43, 45, 48, 49, 50, 51, 52, 53, 56, 57, 58, 59, 62, 65, 66, 69, 70, 79, 103, 154
first secretary, 36
instructions to agents, 160
resigns, 69
visits agencies, 58, 59
death, 69
Perkins, Simon, agent at Warren, Ohio, 163
Perkins, Thomas C., 69
Perkins, William L., first special agent, 156, 158, 166
Perry, Commodore Oliver Hazard, 21
Pewabic, wreck of the, 216
Phelps, Humphrey, agent New York City, 172
"Philadelphia Contributionship," 12, 13
Phœnix Bank, Hartford, investment in stock, 41, 65
Phœnix Fire of London, 7, 162
Phœnix Insurance Company of Hartford, 96, 109
"Phœnix Office," London, 7
Pioneer of Underwriting, 154
Policy, first issued by Ætna, 42
Policy, origin of term, 4
Pond, Caleb, Director, 37
Poor, Moses, agent Washington, D. C., 166
Porcelain manufacture, first, 22
Portland, great fire of 1866, 123
Postage, early, 50
Potter, Charles W., Assistant General Agent, 184
Povey, Charles, insurance pioneer, 9
Pratt, Henry Z., 93, 125
Vice-President, 104
Pratt, Joseph L., Director, 226
Prohibited risks, 82
Prohibition, 21, 25
Proof of Loss, first blank introduced, 98
Protection Insurance Company of Hartford, 68, 177
Providence-Washington Fire Insurance Company, 13
Puritan customs, 25

Quebec Fire Assurance Company, 162

Rand, Daniel, agent at Middletown, Connecticut, 156
Ratchford, E. D. W., agent, 161
Rate-cutting in New York, 74
Rate-fixing, 204
Rates, increased, 70
Rees, Ebenezer S., agent Darien, Georgia, 172

Rees, Henry E., 131, 172, 193, 205, 227
Assistant Secretary (1897), 131
Secretary (1907), 131
Vice-President (1912), 131
Rhode Island, first Ætna agent, 167
Richards, Mark, agent Philadelphia, Pennsylvania, 167
Richmond, Virginia, great fire at (1839), 81
Ripley, Edwin G., 93, 96, 97, 100, 101, 104, 176, 188
Secretary (1853), 96
Vice-President (1854), 96
President (1857), 100, 101
death (1862), 103
Ripley, Franklin, agent Greenfield, Massachusetts, 155, 166
Ripley, Philip, 96
Risk of $17,000, largest to 1821, 54
Risks, classified, 101
Risks, limit of, 51
good and bad, 83
River craft non-insurable, 211
Robins, Ephraim, General Agent Protection Insurance Company, Cincinnati, 177
Robins, Gurdon, agent Fayetteville, North Carolina, 46, 156, 166
Robins, W. B., agent Cincinnati, 168
Rochester, great fire of 1904, 137
Rolling mill, erection of first, 22
Russell & Ziegler, agents New York City, 173

St. John, New Brunswick, great fire, 81, 123
St. Johns, New Foundland, great fire of 1846, 89
St. Louis fire of 1849, 91
"Safe" of the Company, 28, 51
Salamander Society of New York, 74
Salary of President for first six months, 57
Sanborn System of maps, 98
Sanderson, Arthur G., Assistant General Agent Pacific Branch, 192, 195
Sanford, Peleg, early insurer in Hartford, 14
Sanford, Thaddeus, agent at Mobile, Alabama, 65, 159, 166
San Francisco, earthquake and fire of 1906, 138
first Ætna agent, 166, 189
prompt settlement of losses by Ætna, 194
Saunders, Christian, agent at St. Louis, Missouri, 166
Sawyer, Nathaniel, agent Chillicothe, Ohio, 163, 168
School for deaf-mutes, first in U. S., 22
Schools, district, 24
Seldon, Edward, agent Pittsburgh, Pennsylvania, 167
"Selling Letters" by Secretary Perkins, 51, 62
Seminole War, 19
Sering, John, agent Washington, Indiana, 163, 166
Settlement of claims (1822), 59, 60
Sewing machine invented, 22
Seymour, Henry, Director, 37
Shipman, Arthur L., Director, 227
Shipman, Elias, New Haven insurer, 14, 15
Shipman, Nathaniel, Director, 226
Skinner, Roger L., agent New Haven, 156
Slavery, 20

[259]

INDEX

Sloan, Edgar J., Assistant Secretary (1907), 141, 142
  Secretary, 144, 162
Smith, James, agent, 163
Society for Savings, Hartford, 30
South Carolina, first Ætna agent, 167
Southern Agencies, closed, 103
South Sea Bubble, 11
Spanish Influenza, 21
Spanish War, 132
Special dividends, 91
Spencer, Charles L., Director, 227
Spencer, George W., General Agent Pacific Branch, 191, 194
Spencer, Stephen, Director, 65
Steam power, first used in manufacturing, 22
Starr, Frank Farnsworth, Genealogist, 72
Starr, John L., agent, 161
State Bank, Albany, 199
Stagg, Henry, agent, 168
Steamship, first ocean, 22
Stedman, Griffin, Director, 37
Steel-plate engraving invented, 22
Stereotype plate, first, 22
Stewart, David R., agent, 161
Stockholders, the original, Appendix III, 248
Stoddard, J. N., agent Plymouth, Massachusetts, 199
Stonington, Connecticut, fire at, 81
Stoves vs. fireplaces, 57
Street cars, first in Hartford, 71
Stronach, R. E., Marine Secretary, 214
"Sun" Fire Office, London, 9
Surplus decided on, 67

Talbot, Bird & Co., agents New York City, 173
Taxation, oppressive in various states, 200-209
Terry, Nathaniel, 15
Theaters, prohibited risks, 82
Thom, Isaac, agent Louisville, 163, 166
Thomas W. Lawson, wreck of the, 216
Tillinghast, Stephen, agent Providence, Rhode Island, 156, 167
Toronto, great fire of 1904, 137
Town-meeting, 24
Townsend, George E., Assistant General Agent, Pacific Branch, 196
Treat, Selah, 70
Tudor, Samuel, Jr., Director, 37
Tuttle, Miles A., Director, 93
Tuttle, William F., Director, 226

Underwriter, origin of term, 4
United States Bank, reorganization of, 21

Valued policy legislation, 202-203
Van Buren, Martin, Ætna policy-holder, 157
Van Rensselaer, Jeremiah, first General Agent, 74, 163
Vermont, first Ætna agent, 167
Vicksburg, great fire of 1867, 123
Virginia, antagonism to foreign companies, 201
  first Ætna agent, 167

Wadsworth, Daniel, early insurer in Hartford, 14
Walton, John, agent, 161
War Clause, 103
War of 1812, 17, 18
Ward, Lauriston, agent Saco, Maine, 166
Ward, Samuel S., Director, 226
Watkinson, David, 29
Way, John L., Director, 227
Webster, Noah, 45
Weeks, Egbert O., Assistant Secretary, 129, 130, 131, 212
  Vice-President, 129
  death, 129, 213, 214
Welles, Alfred, 95
West Virginia, first Ætna agent, 167
West India Islands, 23
West Indian trade, 23
Western agents, 176
Western Branch, 97, 144, 162, 168, 170, 171, 176-187
White House, burning of, 18
Whittelsey, Roger, agent, 156
Whittelsey, W. F., Marine Assistant Secretary, 213
  Marine Secretary, 214, 221
  Marine Vice-President, 196, 214
Williams, A. A., Special Agent, 165
Williams, Almeron N., Assistant Secretary (1902), 133
  Vice-President (1912), 134, 227
Williams, Andrew N., agent, 159
Williams, Thomas S., 42, 45
Willmarth, A. F., Assistant Secretary, 97
  Special Agent, 165
Winning of the West, 176-187
Wood, Joseph, agent, 156
Woodbridge, Ward, 29
Wyman, William H., General Agent, 183-187

www.ingramcontent.com/pod-product-compliance
Lightning Source LLC
Chambersburg PA
CBHW031421150426
43191CB00006B/348